P9-DDU-862

John Wooden's
UCLA Offense

John Wooden

Swen Nater

Human Kinetics

Library of Congress Cataloging-in-Publication Data

Wooden, John R.
John Wooden's UCLA offense / John Wooden, Swen Nater.
p. cm.
Includes bibliographical references and index.
ISBN 0-7360-6180-0 (soft cover)
1. Basketball--Offense. 2. Basketball--Coaching. I. Nater, Swen, 1950- II. Title.
GV889.W66 2006
796.323'077--dc22
2005033376

ISBN-10: 0-7360-6180-0
ISBN-13: 978-0-7360-6180-3

Developmental Editor: Leigh Keylock; **Assistant Editors:** Christine Horger and Carla Zych; **Copyeditor:** Patrick Connolly; **Proofreader:** Julie Marx Goodreau; **Indexer:** Betty Frizzéll; **Graphic Designer:** Andrew Tietz; **Graphic Artist:** Francine Hamerski; **Photo Manager:** Dan Wendt; **Cover Designer:** Keith Blomberg; **Photographer (cover):** Todd Cheney; **Photographer (interior):** Dan Wendt, unless otherwise noted; **Art Manager:** Kareema McLendon-Foster; **Illustrator (cover and interior):** Andrew Tietz; **Printer:** United Graphics

Human Kinetics books are available at special discounts for bulk purchase. Special editions or book excerpts can also be created to specification. For details, contact the Special Sales Manager at Human Kinetics.

Printed in the United States of America 10 9 8 7 6 5 4 3 2 1

Human Kinetics
Web site: www.HumanKinetics.com

United States: Human Kinetics
P.O. Box 5076
Champaign, IL 61825-5076
800-747-4457
e-mail: humank@hkusa.com

Canada: Human Kinetics
475 Devonshire Road Unit 100
Windsor, ON N8Y 2L5
800-465-7301 (in Canada only)
e-mail: orders@hkcanada.com

Europe: Human Kinetics
107 Bradford Road
Stanningley
Leeds LS28 6AT, United Kingdom
+44 (0) 113 255 5665
e-mail: hk@hkeurope.com

Australia: Human Kinetics
57A Price Avenue
Lower Mitcham, South Australia 5062
08 8277 1555
e-mail: liaw@hkaustralia.com

New Zealand: Human Kinetics
Division of Sports Distributors NZ Ltd.
P.O. Box 300 226 Albany
North Shore City
Auckland
0064 9 448 1207
e-mail: info@humankinetics.co.nz

The efforts of this book are dedicated to three very special people: my wife, Marlene, and daughters, Alisha and Valerie. They are also very dear to Coach Wooden.

—Swen Nater

CONTENTS

DVD MENU

On the main menu you may view the Introduction or Credits or move forward to the UCLA Offense menu.

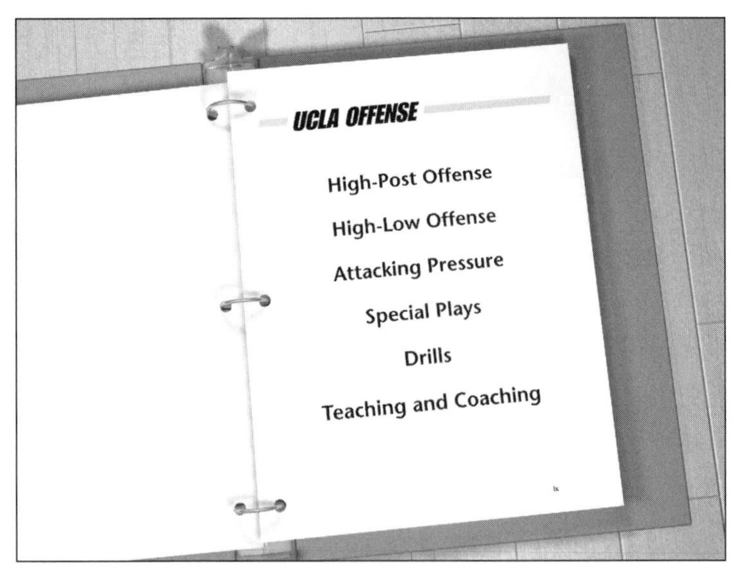

On the UCLA Offense menu, you may select any of the six main segments. Once within each segment, you may use the "Next" button on your DVD remote control to skip to the subsections within each segment. The subsections are listed on the following page.

FOREWORD

AMAZING! It is truly amazing to me that I have the opportunity to write this introductory section to *John Wooden's UCLA Offense*. I say amazing because as a high school and collegiate player I followed the UCLA program and marveled at the accomplishments of Coach Wooden and his teams. His last national championship occurred in the same year that I started as a head coach in collegiate basketball. As I have grown as a coach, I have studied Coach Wooden and have tried to emulate many of the things he did as a coach and as a person. To be given the honor to now write this section is truly amazing to me!

I find it remarkable what Coach Wooden has done throughout his life. In the 30 years since he retired as a head coach, he has continued to give back to basketball, the coaching profession, his former players, and people throughout the world his insights into our great game and how to lead a great life. However, it is truly amazing that now at the age of 95 he has authored this book and DVD that further add to his legacy as the game's greatest coach.

As you would expect, the quality and detail of the information provided in the pages to follow and in the accompanying DVD are superb. Over the years many of us might have lost sight of what an excellent technician and tactician Coach Wooden was in practices and on the sidelines. There is no doubt that he had great players like Lewis Alcindor (Kareem Abdul-Jabbar), Bill Walton, and Sidney Wicks, but even today we must marvel at how he could get five athletes to execute as one on the court. In developing a friendship with Coach Wooden, I've often heard him remark that the team is always bigger than any one individual. He certainly practiced what he preached, and to see UCLA play was inspiring.

Coach Wooden's high-post offense, high-low offense, and the special plays he developed within those offenses have a simplistic genius about them. He carried this throughout his offense, and you can see this same genius in out-of-bounds situations. They reflect his knowledge of the game and what he believes should be the priorities of an offensive unit.

Every tactic hinges on correct execution of fundamentals—the staple of all Coach Wooden's teams. Passing, cutting, and screening are all essential elements underlying the Xs and Os he presents. For that reason, this offensive system is well suited to high school and even middle school levels where it is especially important that players be properly grounded in basic basketball skills.

Many coaches today, whether we are aware of it or not, run some elements of Coach Wooden's offense or the special plays that he developed to augment it. Only when you see the entire system presented as a whole, and at the detail provided here, can you really appreciate the value this book and DVD offer us all. Even if you don't adopt the complete package, you will find many facets of Coach Wooden's offense to implement into your offensive scheme.

In addition to the Xs and Os, please make sure to study the many teaching insights and technical and tactical corrections of common errors players are likely to make when learning and applying the offense. The chapter on the development of fundamentals, the use of drills, and the conduct of practice is a real treasure for any coach who wants to be an effective teacher on the court.

I can remember when Coach Wooden was at one of my practices here at Duke University in his 90s. He still was excited to see young men learning, playing hard, and trying to be one. When he talked to our team you could see that all the players were fixed on every word Coach Wooden had to say. After the practice he made simple comments to me that were great teaching points. He laughed and said, "Mike, you certainly know how to put together a team, and I hope these things will help you." All I could do was to say thanks. On that day he made me a better coach. Through this book and DVD he can help you in the same fashion.

In recent years Coach Wooden has written insightfully on leadership and life priorities. Those books have been valued by hundreds of thousands of people from all walks of life and will be for years to come.

Coach Wooden's lessons to coaches on standards of conduct that should be expected of players to build both personal discipline and team cohesion have been passed down from one generation to the next. He felt it was his responsibility to ensure that a player never criticized a teammate, a scorer always acknowledged a teammate's role in contributing to the basket, and players never taunted opponents. Today's athletes, teams, and the game would gain tremendously if every coach would enforce those guidelines.

Now, to the benefit of every basketball coach and serious-minded player, Coach Wooden provides this book and DVD to share the complete offensive system that his UCLA teams used to achieve unparalleled success. Many elements of the offense are presented here for the very first time, as the Coach was very careful not to reveal any secrets during his coaching career.

John Wooden's UCLA Offense is a rare opportunity for us to soak in the genius and principles of its author. We should all be grateful and try to be true to the Coach in attempting to transfer his knowledge to our teams. If we do, we will all be better!

Mike Krzyzewski
Duke University

ACKNOWLEDGMENTS

In order for a team to create high-percentage shots, five players must work together, each fulfilling a key role to make it happen. Writing a book is no different, especially one about an offensive system that spans several decades, involves many individuals, and requires a prodigious amount of cooperation to teach and learn. Contrary to what some may believe, the coaches are not solely responsible for the success of the offense; they provide the basic structure and teach the skills. The players, through experimentation, inspire revisions and additional options that develop the game into a system tailor-made for each team.

We first acknowledge all of the players of the UCLA basketball program. We learn more from players than they realize, not only about how the game should be played but also about human nature. Coach Wooden made it a point to learn as much about each player as he could so he could help each person reach his potential. But what he learned about players served another purpose. Often, years later, another player, with a personality similar to that of a previous player, came along. What he learned from each player helped those who followed.

Although not directly involved in the book, Don Johnson, former head coach of Cypress College in Cypress, California, All-American basketball player at UCLA, and coach at the community college Swen attended, taught Swen his first offense. When beginning his time at UCLA, Swen learned that what Coach Wooden taught mirrored what he had learned from his previous coach.

All of the UCLA assistant coaches deserve recognition for their contributions. The word *assistant* falls short of defining the irreplaceable roles played in the development of each player and of the teams. These coaches did so much more than assist; they helped lead. Their proactive approach, especially during practice planning and practice review, resulted in many key additions and alterations of the offense. Without the assistant coaches, we never would have attained success.

Although the manager is not directly involved in the creation of the offense, the role of the manager is still indispensable. The manager is given significant responsibility that results in two things that are key to success: economy and efficiency. Managers make it possible for the coaches to concentrate solely on teaching. We thank all the managers for the work they did, not only on the court but off as well.

Special thanks to all of the coaches who received manuscripts and were kind enough to provide feedback. Bob Knight took time out of his summer to provide candid feedback. The information Pete Newell provided added a perspective not only from the development of the post player but also from a man who has witnessed a significant portion of the evolution of the game and competed against John Wooden as a coach. The amount of help Hank Bias (boys' basketball coach at Fairmont High School, Kettering, Ohio) has given cannot be ignored. To date, he has paid Coach Wooden three visits and has twice brought Swen to his campus to work with his boys. Coach Bias offered the use of his players and opened his gymnasium to the DVD shoot. He spent hours on the phone with Swen, offering insight from the perspective of a current high school coach involved in inner-city basketball. And those amazing young men of his spent two long days in a hot gymnasium doing take after take. Their effort was as strong at the end of the second day as it was at the beginning of the first. Thank you, Coach Bias and Fairmont High School players.

Human Kinetics vice president Ted Miller and developmental editor Leigh Keylock were great teachers and leaders. Their vision for the purpose of the book equaled that of the authors. Special thanks also to Doug Fink, Human Kinetics video department director. Before a word was written, Doug envisioned a DVD that would complement the book perfectly. He received professional assistance from many talented production crew members in both Kettering, Ohio, and Los Angeles, California. Please see the credit segment of the DVD to see a list of these talented professionals.

The fine folks at UCLA, who locked all the doors at Pauley Pavilion so the interview and cover photo could be taken, are to be thanked for their graciousness.

Ron Gallimore and John Super of Lesson Lab, Santa Monica, provided the facility used for recording DVD comments and narration. We are indebted to them for their generosity. The doughnuts and coffee they provided were of superior quality.

Finally, the UCLA game footage on the DVD was made possible by John Montague, a curious and dedicated UCLA basketball fan. John led us to the sources for those tapes.

INTRODUCTION

At a coaching clinic years ago, in front of a large audience, one of the attendees asked, "Coach Wooden, what part of the game of basketball is most connected to winning?" to which I replied, "Some say the team that outrebounds the opponent usually wins the game. Some say the team that has the least number of turnovers usually wins the game. Some say the team that makes the most free throws usually wins the game. Still others say the team that shoots the highest field goal percentage usually wins the game. From my experience, I say the team that scores the most points usually wins the game."

I am grateful that the person who asked the question was a good sport. But I believe the point was well taken. Basketball is a sport of scoring. And, obviously, the only opportunity to score is when your team has the ball.

Since writing *Practical Modern Basketball,* a countless number of coaches have requested further information, especially about the offense we used at UCLA. Because of the comprehensive nature and page limitations of that book, it did not provide nearly all the detail needed to understand, implement, and refine the offense. Nor, admittedly, was I inclined to share all of those tactical details while I was still coaching. Now I have decided to present, in this book and DVD, a thorough description and demonstration of the offensive system and what makes it work.

Assisting me in this endeavor is one of my former players, Swen Nater. During his early years in coaching, Swen's teams attempted to run the UCLA high-post offense, but he soon realized that his experience at UCLA and study of the Xs and Os of *Practical Modern Basketball* left some important gaps in his knowledge and teaching of the system. At first, his efforts to develop the offense into a smooth-working unit in which the movements of five players are synchronized met with modest success. So Swen sought solutions to these difficulties during his many visits, and he slowly began to grasp all the elements that make the offense work on the court, with a team, versus an opponent. In time, he developed a fine offense.

In the years since, Swen has also been asked by high school basketball coaches to help them implement the offense with their teams. Most have been interested in the high-post offense, but others—seeking to take advantage of an exceptional post player—inquire about the high-low offense, the system we used at UCLA with the Lewis Alcindor (Kareem

Abdul-Jabbar) and Bill Walton teams. In unique cases, Swen has worked extensively with coaches and their teams during the off-season to help them adopt the offense and get it running proficiently.

Through these experiences, Swen appreciated the importance of knowing not only the Xs and Os, but, equally as important, all the "little things" that make the offense work. He thought other coaches would find great value in a resource that provided this information and direction. When he suggested that we collaborate on a project that goes well beyond the standard descriptions and diagrams, I agreed but insisted on three things.

First, all the plays and all options needed to be included. Each UCLA team had one main play but also many options off of that play. Those alternatives are essential to fitting the offense to a team's particular strengths, addressing each game situation, conquering well-prepared defenses, and providing a variety of ways for the main scorers to score.

Second, the presentation had to go beyond Xs and Os and offer all of the key principles, teaching points, practice drills, and other facets that make the offense successful. Proper execution of this offense requires more than simply showing a player where to go in a play diagram; it involves a solid grasp of and belief in the rationale behind it, an ability to teach it effectively, and a commitment to providing the repetitions and constructive corrections that make it work.

Third, though diagrams are useful, they fail to convey what really happens on the floor. Proper timing of movements can only be shown through a more dynamic medium. Fortunately, our publisher, Human Kinetics, agreed that a companion DVD would augment the written material and static diagrams in a very meaningful way. The enclosed DVD will allow you to see how the offense should manifest itself on the court.

Some may question if the offensive system I used is applicable against today's "sophisticated" defenses. To that I answer with an emphatic "yes." In fact, I believe the system to be perfectly suited to counter all the modern defenses I have seen, and that includes run-and-jump, 1-3-1 trapping, box-and-one, triangle-and-two, and switching man-to-man. The reason is that it is founded on timeless principles of effective offense, principles that are still perfect antidotes for the defensive stunts just mentioned.

But there is no question the game has changed over the years. Today, because of increased athleticism and size, we see more dunks than ever before. And, because of the advent of the three-point shot, the mid-range jump shot has become almost nonexistent.

I am often asked if I would change anything if I were coaching today. Of course I would. For one, I would take full advantage of the three-point shot. Through the years, I had several players who, in any era, would be excellent long-range shooters.

The dunk shot, as emotionally lifting as it can be for both players and fans, is not that important to me. When teaching, I worked hard to keep the emotional level of my players at an even keel, because I believe that for every high there is a low. Yet, a powerful inside presence is important for team success.

A balance between the inside and outside game can prove extremely beneficial for offensive success throughout an entire season. However, good balance is not limited to inside and three-point scoring. In my opinion, the threat of scoring from all positions on the floor is better strategy, including mid-range jump shots. The offenses I used could easily be adjusted to accommodate all types of scoring from all positions. For that reason, I would not change the basic structure of the offense.

Although we used the same basic system throughout my career, we also made many adjustments based on personnel changes from one year to the next. The flexibility of the system allowed us to create scoring opportunities for our best offensive players.

Several examples of the adjustments we made are described in this book, from featuring guards Walt Hazzard and Gail Goodrich in the early 1960s, to center Lewis Alcindor in the late 1960s, to forwards Curtis Rowe and Sidney Wicks in the early 1970s, and then to versatile center Bill Walton after that.

I see coaches who are frustrated because the strategies of some opponents take their teams out of their normal offensive systems, rattle their players, create turnovers, reduce the scoring of their best offensive players, and reduce their teams' offensive production. A reason for this may be, like during my coaching years, that some of the offensive principles have been forgotten. Proper spacing, strong-side vertical penetrating cuts, ball movement through passing rather than dribbling, and weak-side action that is in sync with strong-side action—all these are essential to creating scoring opportunities throughout the game for those who should be the main scorers.

Many of the coaches who consult me explain that their teams have less talent and quickness than their opponents. Try as their players might, they simply can't seem to withstand the pressure applied by defenders. To those coaches I say, we have good news. Why? Because our offensive system is designed to take full advantage of any defense, no matter how aggressive and no matter how quick the athletes.

While the offense you run is important, it's much more critical that you teach well the offense you use. I allotted significantly more time to teaching offense than defense. The execution of offense involves more fundamentals than defense, and the fact that five players are moving an object between them complicates the situation even more. A good basketball curriculum for offense must entail four things:

1. Conditioning—Physical conditioning is necessary to maintain effort and execution throughout the course of an entire game. Mental conditioning is essential for meeting the rigors of practice, being disciplined to fulfill the duties as a member of a team, and handling the pressure of game situations.

2. Skill instruction—Teaching players quick and proper execution of the basic fundamentals is a prerequisite for any tactical instruction. Not even the finest strategic system can overcome poor execution of the basics.

3. Team spirit—A coach must ensure that every individual on the squad is eager—not merely willing—to sacrifice personal glory for the benefit of the team. Selfishness, infighting, ego, and envy will ruin team spirit, and that will be reflected on the floor.

4. Flexibility—Every offense must have a defined structure yet offer many options that allow a team to diverge from that pattern when better scoring opportunities present themselves. Failure to take advantage of a mismatch or one-on-one situation must be corrected as well as failure to execute a play.

We enjoyed a great deal of success during my years at UCLA, but I must be quick to say that a head coach cannot do it alone. I share the credit with all who played a part, and that includes many. Our managers played a key role in helping practice sessions run efficiently and smoothly. My assistant coaches were great teachers and added things I could never have. But the people most responsible for the championships were my players. As every coach knows, you cannot win championships without talent. I am grateful for the many fine individual performances I witnessed through the years, but more important, I am thankful for the sacrifice many of them made so our teams could reach their potentials. I am also appreciative for the reserves who were talented enough to be starters at other universities, but who elected to stay at UCLA to practice hard and help develop the regulars into a powerful machine.

Finally, a word about coaching. This book features an offensive system designed to help teams become more successful when in possession of the basketball. In other words, it is a curriculum for offense. The effectiveness of the teacher will largely determine how well his students embrace what is being taught to them. But to be effective in the long run, a coach must provide an example. Perhaps the role of teacher and coach is best summarized in this short verse from an anonymous author:

No written word, no oral plea,
Can teach our youth what they should be,
Nor all the books on all the shelves.
It's what the teachers are themselves.

It is my sincere hope that you find the content of this book and DVD helpful in fulfilling your goal to be the best prepared and most effective coach you can be for the athletes under your guidance. If these resources contribute to the success of your players and team in some way, the time and effort to create them will have been well worth it.

KEY TO DIAGRAMS

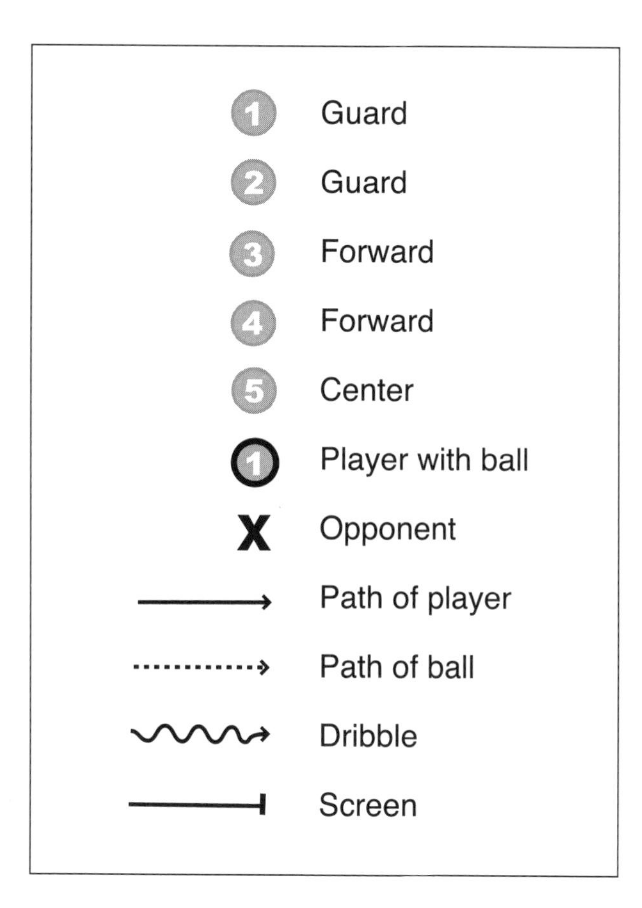

Part I

THE FOUNDATION

Since UCLA won 10 NCAA championships in 12 years (1964-1975), 19 different colleges have won men's Division I basketball titles. Each of those programs favored a particular offensive system of play, distinct in style from the rest, yet apparently effective for their purposes.

Some believed an up-tempo style was to their advantage, while others preferred to slow it down and control the ball. Some were convinced a perimeter attack was the team's strong suit, while others thought their best bet was the inside track. Some gave players freedom to operate freely all over the floor, while others limited players to certain areas of the court where they could be most effective.

Such different styles of play, yet each team was able to claim the championship. How is that possible? The key in each case is that the style of play chosen optimized the skills and physical attributes of the players, and that the style was consistent with the philosophy that the coach believed in and could teach.

In fact, all championship offensive attacks have something in common—the sound principles on which they are founded. Once this foundation is established, it's a matter of effective instruction, much repetition, and precise execution.

In part I of this book, I explain the rationale for developing the UCLA offensive schemes that were so successful for us. Many of these concepts apply regardless of what system or style a program adopts. We considered this framework the solid base from which all specific decisions could be made.

CHAPTER 1

ORIGIN OF THE OFFENSE

Through the years, many coaches have asked what prompted me to devise and teach what would become the trademark UCLA offense. Like most things in basketball, rather than a special spark of genius, necessity was the mother of that tactical invention.

Any review of the game's past confirms that other innovations in the game were spawned by similar reactions of coaches and players to the circumstances of their time. So, a quick look back at the major adaptations that have been made in the game might be helpful in understanding the origin of the UCLA offense and the context in which it was created.

A BRIEF HISTORY OF BASKETBALL INNOVATIONS

The sport of basketball has evolved a great deal since December of 1891 when the physical education chairman of the School of Christian Workers (later Springfield College) commissioned one of his teachers, Dr. James Naismith, to keep the school's athletes physically occupied during the winter months by inventing an indoor game. Dr. Naismith requested that the janitor attach two boxes to the gymnasium balcony, one on each side of the gym. A soccer ball was used, and nine players were allowed on each team.

The number of players participating on each team at one time was soon reduced to five, but the game still resembled a soccer match. The court was divided into three sections: back, middle, and front. Two players occupied the back section, closest to the basket their team was protecting. These players were appropriately called guards. One player occupied the middle section and was named the center. The two forwards operated in the section closest to the opponent's goal and were the only players who made field goals. Once in their zones, all players were required to stay within the assigned lines (see figure 1.1).

When the zone lines were abolished, players were allowed to roam all over the court. However, the guards usually didn't advance to what later became the half-court line. They were used as outlets to help restart the offense. The forwards and center ran a three-on-three game. Eventually, one guard, called the floor guard, became part of the attack. The other stayed back because protecting one's own basket remained a pivotal part of strategy.

Defense was strictly man-to-man, and offenses attacked with rapid passing and player movement. Possessions started from the center jump, and offenses seldom ran what we now call half-court plays because most attacks were quick and high-percentage shots were readily available.

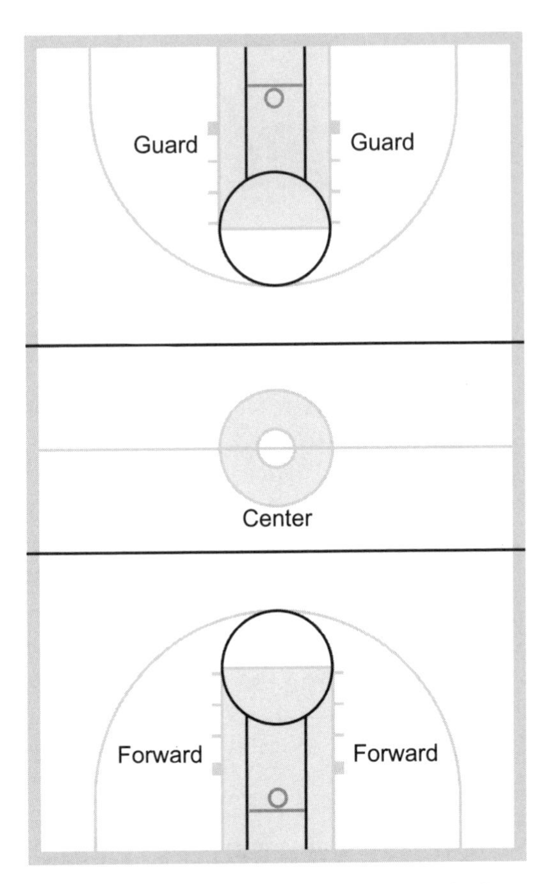

Figure 1.1 Early positioning for guards, forwards, and center.

But as defense became more sophisticated and offenses were less able to free offensive players, screening became a prominent feature of the game. At first, no rules defining legal and illegal screens were established, and consequently, offensive players set extremely physical picks to spring teammates to score.

As a result, zone defense emerged to offset the effectiveness of the screen. Standard man-to-man offenses proved virtually useless against the zone, because cutters and players who received screens seemingly had no place to go where defenders were not awaiting their arrival. Many coaches found a solution in the stall or ball-control offense. They simply spaced offensive players across the entire court and kept the ball away from defenders. However, this reduced scoring significantly, which in turn reduced fan interest and attendance. Something had to be done.

That something was the institution of the 10-second rule. This rule forced offenses to attack a man-to-man or zone defense in the half court. But proactive coaches responded with a strategy of advancing the ball across half court before the defense had a chance to get in position. As

Ward Lambert said (*Practical Basketball*, 1932), "When a successful fast break is obtained, the mass principle of zone defense is destroyed." And the legendary Clair Bee explained this tactic as follows (in his book *Zone Defense and Attack* in 1942): "The cardinal principle in attacking a zone formation requires entering scoring territory before the defense has had a chance to form. This can be most effectively accomplished through the use of a quick break."

Yet, still unresolved was the question of how offenses could be more effective when the fast break wasn't available. The answer for many was a tactic resurrected from the past: screening. Coaches developed ways of using screens against zone defenses, and almost every offensive half-court play involved a screen of some sort. Winning teams were known for their fast break, rapid passing, screening, and player movement to open positions, all of which made for a more interesting sport to watch.

That was the case until teams with a tall, offensively skilled center began using the strategy of simply having the center camp in the middle of the lane, two or three feet from the basket, for as long as necessary until his teammates fed him the ball. George Mikan (DePaul) and Bob Kurland (Oklahoma A&M) were two centers of that era whose hook shots were nearly unstoppable. The dominance of players such as Mikan and Kurland, and the congestion caused by such lane-clogging centers, led to the advent of the three-second rule.

No longer able to position their centers in the lane with impunity, coaches moved their big men either to the low-post or high-post area. However, the repositioning of the center did not diminish his role as a medium for ball movement; he continued to receive the ball, although at different positions. Centers who were not skilled away from the basket remained close to the basket. The offense was initiated by perimeter weaving and ball movement with an occasional pass into the low post (see figure 1.2). Those centers who could operate farther away—ballhandling, shooting, and driving—moved up the lane to the side-post or high-post areas. The mission of opening up the lane was accomplished, and more scoring resulted. Thus, the high-post offensive style of basketball was born. In the high-post offense, the talented center

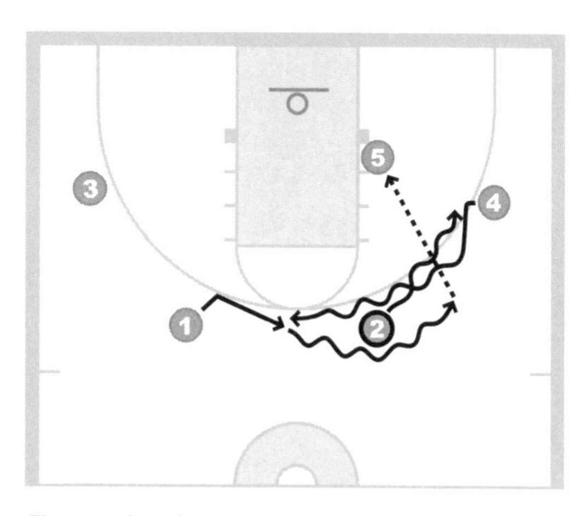

Figure 1.2 The center remaining close to the basket, with offense initiated at the perimeter.

was almost exclusively used as the primary receiver for initiating the offense (see figure 1.3).

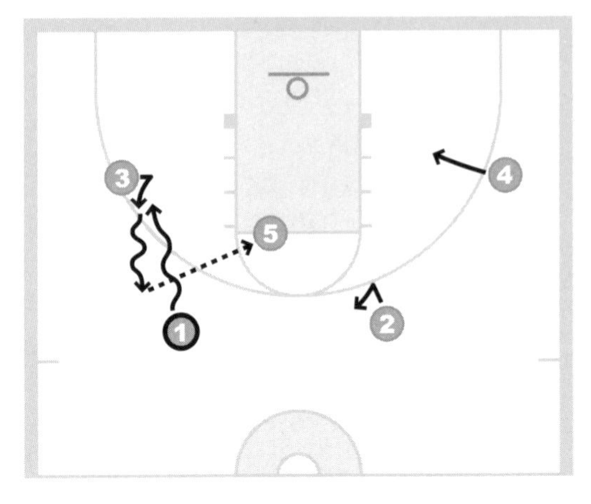

Figure 1.3 The center as the primary receiver for initiating the offense.

EARLY HIGH-POST OFFENSE

The high-post set opened up the lane and allowed teams to excel if they had a center with good ballhandling and passing skills. Early high-post offenses used little screening and a lot of cutting, and most half-court plays during this era began with a pass to the center at the high post. Positional responsibilities were very specialized. Guards were responsible for initiating play to the center, for balancing the floor, and for protection. Centers handled the ball away from the basket, looked for open teammates, and made individual moves. Within their areas, forwards and floor guards maneuvered to get open, while the other guard remained close to the half-court line. Triangles and spacing, as well as quick passing and cutting, were the means for running plays.

Guard-to-Center Entry Pass

The entry pass to the center was almost always made by a guard. This pass was followed by both forwards reversing toward the basket and coming back out, allowing for perimeter passing or a series of lateral perimeter cuts and handoffs, sometimes called a "weave" (see figure 1.4, *a* and *b*). For a time, weaves were effective if

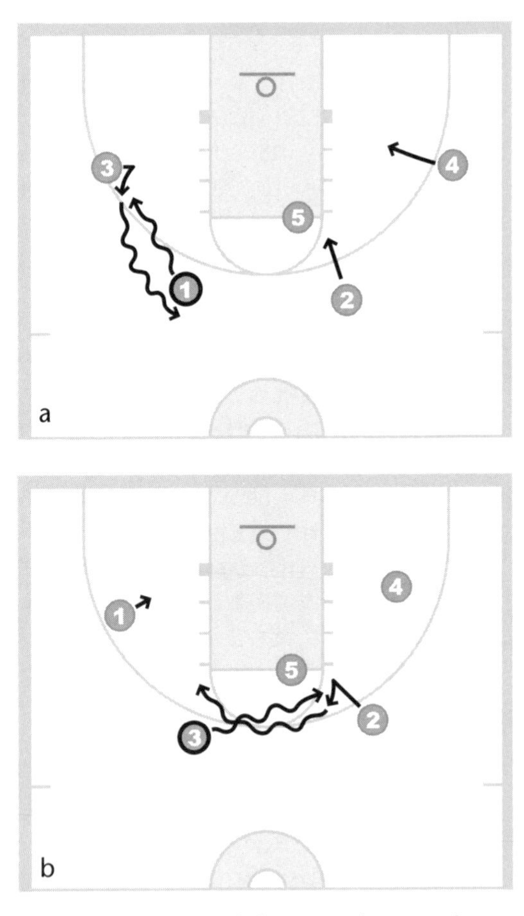

Figure 1.4 Weaves following the guard-to-center pass.

players were patient when looking for a driving or cutting opportunity. However, in short time, they became easily defensed; defensive players sagged toward the basket, eliminating cutting and driving.

Guard-to-Forward Entry Pass

Smart defenses also figured out that denial of the pass to the high post would diminish the offense's options. However, the counter for high-post denial came quickly; the guard-to-forward pass emerged as a second entry pass. Wise high-post centers delayed their backdoor cut until the forward received the ball. This sealed the defense. But, most of the time, the backdoor was not available. However, a supplementary method of entry was. Staying with the principle of penetrating the defense early after the entry pass, the passing guard cut directly to the basket on the strong side (see figure 1.5).

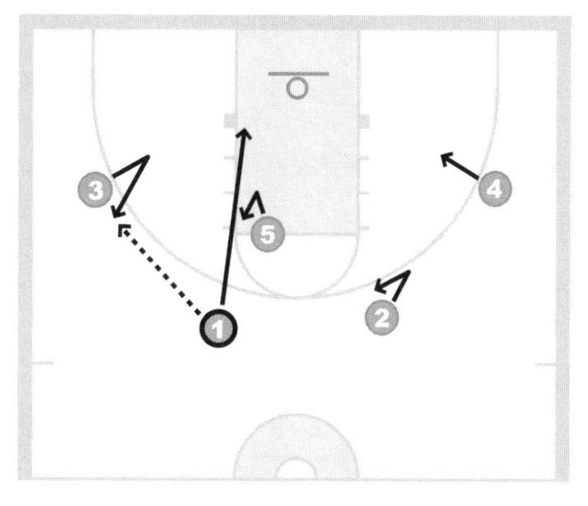

Figure 1.5 The guard (1) cuts directly to the basket after passing.

Ball-Screen Entry

In time, in order to prevent offenses from operating as they wished, defenses began to deny the guard-to-forward pass as well. This made it necessary to create still another method for initiating play. Since the center was in proximity to the guard, it made sense for him to quickly step out and set a ball screen (see figure 1.6). Now the guard had three options for initiating play: a pass to the high post, pass to the forward, and the ball screen. At first, the ball screen was used as an option when the guard-to-forward, or guard-to-center pass was not available. However, because of its effectiveness, in particular the quick penetration it provided, it evolved into a viable primary option for some teams.

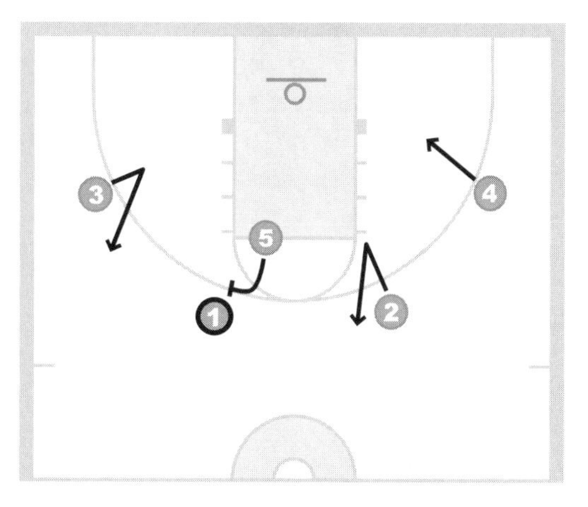

Figure 1.6 The high-post player setting a screen for the guard.

NO STRETCH OF THE IMAGINATION

In the early 1930s, Purdue University had fine players, including the most talented post player in the nation, Charles "Stretch" Murphy. From the low or mid post, his pass-faking, driving, and jumping abilities were superb and caused serious challenges for defenses. Incidentally, although he never thought to dunk the ball, he could have easily done so.

But it was Murphy's skill at the high post that was most valuable to the Boilermakers. His driving and shooting abilities required his defender to maintain complete concentration on him. Head coach Ward "Piggy" Lambert took full advantage of this by using a cutting attack. Cutters and drivers were successful at completing inside penetration because no tall player was there to help.

EVOLUTION OF THE OFFENSE

As a young high school coach in Dayton, Kentucky, my first offense was identical to what we used when I played at Purdue in the early 1930s. Although screens were used at times, for the most part, the offense was initiated with a pass to the high post or the forward, followed by sharp cutting to the basket. At the time, I believed the difficulties we had executing the offense were because of deficiencies in our personnel. Then I made an adjustment that helped a great deal.

UCLA Cut and Ball Reversal

I added the high-post screen, after the guard passed to the wing (see figure 1.7). I had two reasons for this: (1) to provide for an inside scoring threat to initiate the offense—something I felt, and still feel, strongly about—and (2) to allow the forward to pass the ball to the high post if the cutting guard wasn't open. I wanted the ball at the high post so the center could immediately look to the weak-side forward positioned in the lane.

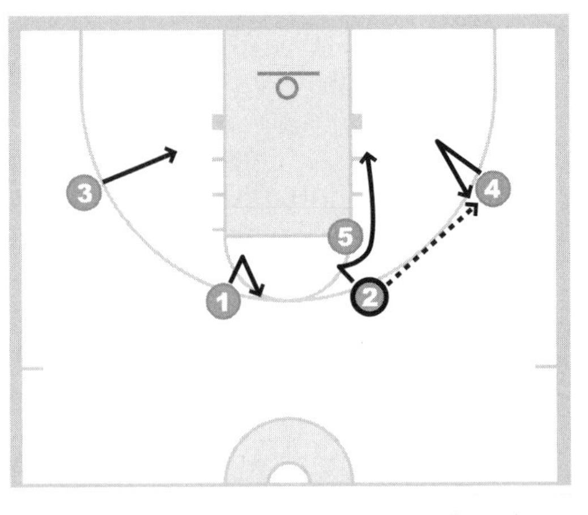

Figure 1.7 The high-post screen, after the guard-to-wing pass.

Side-Post Game and Ball Reversal

At South Bend Central High School in Indiana, my next teaching and coaching assignment, I added another option I think improved our offense—the side-post game. As successful as the pass from the forward to the high post was, after the UCLA cut, there were occasions when the forward was unable to pass to the cutting guard or to the center at the high post. His only option was a pass back out to the other guard. This usually resulted in resetting the offense. I wanted immediate action on the other side. I had to come up with something that would quickly attack the weak side and keep the ball moving. The result was what is known as the side-post game. When the forward passed out to the guard, the weak-side forward came to the high post to receive the pass from the guard, and the guard cut off this forward, looking for the handoff (see figure 1.8).

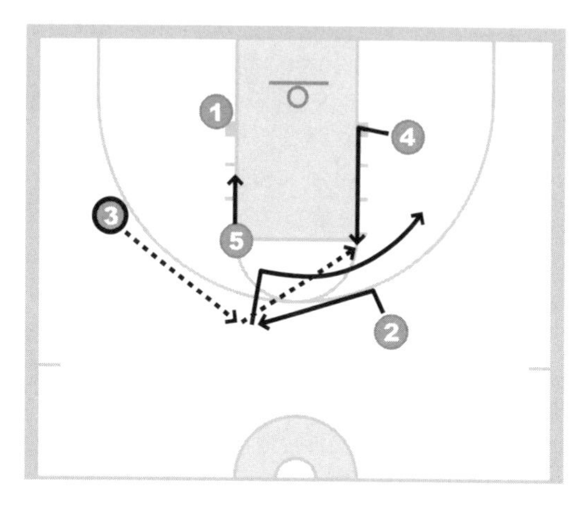

Figure 1.8 The weak-side forward comes to the high post to receive the pass, and the guard looks for the handoff.

To keep weak-side defenders occupied away from the side-post action, and to provide another scoring option, I added a double down screen on the other side. If the high-post forward chose not to explore the side-post option, or if a weak-side defender became too concerned with stopping the side-post play, another scoring opportunity would present itself (see figure 1.9).

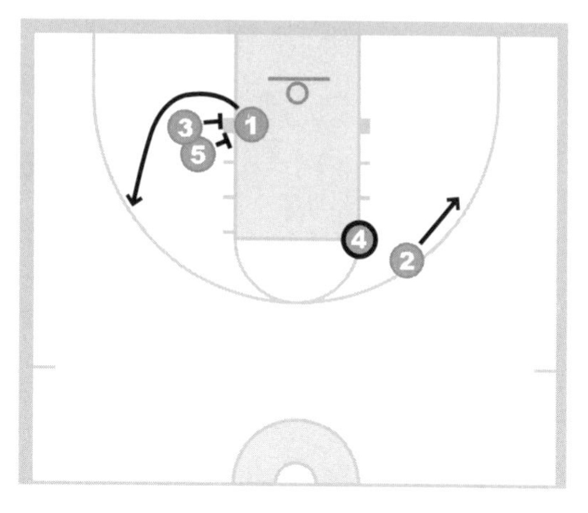

Figure 1.9 The double down screen on the weak side.

Guard Reverse

Something I learned early on was that the offense worked best when it was initiated by moving the ball from strong side to weak side by a guard-to-guard pass, followed by a pass to the forward. Since weak-side players generally sag toward the ball, quick ball movement ensured a guard-to-forward entry pass. For most of my teams, I preferred to start the offense this way because the guard-to-forward pass was immediately followed by a vertical cut—the UCLA cut. This worked well for some time. However, while I was at South Bend, one opposing coach was wise enough to have the second guard's defender play the passing lane, preventing us from swinging the ball. As a result of this weakness in our offensive attack, the guard reverse became part of the offense.

I taught our weak-side forward to watch how the defense was playing the guard on his side and, if he saw pressure, to come immediately to the high post to receive the ball. I told the weak-side guard who was being overplayed to cut to the basket, looking for the backdoor pass from the forward (see figure 1.10). However, I didn't want the offense to stop there; we needed another immediate scoring threat to follow the backdoor play. Therefore, if the guard did not receive the ball, he continued through and came off a double screen, set by the center and forward, on the other side (see figure 1.11). The guard who passed the ball to the forward replaced the cutting guard to balance the floor and provide defensive protection. The guard reverse worked extremely well, and when used occasionally, it continued to do so for the rest of my coaching career.

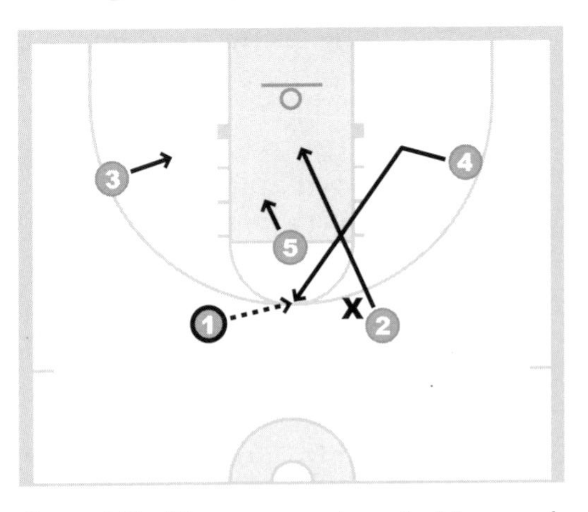

Figure 1.10 The pressured weak-side guard cuts toward the basket, looking for the backdoor pass.

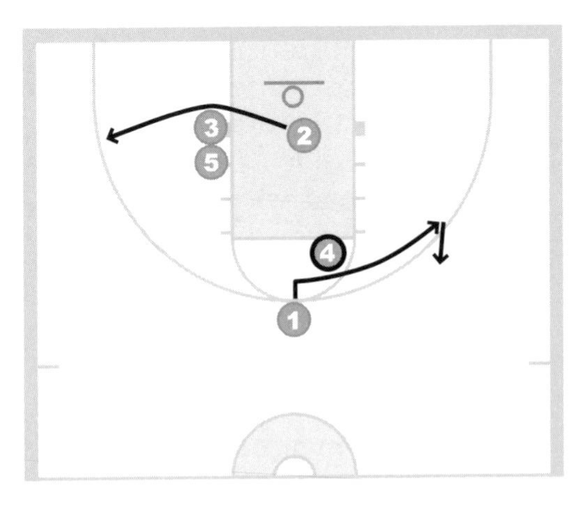

Figure 1.11 The guard (2), having not received the pass, comes off a double screen set by 3 and 5.

In the 1910s and 1920s, Dr. Walter E. Meanwell, Hall of Fame coach of the University of Missouri and the University of Wisconsin, strongly believed in backdoor action. One of his plays clearly demonstrates attacking the defense with a high set, passing the ball to the high-post area, and reversing players to the basket.

Guard 1 brings the ball into the frontcourt while 2 balances the floor in the two-guard front. The forwards, 3 and 4, sprint down the wings below the free throw line extended and come up to the two elbows of the lane. The center, 5, cuts straight toward the basket and then comes to the high post at the correct time. Player 1 passes to either one of the forwards (in this case 3). Player 3 "slap passes" the ball to 5, who arrives in time to catch the ball, and both 3 and 4 reverse to the basket, looking for the backdoor pass (see figure 1.12).

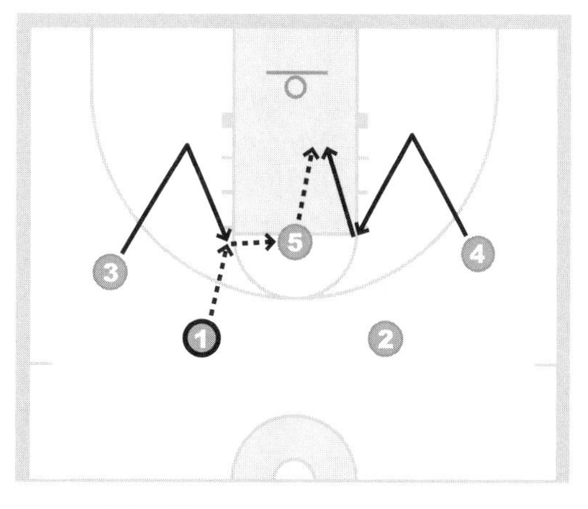

Figure 1.12 The center receives the pass, while 3 and 4 reverse to the basket.

Pete Newell, coach of the 1960 national champion University of California at Berkeley and one of the finest teachers I have seen, often began a game with a guard reverse. An opposing coach was usually well aware of this strategy; it was infamous among coaches. But no matter how many times the opposing coach warned his players during the previous week of practice or even immediately before the game, the play always seemed to work.

Additional Adaptations

After adding the guard reverse, the general structure and movement of the offense were pretty much complete, and with various adjustments to place talented scoring players where they belonged, our offense was able to handle any defense I had seen. However, through the years, I continued to pick up ideas, and I implemented some of them. I also adjusted the offense from year to year based on my personnel, although I never compromised the principles of triangles, spacing, and defining specific and limited roles for the players.

For example, when Lewis Alcindor (now known as Kareem Abdul-Jabbar) joined our team, I didn't think that having him start at the high post was in our best interest nor his. Although the high-post offense would bring him to the low post eventually, I didn't want him handling the ball up there at the high post; we had other players who could fulfill that responsibility better.

With Lewis at the high post when the UCLA cut occurred, his defender would surely sag and stop the cutting guard from scoring if he received the pass from the forward. In addition, I didn't feel comfortable having him pass to the ducking weak-side forward. I wanted him close to the basket for scoring and rebounding reasons.

Determined to create an offensive system that would take full advantage of Lewis without diminishing the offensive effectiveness of the other players or sacrificing principles such as ball movement and flexibility, I came up with a variation of the high-post offense that we called the high-low offense (see figure 1.13). Although it did not have the degree of player movement I wanted, it was effective, both against zone and man-to-man defenses. Only two of my teams used that offense: Alcindor's and Walton's. The rest used selected plays and versions of the high post.

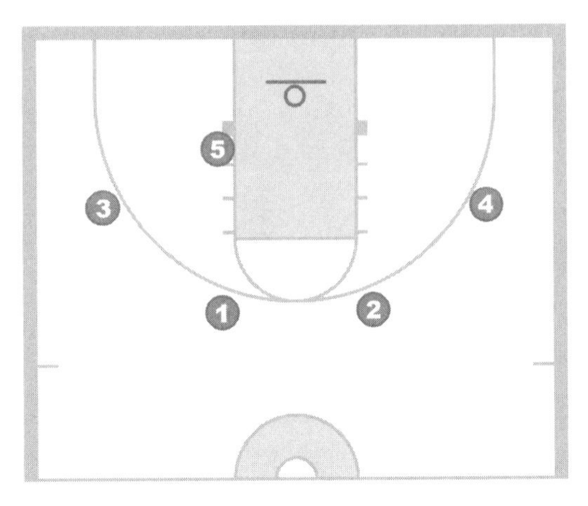

Figure 1.13 High-low offense alignment.

COMPARISONS TO THE OFFENSE

In recent years, two types of offenses, both successful, have emerged: "flex" and "motion." With the high-post offense as a model, we will analyze both types and identify their strengths and weaknesses. Before we do, we need to define *flex* and *motion* because several versions of each exist, some more sound than others when it comes to staying within solid principles. We will define both types in their *original* and orthodox forms. As we do, we believe the superior integrity of triangle offense (such as the high post) as it relates to being a complete system will surface.

Flex Offense

The main player and ball movements of the traditional flex offense are shown in figure 1.14, *a* through *c*. The concept is to achieve repeated ball reversal through screening players from the weak-side to the strong-side low-post area and down screening on the side away from the ball. This type of activity, sometimes referred to as "screening the screener," is designed to create opportunities for high-percentage shots through defensive error, switching, and mismatches.

Flex offense offers excellent floor balance, continuity, strong-side to weak-side ball reversal, and inside scoring threats. However, a deficiency in vertical cutting and its predictable pattern leave it prey to prepared defenses that may use switching to maintain passing-lane pressure.

Theoretically, this offense does not penetrate the middle with a pass to the high post, which, in my opinion, is a key to an effective attack.

The basic flex pattern gives each ball handler two passing options at most, whereas triangle offenses offer at least three, sometimes four. However, passing options in the flex offense are sequential.

Three even greater concerns are lack of an immediate ball reversal attack, weak-side action, and rebounding balance. In the high-post offense, when the ball is reversed from strong side to weak side by the forward's pass back out to the guard, the ball is quickly advanced to the side post (high-post weak-side elbow), and an immediate two-player attack occurs. The flex simply reverses the ball from forward to guard to guard to forward, followed by the weak-side back screen.

That leads us to another related concern—inefficient weak-side action. To create a high-percentage shot on the strong side, weak-side defenders must be kept busy guarding weak-side players. The flex simply offers an interchange of two players—the players occupying the guard position and the forward position; this is, at best, activity with little achievement. In a high-post triangle offense, while the side-post option is in progress, a double screen is occurring on the other side. Any strong-side help by a weak-side defender will allow an alert team to find the weak-side opening.

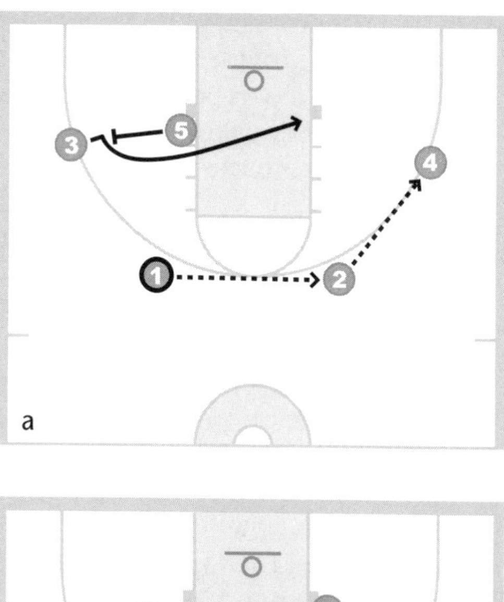

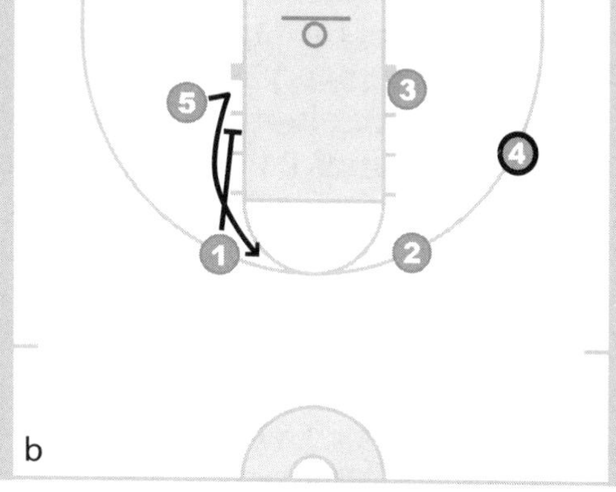

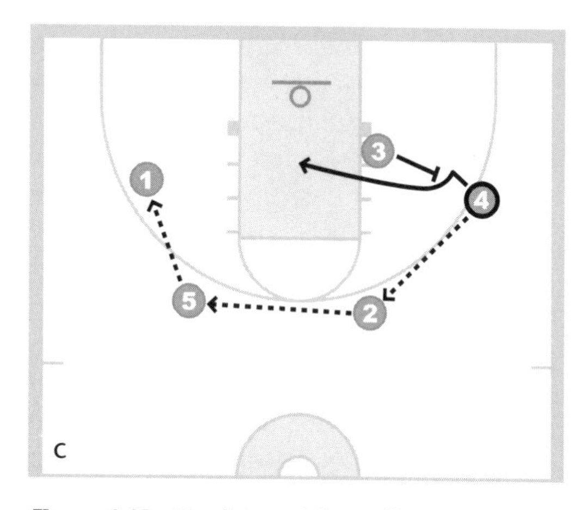

Figure 1.14 Traditional flex offense sequence resulting in ball reversal.

It has been said, "Never say never and never say always." However, in order to provide proper inside rebounding when any shot is taken—which is part of rebounding balance along with covering long rebounds and protecting against the fast break—a team should "always" have three players close to the basket. In the flex offense, if the ball is passed to the player coming around the weak-side back screen, only that player and the screener are in offensive rebounding position, and it is questionable if the screener is in good position at all. When a shot is taken in other options of the flex offense, more rebounders may be in position, but never consistently and sufficiently. The triangle offense is designed to properly position rebounders when any shot is taken.

Like the high-post offense, the flex offense has evolved, and some variations offer less violation of sound principles. In fact, the following play (found within a contemporary flex offense) resembles the UCLA cut option of the high-post offense and has been very effective. However, you may notice a weakness in rebounding balance after the weak-side screen.

1 passes to 3 and cuts off 5, who has come to the high post. Player 3 passes to 5, and 5 looks for 4 ducking in the low-post area on the weak side. If 4 does not receive the ball, he moves to the weak-side short corner, and 5 passes to 2 (see figure 1.15*a*). Player 1 back screens 3 to the basket (the "flex cut") and immediately receives a down screen from 5 (see figure 1.15*b*). The center (5) and strong forward (4) are completely out of rebounding position if 3 receives the ball or 2 happens to shoot an outside shot.

Having three inside rebounders when *any* shot is taken is pivotal to success (see chapter 2). Additional offensive rebounds can make the difference between a win and a loss.

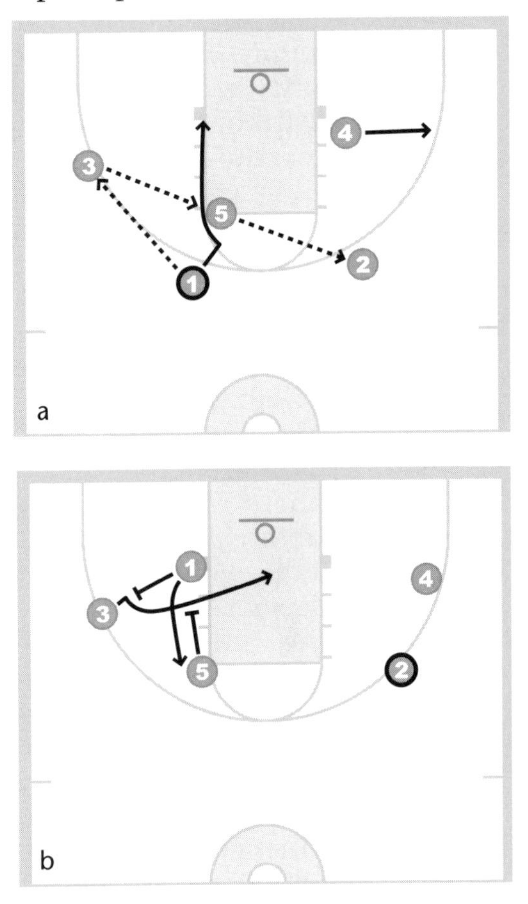

Figure 1.15 The flex offense shown here results in 5 and 4 being out of rebounding position.

Motion Offense

Although many fairly sound variations exist today, in its orthodox state, motion offense is a system where all five players are engaged in constant cutting, screening, and passing as the ball is reversed from one side of the half court to the other. Even the post player has freedom to post up, move across the lane, move to the high post, back screen a weak-side teammate to the strong side, or down screen for a shooter. Players are instructed to avoid being stationary at any time and to be engaged in continuous movement and activity, getting teammates open and looking for openings themselves.

Beginning with a one-guard front—with one guard and one forward on the wings and two post players inside—1 passes to the forward, 3, and screens away for the other guard, 2, to come to the point. Player 3 looks inside for 5 as 4 back screens for 1 (see figure 1.16*a*). Player 3 passes the ball out to 2. Player 5 back screens for 3, while 4 sets a down screen for 1 (see figure 1.16*b*).

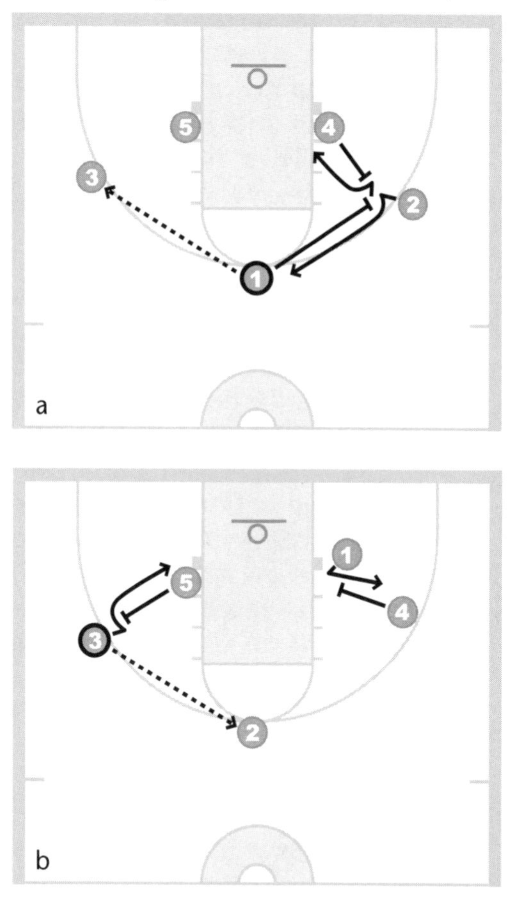

Figure 1.16 The motion offense initiates with a one-guard front and continues with 5 and 4 screening for 3 and 1.

Strengths of a motion offense are unpredictability, ball reversal, and constant vertical and horizontal penetration. However, this type of system (five-man motion) requires all players to be "jacks-of-all-trades." In a triangle offense, players are strategically placed in positions and plays where they are specialized to use what they are best at. In my opinion, this is generally more efficient. In this brand of motion offense, ball handlers have limited passing options, especially consistent, consecutive passing options. For example, with 2 in possession of the ball at the top of the key, if 5's back screen and 4's down screen are executed simultaneously, he may miss the open man.

In the previously described motion play, the immediate attack of the weak side is nonexistent. Compared to the high-post (triangle-style) offense, there is excessive activity without achievement. For levels of basketball where there is no shot clock, this may work, providing the players have the patience and discipline to find the high-percentage shot. But at higher levels, the offense may be scrambling for a good shot as the shot clock nears zero.

Perhaps the most significant difference in value between the motion and triangle offense is the development and effective use of the low-post player. Because weak-side activity, at least in part, works independently from the strong side in a motion offense, a weak-side cutter may interfere with a strong-side low-post player who is making an offensive move. In addition, if weak-side movement has too much variation, the post player will have a difficult time making good passes to cutters and shooters.

Another concern is quick ball reversal. If weak-side players are engaged in screening and cutting when the ball needs to be reversed, timing will be off. There is a purpose for ball reversal, and it is not to reset the offense. Ball reversal must immediately attack the weak side.

Some motion offenses have the post player involved in perimeter action such as back screening and even handling the ball. This may be acceptable if that player is not a skilled low-post player and lacks the potential to become one. However, to fully develop and take advantage of a strong inside player, he must be positioned inside, and the offense must be designed to get him the ball in at least three locations (through offensive options). When he receives the ball, he must have ample operating room, and through good weak-side action, he should have passing options to cutters and outside shooters.

The concerns just described relate to motion offense in its purest form. However, many reasonably sound motion systems exist today, some closely resembling triangle-type offenses, at least to a degree. Following is an example of a contemporary "motion" offense that is more of a pattern rather than freelance, maintains good spacing, and has *fairly* good rebounding and defensive balance when a shot is taken.

1 passes to 3 on the right wing and interchanges with 4, who comes to the high post. Then 3 passes to 4 (see figure 1.17*a*). Player 3 down screens for 5 on the strong side, while 1 sets a back screen for 2 on the weak side (see figure 1.17*b*). If he does not receive the ball, 5 immediately rescreens for 3. Although this action can, and does, create open inside and outside shots, there is no "low-post" player nor complete triangle inside rebounding.

In summary, there are important conceptual differences between the two competing styles of offense and the high-post offense in the following five areas: economy, passing options, ball reversal, individual initiative, and rebounding and defensive balance.

Because the nature of the triangle offense involves each of the five players doing his "part" and not overlapping with another's responsibility, the system is set up to be extremely economical. Each player is part of a five-person synergy and is therefore assigned a complementary job description designed to fulfill a specific function to make the whole work without a hitch. A fair comparison of how it works is a NASCAR pit stop where the coordinated efforts of all teammates service the race car effectively and in the shortest amount of time possible. The degree of offensive efficiency is directly proportional to role differential and inversely proportional to the amount of role overlap.

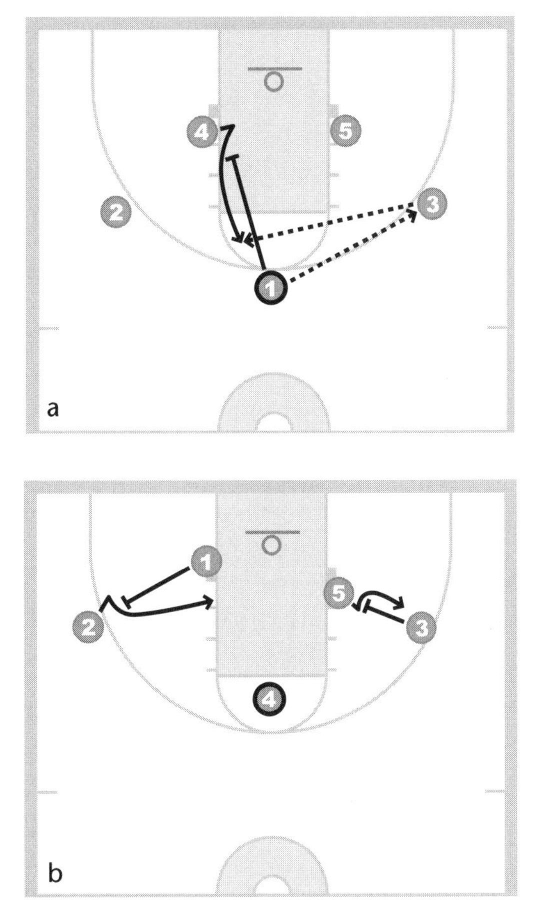

Figure 1.17 This version of the motion offense offers better rebounding and defensive balance than the traditional version.

In the high-post offense, new triangles are formed when the ball is transferred from one player to another. Therefore, each ball handler has at least three passing options, all in succession. This can only occur when players are in ready position to move into those triangle positions.

For ball reversal to accomplish something, it must be done with an immediate attack to the weak side, not simply a pass from the strong-side wing to the guard to the other wing. The side-post game is a quick method of weak-side attack while the defense is shifted toward the strong side. Motion and flex offenses usually move the ball around the perimeter to the weak-side wing and then attack, allowing the defense to regain position.

In the triangle offense, every time a shot is taken, rebounding balance exists (see chapter 2). There are no exceptions because the offense is designed to be balanced at all times—when a shot is taken and even in the event of a turnover.

Because of proper spacing, quick ball movement, and good weak-side action, the triangle offense provides better opportunities for individual initiative. Not only are basket cuts more effective, but one-on-one moves are as well, not to mention the passing options available for the one-on-one player if defenders leave to help. Inconsistent and improper spacing stifles timing and, therefore, reduces the effectiveness of individual moves.

I want to emphasize that there are almost as many versions of flex and motion offenses as there are coaches who teach them. Although their original and pure forms are not, in my opinion, completely sound offenses, some versions *are* very sound, and the coaches who teach them do an extremely good job. It is not so much the type of offense you run but how well you teach it, as long as it has balance, the players are fundamentally sound, and it is based on sound principles. It is not the Xs and Os that make an offense work to create high-percentage shots; it's attention to the details that results in the proper pass at the proper time, the quick shot, and the correct cut at the correct time.

In my opinion, Bobby Knight (Texas Tech) and Mike Krzyzewski (Duke) are excellent teachers in all areas of the game, including the details. In regard to offense, both use a type of motion offense and do a great job with spacing, vertical cutting, the priority of passing, efficiency, post play, rebounding balance, and defensive balance.

CLOSING POINTS

I believe that the overall balance, spacing, ball movement, opportunity for individual initiative, and flexibility to allow for adjustments that take advantage of particular talent all helped my players believe in our system. Placing players in positions where they are most effective and providing opportunities for them to use their talents are the first steps toward getting them to believe.

The next step is for each player, whether an All-American or a reserve, to accept a role that best allows the team as a whole to function at its peak potential. This is something I strongly believe in and always strove for. If a player did not conform, no matter how talented he was, he had a good seat at the games.

Each of the following chapters dealing with specific offensive plays will feature one main play followed by additional options that are available. Those options were created specifically by and for particular UCLA players. Each coach must determine what plays and options are best suited for his players. He may select some presented in this book and DVD, or he may create his own. The possibilities are limited only by the coach's creativity. However, he must be ever conscious to avoid getting caught up in creating a cunning play and forgetting about the sound principles presented in chapter 2.

CHAPTER 2

PRINCIPLES FOR OFFENSIVE SUCCESS

In the simplest terms, the object of the game of basketball is to outscore the opponent. Therefore, it follows that a prime objective of a half-court offense should be to create high-percentage shots.

What defines a high-percentage shot for one team may differ from another. A squad with several accurate perimeter shooters, for example, will view the three-point shot as a good option in its offense, whereas a team with strong inside scorers will orient its efforts toward getting the ball inside. Agreement among the coaching staff and players on what types of shots give the team the best chance to win is essential for a cohesive and effective offensive attack.

The UCLA offense, with the assistance of the abilities of the players, produces what should be high-percentage shot opportunities that will allow any type of team to be successful. However, as with any offensive system, no Xs and Os devised on paper have ever scored a single point on the basketball court. Before an offense can be consistently productive, the players must be in good condition, well grounded in the fundamentals, unselfish, and able to execute as a smooth-working unit.

In addition to those essential prerequisites, the offense must be based on sound concepts. I have identified 10 key principles that together provide a structure to facilitate team play yet also create opportunities to maximize the talents of specific individuals on the squad:

- Spacing
- Triangles
- Penetration
- Passing
- Strong/weak side balance
- Flexibility
- Timing
- Equal opportunity
- Rebounding balance
- Defensive balance

I'll explain the significance of each principle in the forthcoming pages, though some of the concepts are likely already familiar. At first glance, the inclusion of rebounding and defensive balance may seem strange in a list of offensive principles. However, their significance will also be explained if it is not readily apparent.

The 10 principles of half-court offense presented in this chapter are the cornerstone of the UCLA offense and are essential for the success of any offensive system. Because talent changed from season to season, the plays and options were modified through the years, although the basic structure of the offense remained. However, in all situations, these core principles remained intact.

SPACING

The strong side usually consists of three players with the two weak-side players refraining from being spectators by remaining active to keep their defensive men busy and staying ready to help reverse the basketball. Although player movements such as down screens, splits off the post, and interchanges will disrupt spacing at times, those strong-side players should be spaced approximately 15 feet apart when a pass is made. For example, weak-side double screens and position interchanges will be momentary departures from this 15-foot spacing rule. However, when the ball is reversed by a pass to the high post or opposite side of the floor, 15-foot spacing is reestablished. Players 3 and 1 are engaged in a two-man game on the strong side, with 3 holding the basketball. On the weak side, a double screen is occurring (see figure 2.1*a*). After 3 elects not to hand the ball to 1, 2 comes off the double screen, and 4 immediately moves to the high post to create 15-foot spacing on the strong side (see figure 2.1*b*).

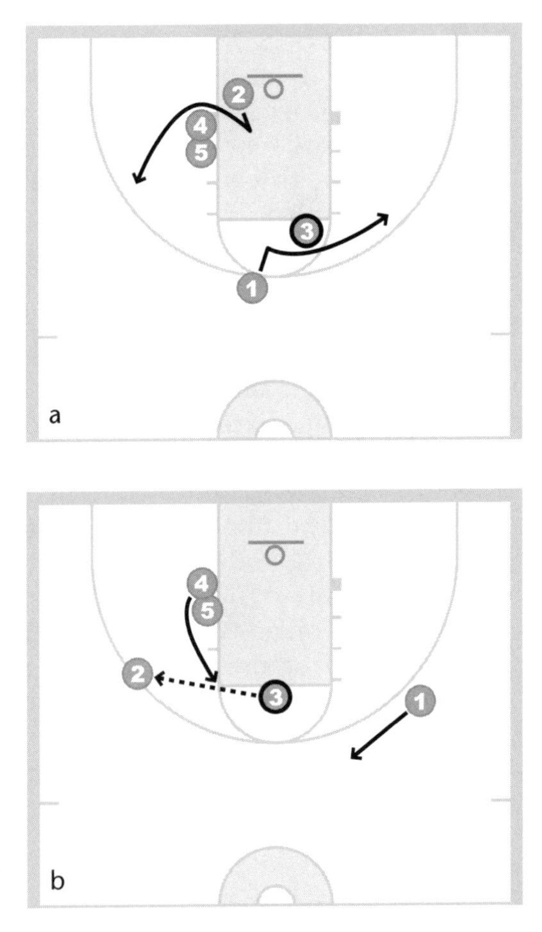

Figure 2.1 *(a)* This action temporarily departs from 15-foot spacing, but *(b)* after 2 comes off the screen and 4 moves to the high post, the 15-foot spacing is back in play.

Proper spacing is important for at least two reasons: It facilitates safe passing and provides operating room for the player with the ball. A pass more than 15 feet is in the air too long and is subject to interception. A pass less than 15 feet may be difficult for the receiver to handle. Fifteen feet is adequate for a good one-on-one player to make an individual move (such as a drive or a maneuver for a jump shot) with limited additional defensive help, and it leaves room for him to make a pass to an open man if he is stopped.

Proper strong-side spacing is important for any team, but for Lewis Alcindor and Lynn Shackelford, it was indispensable. Both players were strategically placed on the same side of the floor. Lewis, a fine low-post offensive player, needed room to operate. Lynn, a tremendous outside shooter, needed enough space to get his shot off. Lynn often passed into Lewis, followed by his defender dropping down to double-team. Fifteen-foot spacing was sufficient for Lynn to get an open shot when Lewis passed the ball back out. One of them usually had a high-percentage opportunity. The only recourse the defense had was to double-team Lewis from the top or weak side. However, players were trained to get open, and Lewis was exceptionally good at finding the open man.

TRIANGLES

What has become known as "triangle offense" has received much publicity ever since the world champion Chicago Bulls made the label famous in the 1990s. Assistant coach Tex Winter was responsible for its implementation. However, few fans realized that Tex was teaching this type of attack as head coach at Marquette University (1951-1952) and then at Kansas State (1953-1958) long before its recent popularity.

And, in fact, Tex's offensive knowledge was influenced significantly by those who coached him, such as USC coach Sam Berry. Indeed, if reliable sources are correct, it may well be that the origin of the triangle offense can be traced back to the advent of the game itself.

Most coaches are familiar with the purpose of creating triangles within an offensive attack: Adding a third receiver produces more and better passing angles and scoring opportunities than a simple two-man game. But just as important is how those triangles are formed.

A stationary triangle where all three players arrive at the same time is of little value. However, if, for example, the ball is on the wing with a low-post player getting open to receive, and another player is arriving at the high post on the strong side after the wing player has had time to consider the pass to the low post, the passer now has two passing options in *succession*. If the pass to the low post is not there because of defensive pressure, the logical next option is a pass to the high-post player, who can deliver the ball. It is important to understand that the pass to the high post will not be possible if that player is stationary. However, if he is quickly moving to that area from the weak side and at the right time, he will most likely be open to receive the ball.

Bill Walton was occasionally fronted at the low post. With the ball at the wing in the hands of Henry Bibby, Keith Wilkes (later Jamaal Wilkes) would recognize the overplay and fake a quick backdoor cut from the weak-side high-post area where he was positioned in the 1-3-1 set. Keith would then return to the ball-side high post to receive the pass from Henry and deliver it to Bill, who sealed his man away from the basket (see figure 2.2).

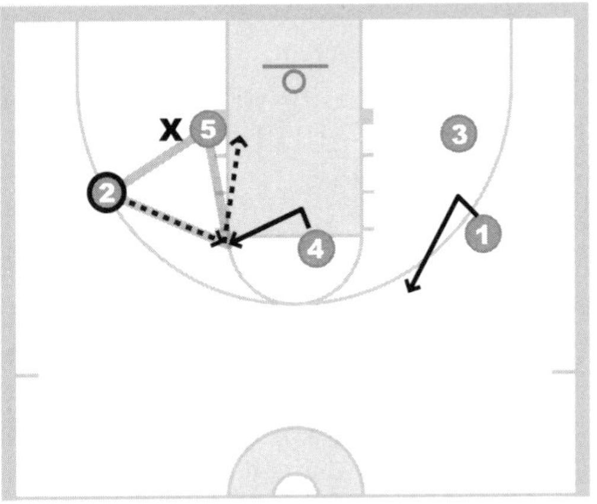

Figure 2.2 Players 2, 5, and 4 form a triangle to get the ball inside.

In the course of an offensive play, strong-side triangles are formed, dissolved, and re-formed in other ways and in other areas of the half court. As we will see in chapter 8 on half-court pressure release, when the weak-side guard is pressured, the weak-side forward should be ready to come to the high post and receive the pass (see figure 2.3). What this action does is create a new triangle to provide a better passing angle to the pressured guard—a backdoor pass for the layup. Whereas the guard with the ball cannot deliver the pass, the forward can.

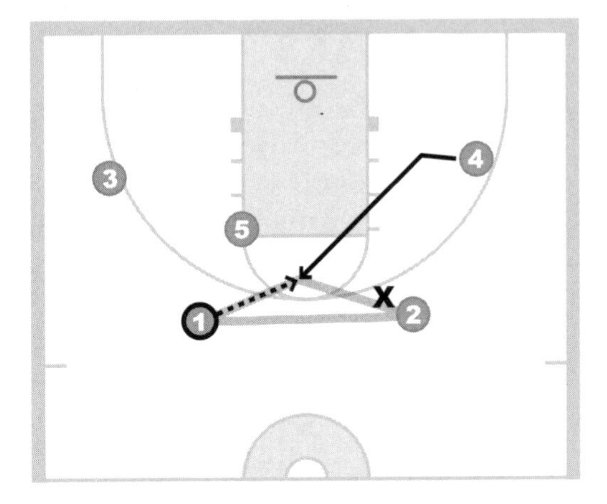

Figure 2.3 This triangle formed by 1, 2, and 4 provides a better passing angle to 2, who is pressured.

Against good teams, an offense usually cannot run the play it wants to; through scouting and game adjustments, opposing coaches will shut certain passing angles down. For offensive success, a coach must teach the creation and re-creation of triangles as the defense calls the play.

the contrary, if ball reversal is limited to passing along the perimeter, delaying an attack on the new side of the floor, weak-side defenders will know they can provide strong-side help and have plenty of time to adjust, when the ball is reversed.

FLEXIBILITY

Defenses change from game to game, and some change from one possession to the next. Therefore, an offense must be capable of adapting to meet every challenge that a changing defense might present. Mechanical offenses where players are forced to follow set patterns are easily defensed. Giving players freedom to break from the pattern helps make an offense flexible, unpredictable, and effective against a variety of teams through an entire season.

To encourage players to be resourceful, the offense must be flexible enough to provide a sufficient number of options to counteract all possible defensive maneuvers. The coach must provide a system of play options and an atmosphere of trial and error and risk taking during the practice sessions. Individual innovation must also, however, take place within the guidelines for proper spacing, ball movement, and so on; otherwise, the offense will likely stall and possessions will terminate at the hands of a single player's attempt to be creative. The team and individual players should get a good sense of when (and when not) to improvise through successes and failures experienced on the practice floor. As the players work within a flexible offensive system, plays that work will emerge, and the ones that don't work will magically disappear.

Although Lewis Alcindor was restricted to the low post, Bill Walton was not. The decision to keep Lewis low had nothing to do with inability but had everything to do with keeping him close to the basket. However, in a practice session, Bill proved his value as a high-post player when, seeing pressure on the wing player on his side, he raced to the side-post elbow, received the pass from the guard, and delivered a perfect backdoor pass to his teammate (see figure 2.5). If he had not felt free to improvise, that play would probably never have existed.

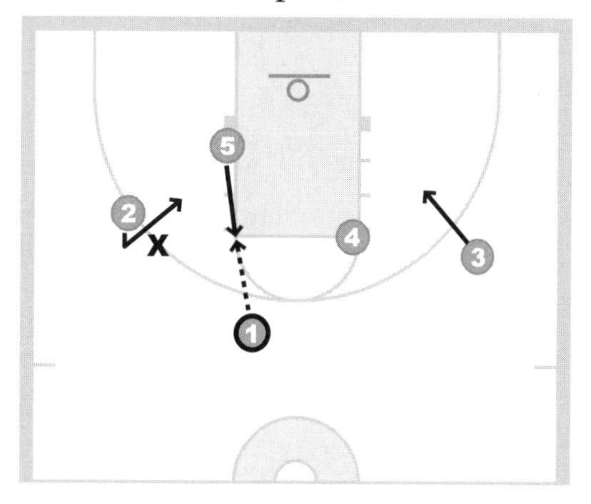

Figure 2.5 This play emerged from Bill Walton's ability to play at the high post.

TIMING

Creating a smooth-working unit is an ultimate goal of any offense. This is accomplished through players practicing and playing together enough so each player will become familiar with the particular skills, tendencies, and preferences of the others.

Bill Walton and Keith (Jamaal) Wilkes played the low-post and high-post positions of the high-low offense for four straight years. Their primary play was for the basketball to go to Bill in the key, via Keith at the high post. The success of the play was completely contingent on timing. It took a little more than one year for the two to learn each other's idiosyncrasies, but once they did, Bill knew when Keith was ready to pass, and Keith knew when Bill was ready to receive. For any play to work effectively, ball movement and player positioning must be coordinated and timed to near perfection. A late or early pass or cut, particularly against a good and quick defense, will surely result in missing the scoring opportunity the play was designed to create. Precise timing is necessary for successful strong-side action, weak-side action, and the integration of the two as the ball is reversed.

The coordination of the players' timing must get to the point where they think as twins, whether the play calls for a pass from guard to guard, guard to forward, wing to low post, wing to high post, high post to cutting guard, or high post to flashing forward. Again, this split-second timing can only be developed by working the players together enough so they will react to the particular peculiarities, physical abilities, and movements of their teammates. In other words, repetition is necessary for the players to become accustomed to each other.

I will attempt to convey timing in the plays described in this book, but text is an insufficient medium for illustrating proper timing. The companion DVD provides much better examples.

EQUAL OPPORTUNITY

Most teams contain a player or two who are natural scorers, athletes who can create and make shots within the flow of the offense. Other players require more daylight between themselves and the defender but are capable of hitting the open jumper or layup. Both types of players are important for team execution.

For example, Walt Hazzard, a great ball handler on the first UCLA championship team, was a "go to" player. He was capable of making the one-on-one move to score. Keith Erickson, though skilled in other areas, was not as effective at the individual move. However, he was capable of making the 15-foot jump shot. Another of Keith's responsibilities was offensive rebounding. His limited scoring role enabled him to place more concentration on going to the offensive boards, something he was very good at and something that was a value to the team.

An offense that places the basketball only in the hands of its more-gifted scorers and freezes out the others is doing the entire team a disservice. Such an offense becomes predictable, is limited in its options, and is therefore easy to defend. Conversely, an equal opportunity offense where scoring opportunities are more equally distributed across players over the course of several games is more difficult to stop.

That doesn't mean that all players should average the same number of points per game. It does mean that every player on the court must be a contributing member of the offensive attack, even if a player's contribution is mostly by passing, cutting, and screening to allow the main scorers to get good shot opportunities. And, when called on to score (when open or when higher-scoring teammates are out of the game), each player should be capable of doing so.

Another appealing aspect of an equal opportunity offense is that it typically improves ball movement, which in turn leads to more open shots. When players believe that they are a viable option on each possession, and that everything they do will positively or negatively affect that trip down the floor, it increases the speed of their passes, the crispness of their cuts, and the solidity of their screens. In short, they know they have a stake in the team's offensive production. As a result, unlike team members who view themselves as simply supporting actors for star players, they are fully engaged in the effort to help their team score every chance they get.

REBOUNDING BALANCE

Offense does not end until the other team gains possession of the basketball. After any shot attempt, players must make the effort to obtain offensive rebounds. To maximize the chances, we insist that when any shot is taken, we have three inside players surrounding the basket, a long rebounder moving to the free throw line area, and a protector going back toward the half-court line (see figure 2.6). (If the shot is taken from the outside, the shooter will always become the long rebounder.)

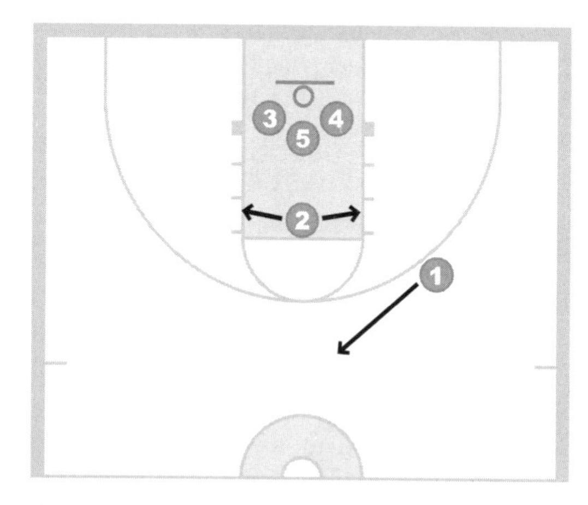

Figure 2.6 This alignment provides for ideal balance during rebound situations.

Rebounding balance is essential for increasing the chances of obtaining offensive rebounds and, therefore, additional shots. Consider this: If team A and team B shoot the same percentage from the field and make the same number of free throws, the difference in the score could very well be determined by which team had the most attempts. An offensive rebound gives a team another chance to convert on the same possession and usually leads to a high-percentage shot. This must be a point of emphasis for every coach, and players should be reminded frequently of the importance of rebounding to the success of an offensive attack.

No UCLA player was better at anticipating the long rebound than Henry Bibby. Because he often took the outside shot, he was often responsible for the long rebound. Positioned just below the free throw line, he had a keen sense for anticipating the bounce of the ball, and he often grabbed rebounds that bounced over the heads of the inside rebounders.

Curtis Rowe was a forward who was extremely cunning at gaining inside offensive rebounding position, even though he was not blessed with the quickness of some other players. A simple fake into the key often caused his defender to give up the weak-side rebounding spot. Curtis was quick to take that A position.

Consistent rebounding balance will result in increased offensive rebounds, but there is another purpose for this alignment—defensive balance.

DEFENSIVE BALANCE

If the opponent obtains the rebound, the rebounding balance alignment also serves as defensive balance. A defensive rebound is generally followed by an outlet pass and perhaps a secondary pass that advances the ball up the floor. The long rebounder is in position to defend a player who receives the first pass because he knows he has help from the protector. The protector defends any long pass to his area or discourages any such pass. If he is not needed to defend an offensive ball handler, he serves as a basket protector until the tall defenders arrive. Simultaneous with the action of the long rebounder and protector, the three inside rebounders sprint back to relieve the protector from protecting the basket and to match up with their defensive assignments.

In all fundamental skill and offensive drills, offensive rebounding positioning and defensive balance should be given equal billing with shooting, screening, passing, and ballhandling. If not, players will assume that they are of secondary importance and, perhaps, optional.

CLOSING POINTS

It is the cumulative effect of doing a lot of little things correctly that eventually makes a big difference in competition. Individually, the 10 principles outlined in this chapter might not seem so significant, but when combined, they can make an offense almost indefensible.

When observing the later rounds of state high school or college basketball tournaments, it is apparent that most teams have employed all, or most, of the principles presented in this chapter, yet some teams execute better than others. What then is the difference between the winners and losers? What caused that errant pass, missed shot, or fumbled ball? The answer is found in the areas of fundamentals and attention to detail.

Without the ability of all players to quickly and properly execute the fundamentals of basketball at high speed and without conscious thought, following the principles of effective offense won't make much difference. All of these principles are dependent on quick, timely, and accurate passing; aggressive receiving; sharp cutting; proper pivoting; skilled dribbling; and quick shooting (with passing and receiving being the two most important fundamentals). Any coach who does not understand that his primary responsibility is to create fundamentally sound players doesn't get it. Neglecting this most essential area will surely result in any team not nearly reaching its full potential.

The attention to details—such as faking without the ball, developing perfect timing on the backdoor pass, making sure all players handle the ball and have scoring opportunities, insisting the outside shooter goes to the free throw line area to become the long rebounder, and teaching definitive penetrating cuts—can be the difference between a season of success and one of failure. In fact, it often is.

Part II

HIGH-POST OFFENSE

Our 1948 to 1949 UCLA team was predicted to finish last in what was then called the Pacific Coast Conference. However, that team surprised everyone outside of the program by winning the league that season. From that year through the mid-1960s, UCLA teams were known for achieving beyond expectations.

Even the 1963 to 1964 national championship squad was not favored to win several of its games that season. Lacking a dominant scoring post player, we relied heavily on the excellent play of our guards, Walt Hazzard and Gail Goodrich. Center Fred Slaughter was a fine screener and passer. And forwards Keith Erickson and Jack Hirsch were unselfish players who were especially adept offensive rebounders. That team executed the offense very well, with Hazzard, an extraordinary driver and passer, penetrating and creating plays for teammates, and Goodrich consistently making perimeter shots. As with each Bruin team in the preceding 16 seasons, the players discovered how to maximize their individual and collective talents within the framework of the high-post offense.

Subsequent UCLA teams, as well as other college and high school teams, that have been committed to the high-post offense have been successful when they have properly learned and employed it. This part of the book explains in detail the key elements of the offense and how it is to be executed. The primary plays, effective options, and possible individual variations presented reflect just how multidimensional the offense can be. And that versatility makes it extremely difficult for opponents to defend.

Your team might not win the conference or a state or national championship this season using the high-post attack, but it will be on the right track. Just keep working at it.

CHAPTER 3

GUARD TO GUARD TO CENTER

Most offenses have a trigger point—a desired place and way in which they are initiated. The same is true of the high-post offense.

We always prefer to begin the offense with the guard-to-guard pass. Weak-side defenders tend to sag toward the ball in order to provide help to the strong side, which leaves substantial space between themselves and their assignments. If the ball is moved quickly (faster than the defense can shift), the guard-to-guard pass almost always makes the guard-to-forward pass possible. In addition to the pass to the forward, the second guard has another option: a pass to the center at the high post.

The sequence goes like this: Guard 2 should make a good fake toward the basket, then pop out to receive the ball from 1, about two or three feet farther away from the basket than the passer (see figure 3.1). Immediately after 1 passes to 2, 1 fakes away to the wing on his side to prevent his defender from dropping down to help on the high post if the pass goes there.

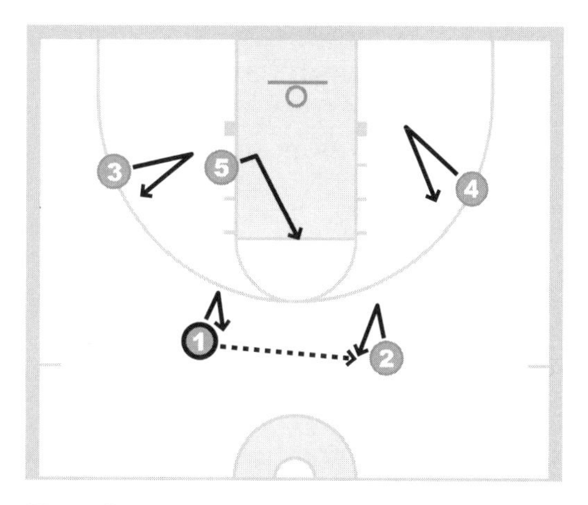

Figure 3.1 Guard 2 fakes toward the basket then pops out to receive the pass from 1.

The center (5) is never stationary. He always starts well below the free throw line and makes his move to the high post at the right time to receive a pass from 2 (see figure 3.2), coming to a two-footed jump stop when landing, which leaves either foot as a potential pivot foot. The timing is crucial if the entry pass to the center is to be completed. Players 2 and 5 are faking and cutting in sequence. They don't cut simultaneously or 5 will arrive at the high post too soon. Player 5 must wait for the right moment. This timing should be perfected in practice sessions that emphasize 5's responsibility to read 2's actions and make the move exactly when he is needed.

In most instances, the pass from 2 to 5 will be in the form of an air pass. If the defender's hands are down, 2 will fake down and pass up (the air pass), using a two-handed overhead pass. However, occasionally the bounce pass will be appropriate. If the defender's hands are up, 2 will fake up and make the one-handed bounce pass, by the defender's knee. The jab fake with the foot, shoulder fake, or head fake can be used to set up the pass. Little movement is needed to make the defender react and create an open passing lane. For example, an effective head fake can be made simply by throwing the chin toward the floor to set up the air pass, or up toward the target for the bounce pass.

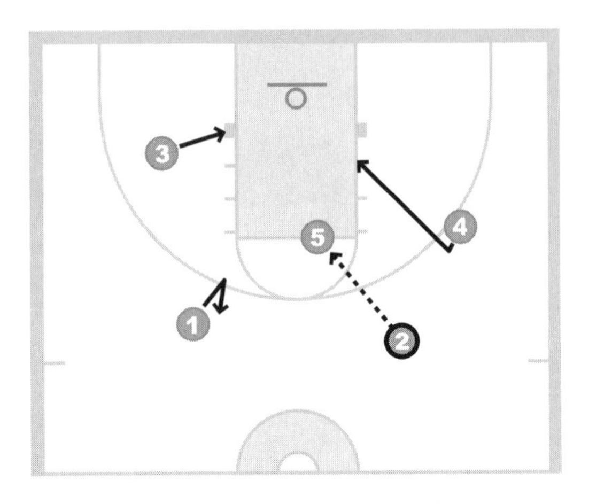

Figure 3.2 Player 5 must perfect his timing to arrive at the high post at just the right time to receive the pass from 2.

Players should learn to pass the ball *by* their defenders, not over or around them. They should also be taught not to stare at their intended target. Such telegraphed passes will often be intercepted by alert, cunning defenders. So 2 must be deceptive when passing, using peripheral vision to stay aware of 5's movements and the defender's position, yet disguising his intentions.

With the entry pass to 5, the offense can initiate a variety of plays from the high post. First, we will review the main play.

BASE PLAY

As the ball is passed to the center, both forwards should reverse quickly toward the block, calling for the ball. The strong-side forward has the best chance of being open since his defender will most likely be higher in the passing lane than the weak-side forward's man; therefore, the center will turn to look for the strong-side forward first. Player 5 drops his outside leg and looks for the backdoor pass as shown in figure 3.3, *a* through *c*. He should use the bounce pass because it is more difficult for the defender to reach than the air pass. To start with, 1 and 2 meet above the top of the key—not too close to 5 because their defenders may attempt to divert 5's attention—and flare to their respective wings, creating triangles and good spacing with the forwards and center (see figure 3.4). Additional cutting options for the guards will be presented later.

If 4 is not open, 5 makes an inside pivot, or "reverse" pivot—swinging his nonpivot foot behind him. Player 5's next look is to the weak-side

Figure 3.3 Player 5 drops his outside leg and looks for the backdoor pass.

forward (3), who has also reversed to the basket. After reaching the block, 3 has used proper footwork to step in front of his defender in the key. Player 3 should time his move into the key so he is open after 5 has looked for 4 and has turned toward him. If his timing is good, the pass should arrive before 3's defender has a chance to reestablish good defensive position.

As with any offensive move, the effectiveness of 5's pass to 3 requires good faking to set up the pass. The choice of a bounce or air pass is determined by how the defense reacts, but any fake and pass must be executed quickly. And, it's best to use just one fake and then the pass—not several fakes preceding the pass.

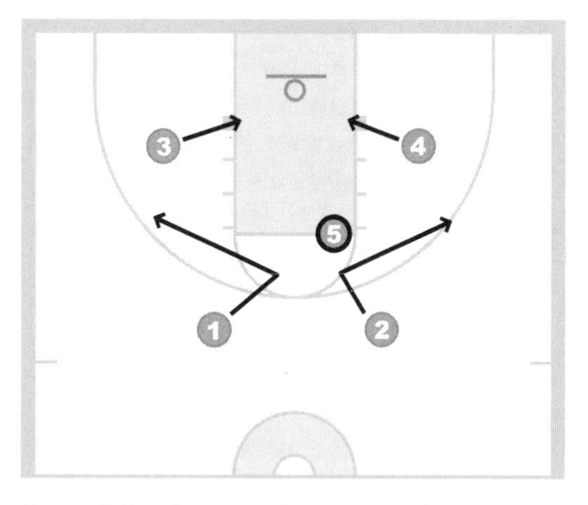

Figure 3.4 The guards meet at the top of the key and flare to the wings, which creates triangles and proper spacing with the other players.

The strong-side forward (4), who has made the backdoor cut, should be active and working for low-post position. The center knows in advance which of the two is the better low-post player and should focus his attention to that side of the floor. Ideally, the better low-post player should be positioned on the weak side, or the side where the play was initiated, because the passing angle is better than on the strong side.

If the center is going to be used as a backdoor passer and a passer to players who have flashed into the key, he must also be a good 15-foot shooter and, preferably, be able to take one or two dribbles for a short jump shot. When catching the pass, if his defender is playing close or leaning and reaching to the outside, the center can drop his inside leg to seal his defender and then drive toward the basket. With strong inside forward play, the defensive center will occasionally drop to help, leaving the center open for the jump shot from the free throw line.

But some teams may play the center extremely tight, even after he has turned to face the basket, in an attempt to "crowd" him and hinder his ability to pass. In this situation, he must be trained to fake the shot and take no more than two dribbles into the key for a jump shot. Without these options for the center, inside play will be less effective.

When 5 turns to look for the forwards, 1 and 2 are at the wings after meeting above the top of the key and flaring. The center's next look is to the guards on the wings.

The time it takes for both guards to reach their side positions is about equal to the time it takes for the center to explore the passes to the strong-side forward and weak-side forward. Again, as with the forward in the deep post, the center must know in advance which of the guards is the better shooter and should get the ball there if that guard has managed to get open.

The players are now focused on getting the ball inside. Generally speaking, perimeter shots should come as a result of the pass back out from the inside. Occasionally, one of the forwards may be overplayed at the low post. In that case, the guard on that side, 1 for example, anticipating the overplay on 3, fakes toward the basket and comes back out at a good passing angle to the forward. Player 5 hits 1, who then hits 3, who has sealed his defender toward the top of the key, creating space for the pass from the guard (see figure 3.5). Player 1 leads 3 with a pass toward the block as shown in figure 3.6.

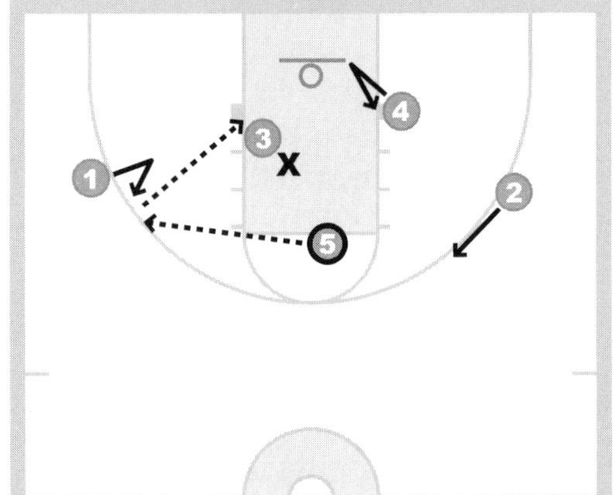

Figure 3.5 Player 3 is pressured, so 1 fakes toward the basket and comes back out to receive the pass from 5 and then passes to 3, who has sealed his defender toward the top of the key.

Figure 3.6 The pass toward the block.

Player 1 will make the appropriate type of pass based on the position of his defender's hands and the position of 3's defender. If his defender's hands are down, he fakes down and uses a two-handed overhead pass into the forward, as shown in figure 3.7. If the hands are up, he fakes up and delivers the bounce pass. If 3's defender is approaching the direct passing lane, the bounce pass will be a better choice because it will be more difficult to intercept.

Figure 3.7 A two-handed overhead pass is called for here, because the defender's hands are down.

If 5 passes to 2 instead of 1, a mirror image of the 1, 5, 3 triangle would result on the other side of the floor with 2, 5, and 4. Personnel will determine which options are viable and which are not.

After passing to 1, 5 cuts down the lane, calling for the ball and heading for the block. Player 4 sets his defender up by faking a cut across the bottom of the key and using 5's screen at the block to get open. This weak-side action helps prevent defensive help on the strong-side block. Screens work best when the player who receives the screen is taking responsibility for getting open. The best time for 5 to cut may not be immediately after he has passed to 1. It depends on when his defender drops to help on 3. He may make his cut after 3 has received the post pass. Player 4 comes to the elbow area looking for the pass from 1 or from 3 if 1 passes there, and 2 moves toward the center of the court as protector and a potential receiver to reverse the basketball (see figure 3.8).

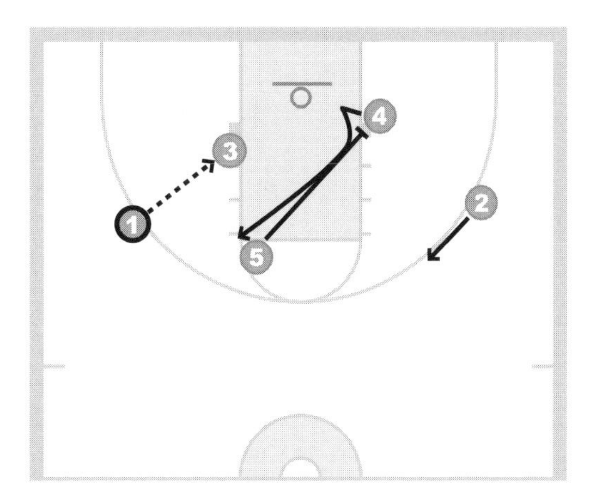

Figure 3.8 Player 5 times his cut toward the block for when his defender is helping on 3. He screens for 4, who comes to the elbow to be ready for a pass.

FOUR-OPTIONS SET

The offense is now in the four-options set (see figure 3.9). Throughout all plays and options of the high-post and high-low offenses, after two or three passes, all plays arrive at this formation. Players are positioned at the strong-side wing (with the ball), low post, high post, weak side, and above the key.

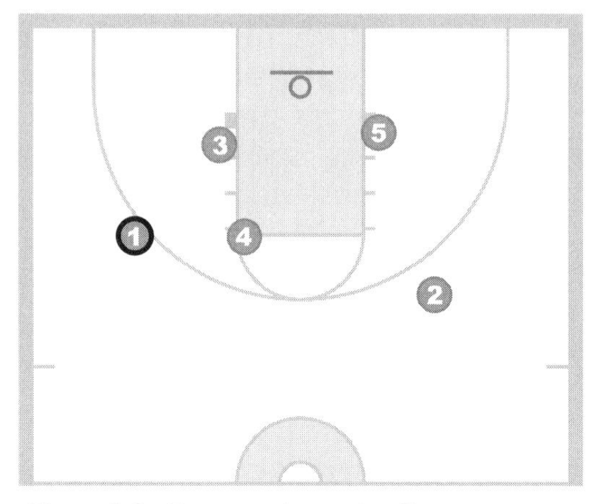

Figure 3.9 Four-options set alignment.

In this case, the options available really hinge on timing, or how the offensive movements are executed sequentially. Each phase of the progression should be open immediately after the preceding option has been explored—no sooner and no later.

In addition to the one-on-one move, 1 has four options, which are presented here in the order they should occur.

- **Option 1: Low post**—1 fakes and passes to 3 on the deep post; 3 has timed his turn so that he is open when 1 is ready to pass. When 3 makes an offensive move, 4 cuts to the basket, calling for the ball in order to look for a pass from 3 and to prevent his defender from helping on 3. If 3 takes the shot, 4 assumes rebounding position along with 5. Player 1 repositions himself on the perimeter to create a passing angle should his man drop to help on 3. He becomes the long rebounder if 3 shoots. Player 2 heads toward the top of the key as the protector, but not all the way to the strong side (see figure 3.10).

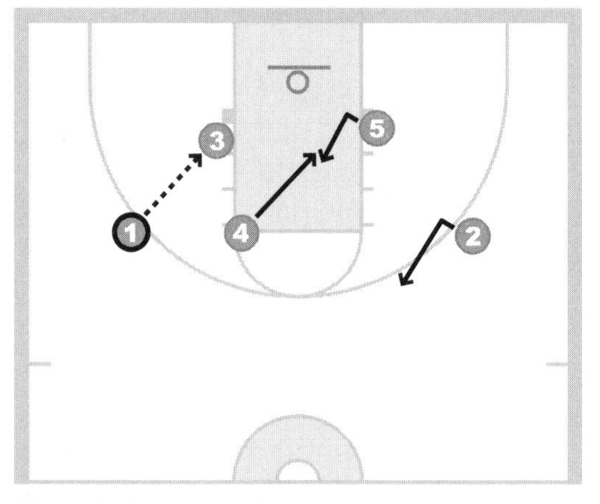

Figure 3.10 In the low-post option, 1 passes to 3.

- **Option 2: High post**—Because 3's defender is fronting, 1 cannot pass to the post and uses the triangle to pass to 4 on the strong-side high post. To get open, 4 makes a fake cut toward the basket and comes back out. Player 3 seals his man away from the basket, and 4 fakes and looks for him underneath. Player 5 works for offensive rebound position. Player 1 is the long rebounder, and 2 is the protector (see figure 3.11).

Player 4 has another option when receiving the ball—a pass to 5, who flashes into the key. This option may take priority if 4 senses that 3 is not open and is aware that 5 has an inside advantage (see figure 3.12). In fact, because 5's defender will likely be sagging toward the strong side, anticipating the pass from 1 to 3, 5 can make good use of the spacing to flash into the key at the correct time. When he sees 4 looking 5's way, 2 fakes in and moves to the wing to create the 4, 2, 5 triangle, in case 5 is overplayed and he is needed to get the ball in.

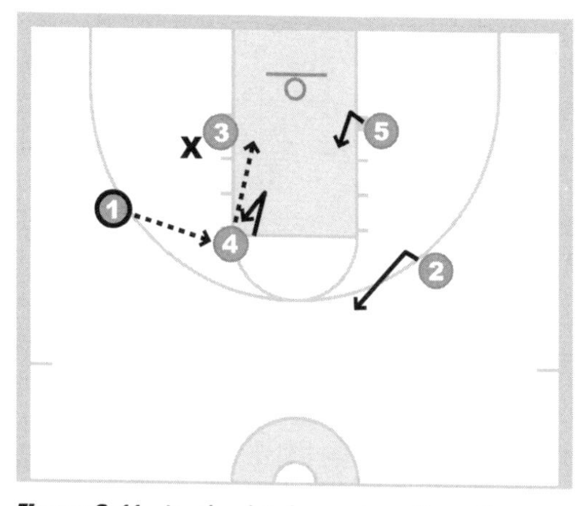

Figure 3.11 In the high-post option, 1 uses the triangle to get the ball to 3 via 4.

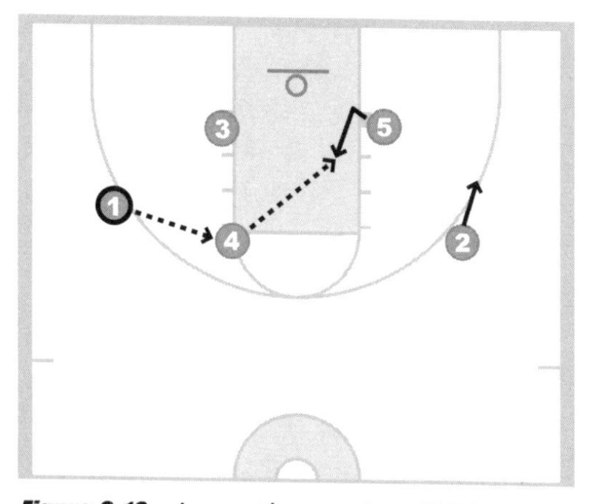

Figure 3.12 As another option, if 3 is not open, 4 can pass to 5.

- **Option 3: Out to the guard**—1 passes to 2, who has watched him explore the first two options without success. However, the rationale for his pass to 2 may be that he sees a better situation on the weak side. Player 2 has faked toward the basket and come back out to the free throw lane extended, above the key and on the strong side. Player 5, seeing the pass from 1 to 2, fakes across the key and comes to the side post, or the weak-side elbow (see figure 3.13). Player 2 passes to 5, takes his defender toward him, and makes the appropriate move to get open. He can receive a handoff pass going over the top, reverse to the basket if his defender anticipates the cut over the top, or pop out for the jump shot if his man goes behind the screen. When he receives the ball in any position, he may make the one-on-one move if he has an advantage. In other words, the side-post game should never be run haphazardly; a legitimate

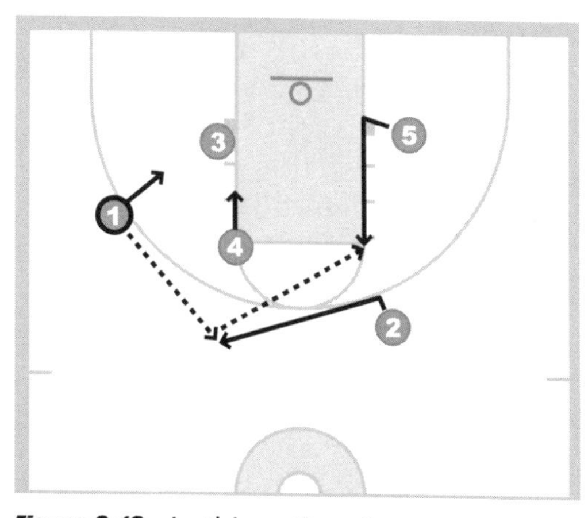

Figure 3.13 In this option, 1 passes to 2, who has faked toward the basket and come back out; then 2 passes to 5.

attempt to score quickly should occur each time. Side-post play is more easily defended if weak-side action is not generating scoring opportunities, allowing weak-side defenders to sag and help. But near perfect timing is essential. Player 3 and 4 set a double screen for 1 on the weak side, with 3 on the bottom side (see figure 3.14). Player 1 should come off the screen when 5 has explored the side-post game and is ready to pass.

Of course, the possibility of an attempt to score from the side-post game always exists, in which case the double screen serves as a method for rebounding balance, if a shot is taken, or for recreating triangles, if it is not (see figure 3.15).

- **Option 4: Dribble up**—As 2 comes to the strong side to receive the pass and is overplayed, 1 dribbles directly and aggressively at him. Player 2 makes a reverse cut down the lane and toward the basket, looking for the backdoor pass and the score. Players 3 and 4 set a double screen, with 3 on the low side (his foot closest to the baseline is on the block). It is likely that 5's defender will be distracted by the cutting guard. At the moment he turns his head, 5 sprints off the double screen for the pass from 1 and the open shot (see figure 3.16).

The positioning of the guards, forwards, and center in the previous example of the four-options set may seem awkward, especially in the case of the post player who is coming off a double screen for

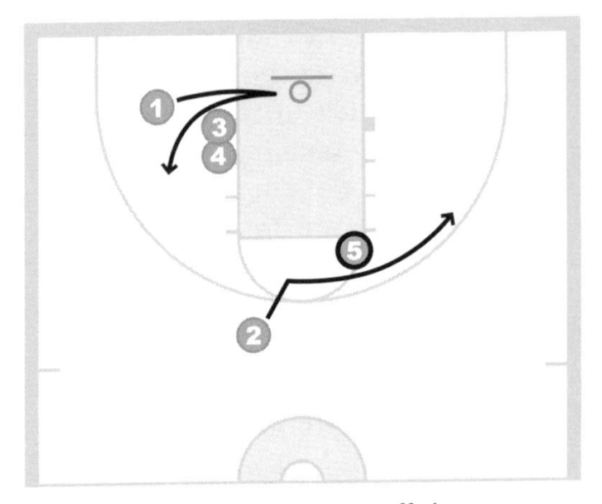

Figure 3.14 Player 1 comes off the screen set by 3 and 4 and becomes available.

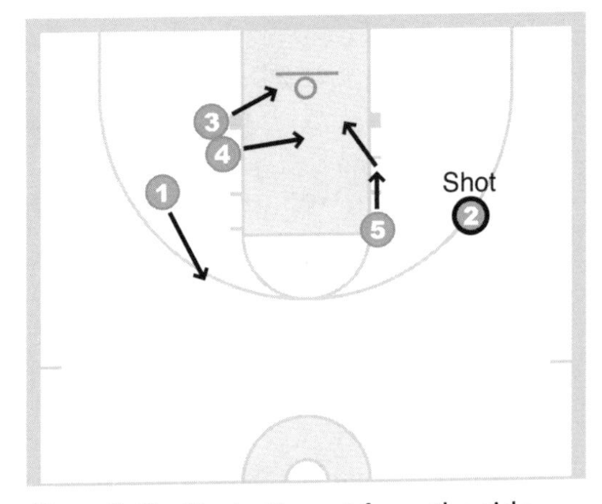

Figure 3.15 Shot attempt from the side-post game.

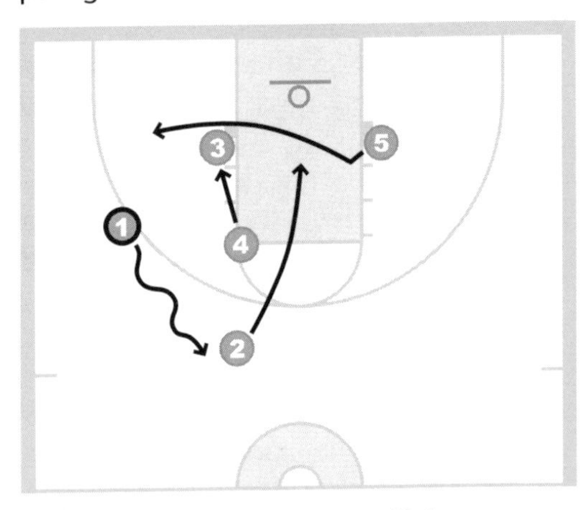

Figure 3.16 Player 5 comes off the screen to get open for the pass and shot, his defender likely distracted by 2's cut.

an outside shot. Many coaches prefer to have their center remain in the post area. The four-options set occurs in every play and option. Employed options should be selected based on personnel.

ADDITIONAL OPTIONS

The following options of the guard-to-center pass were all used by UCLA players. Few were first used during a game; most emerged as good options during the practice sessions where the players were free to improvise and invent creative ways to score. The reserves (those who did not see game time but played a lot of defense during practice) were well versed in the UCLA high-post offense and were therefore well prepared to divert the play when playing defense. It was during times when the defense anticipated the play and tried to put a monkey wrench in it that the regulars adjusted and learned new ways to execute.

Guards Cross and Flare

Limiting guard movement to flaring (after the pass to the high post and the forwards reversing) will result in neither one being open for very long; the defensive guards will quickly adjust to a pattern or routine. Taking advantage of this, a variety of guard cuts, all based on reading the defense, must be available to keep the defense honest.

Player 1 passes to 2, who passes to 5 at the high post. With 2 making his cut first, both guards head toward the center and, instead of flaring, cross in front of the center to the other side of the floor they started from (see figure 3.17). The same options are then available.

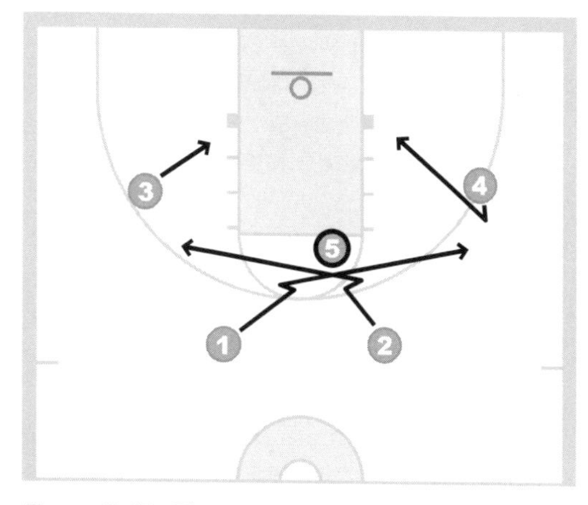

Figure 3.17 The two guards cross in front of the center to the opposite sides of the floor.

Guards Cut Down the Lane

This option should be used occasionally. After the passes from 1 to 2 to 5, the guards immediately cross above the center, with the nonpassing guard cutting behind the passing guard. If the defensive guards are shadowing their assignments instead of moving to the perimeter ahead of them, the offensive guards are wise to cut down the lane (see figure 3.18). As always, guard movement follows the forwards reversing sharply and looking for the backdoor pass from the center, with the center looking over his shoulder for the strong-side forward first. After receiving the pass, the center pivots to look for an open forward or guard inside or the one-on-one move.

If 3 and 4 are good inside offensive players, 1 and 2 should cut down the lane and come out to the wings around the forwards as they are maneuvering for inside position (see figure 3.19). A screen may not be available as the forwards are reversing and posting up. Nevertheless, there are plenty of obstacles for the guards to use to get open on the wings. If they sense a mismatch in size or skill, the flexibility of the offense allows either of the guard and forward combinations to decide who will post up.

Whether forwards screen guards or guards screen forwards, the center's first look is for inside players getting open. Skilled screeners learn to "slip screen," moving into the lane before the screen is completely set because they see an opening. An opening to move into the key can be created when the defender guarding the player using the screen goes over the top of the screen to catch up to his assignment. This cut leaves a momentary space for the forward to move (see figure 3.20). Therefore, the center's first passing option is always inside to the forwards. The second option is to the guards, who have moved to the perimeter, completing the triangles.

After a pass to the perimeter, 5 cuts down the lane, calling for the ball, and screens for the weak-side low-post player, who fakes baseline and comes to the free throw line area. The offense is, once again, in the four-options set.

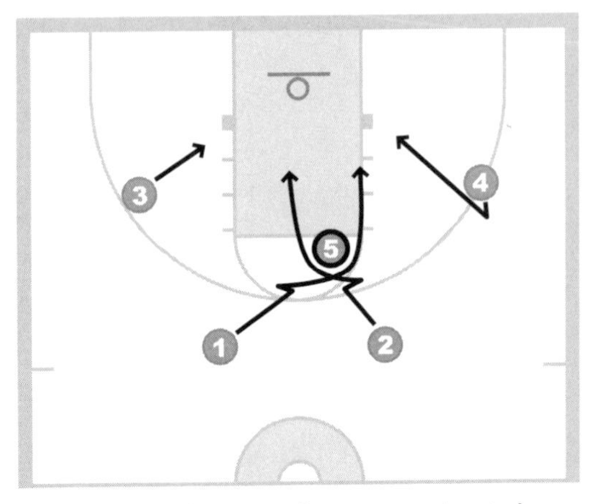

Figure 3.18 The guards cross and cut down the lane.

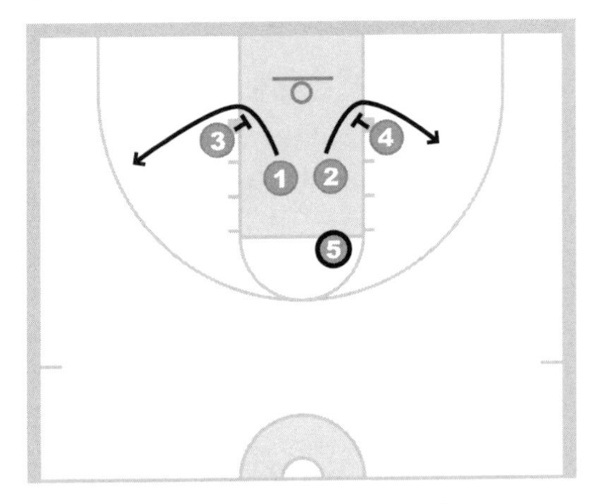

Figure 3.19 After cutting down the lane, the guards come out to the wings around the forwards.

Figure 3.20 An opening into the key makes the forward available for the pass.

One Guard Cuts Down the Lane

Because a decision to cut down the lane is determined by how the defense is playing the guard, it is very possible, and permissible, for one guard to cut and the other to stay on the perimeter. Player 1 passes to 2, who passes to 5 at the high post. Because he delivered the pass, 2 cuts toward the center first. If he senses that his defender is anticipating a cross by moving toward the opposite side of the court, he cuts toward the basket, looking for a pass from 5. Player 1 did not sense the same opportunity and stays out as the protector, but he keeps his defender busy by cutting toward the weak side. As always, both forwards have reversed. Player 4 may elect to down screen for 2, who uses the screen to get open on the perimeter (see figure 3.21). The offense is now in the four-options set.

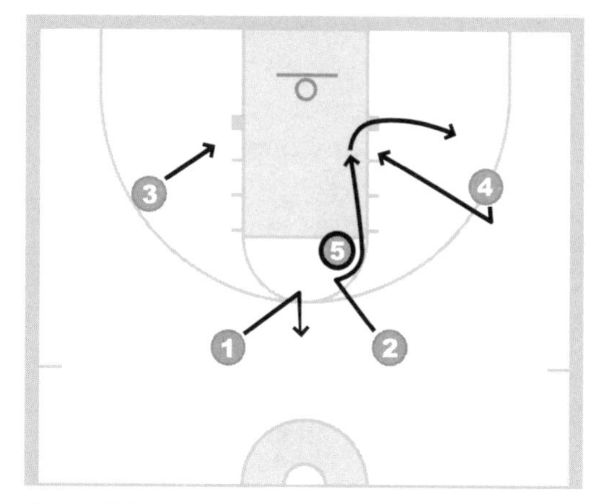

Figure 3.21 Player 2 senses an opportunity and cuts toward the basket.

Forward and Guard Screen

The flexibility of the high-post offense allows for a good shooting forward to get open. Player 1 passes to 2, who passes to 5, who looks for the backdoor pass to 4. Player 4 continues through the lane and comes off a screen set by 3. Player 2 screens for 1, who cuts to the opposite low-post area vacated by 4. Player 1 moves out as a protector (see figure 3.22).

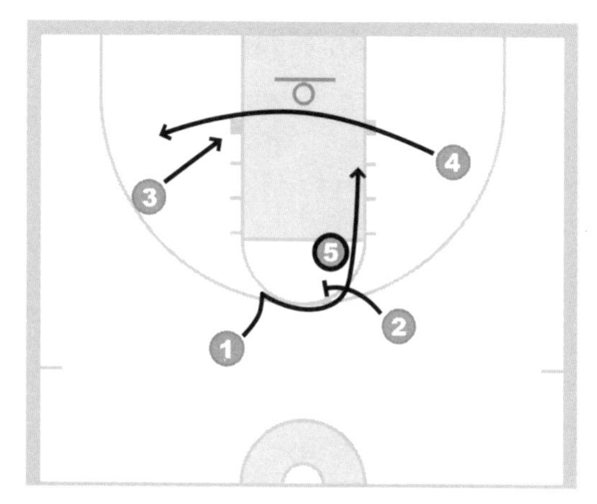

Figure 3.22 Players 3 and 2 screen for 4 and 1.

If 5 passes to 4, he interchanges with 1, and the offense is in the four-options set (see figure 3.23). Player 5 may also choose to pass

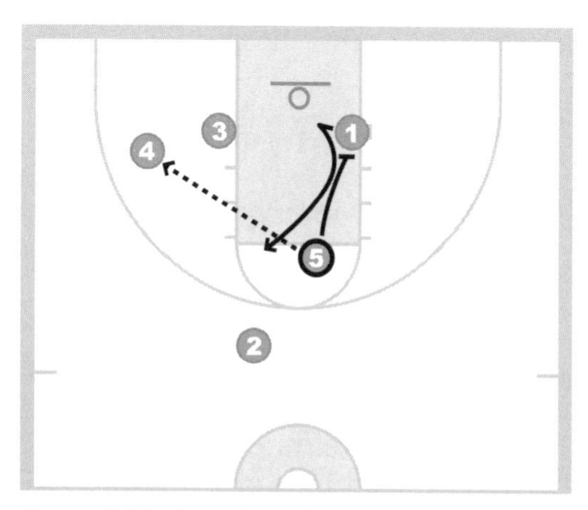

Figure 3.23 In this option, 5 passes to 4 and interchanges with 1.

to 3, who may be open in the lane after the screen, or before it if he decides to slip screen.

If 5 decides to pass to neither forward, he passes the ball out to 2, moves down the lane, and screens for 1, who comes to the free throw line area (see figure 3.24). Simultaneously, 4 turns toward the low post and screens for 3, who comes out for the outside shot. Player 4 should time his move so 1 receives the pass from 2 just prior to 3 being open on the perimeter.

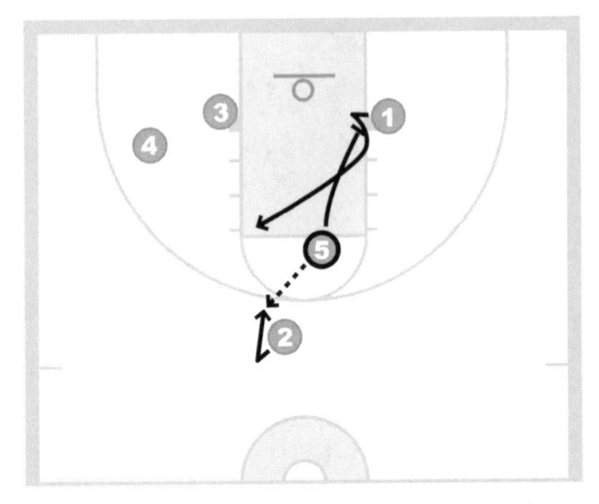

Figure 3.24 If 5 doesn't pass to 3 or 4, he passes to 2, then screens for 1, who gets available for the pass.

Forwards Cross

When 3 and 4 reverse, after the pass to 5, the two forwards may cross and assume opposite low-post sides (see figure 3.25). The guards may flare, cross, or cut down the lane. However, both guards need not do the exact same thing. One may cross while the other remains up top. The same is true for the forwards. Because making plays is all about reading the defense and reacting, the forwards are not limited to both crossing. One may stay on his side while the other comes around him to the other corner.

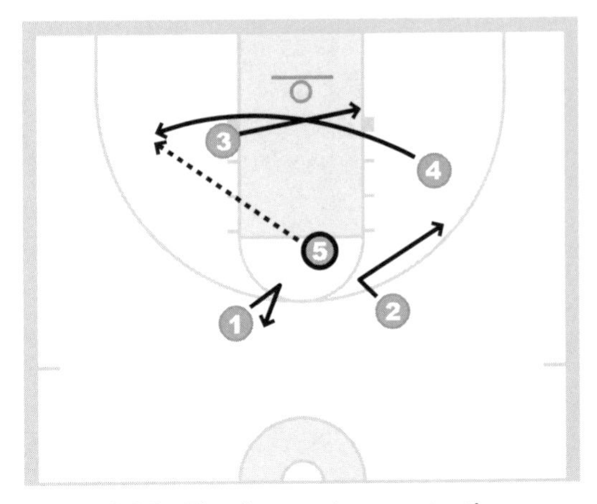

Figure 3.25 The forwards cross to the opposite low-post sides.

FORWARDS AT THE FOREFRONT

The guard-to-guard-to-center plays worked well for the 1970 and 1971 teams led by All-American forwards Sidney Wicks and Curtis Rowe. Both were excellent post players and weak-side rebounders, though Wicks was a step quicker. If the guard-to-guard pass was made in the left-to-right direction, we preferred to have Wicks line up on the right side to exploit his quickness on the backdoor, but if Rowe was there it didn't make much difference; that left Wicks to post up on the weak side, which was probably our highest percentage option.

Wicks had a knack for keeping his defender busy on the weak-side block, deceiving him into thinking he was cutting across the key or simply not interested in scoring. But we made it a point to hit the high post whenever possible and look for Wicks on the duck move. Once in possession of the ball, he used a variety of fakes and an assortment of moves for easy scores. His favorite was a quick pivot for a fall-away jump shot. He often followed it with a pivot, shot fake, and drive for the layup. If double-teamed, he demonstrated his unselfishness and found the open man.

© Corbis

When Sidney Wicks drove to the basket, he usually scored, no matter who was guarding him. Here, Sidney scores against the seven-foot-two Artis Gilmore in the 1970 championship game.

When the center on that squad, Steve Patterson, passed to the wing and then cut down the lane calling for the ball, Wicks or Rowe would pop up to the high post. If the defensive forward and center switched on the down screen, Steve was left with a mismatch inside, while Wicks or Rowe had a quickness advantage at the free throw line area.

Occasionally, after reversing the ball, Wicks would continue through the lane and come off a screen set by Rowe. Wicks was very effective on the wing, especially if he had a quickness advantage as he usually did. Together, that forward tandem, teaming up within the structure of the offense, was very tough to defend.

The guard-to-center pass was perhaps used even more when Steve Patterson took a rest and Wicks played the center position. Wicks was quick to discern if he had a quickness advantage over his defender, and he often caused havoc for the defense with shot fakes and quick drives for layups.

CLOSING POINTS

The forwards post up, guards flare is the primary play, but guards and forwards should be free—in fact, encouraged—to improvise by reading the defense and making the appropriate cut to get open. Emphasize this creativity in practice sessions, where effective maneuvers will be discovered through exposure to likely defensive tactics and through trial and error.

Players should take advantage of what is open or they will become methodical. Intelligent, not foolish, gambling is essential to prevent the offense from becoming too predictable and easy to defend. Some players may be inclined to take too many liberties with this freedom, but their spontaneity should not be squelched completely. The offense simply won't function well if limited to preprogrammed, robotic movements that can be scouted and stopped by the opponents. The potential for surprise is a critical element in this attack, because it forces opponents to defend all options, both the known and the unknown.

CHAPTER 4

GUARD TO GUARD TO FORWARD: OUTSIDE CUT

Another play in the high-post offense is designed to free the forward (3) for an open shot from the baseline. In this case, deception and a double screen are the primary means of springing 3 from the defense. Faking and timing are of utmost importance in making this play in the offense work.

BASE PLAY

The play starts with 1 passing to 2, who quickly passes to 4. Player 2 cuts toward 4 and continues around him, ending up close to, but not on, the low-post block (see figure 4.1). He must get there quickly because we don't want 4 to hold the ball for very long. Player 5 works to get open at the high post, causing 3's defender to think 3 is going to post up in the key. But the play calls for 1 to come back to get the ball at the free throw lane extended above the key and on the strong side.

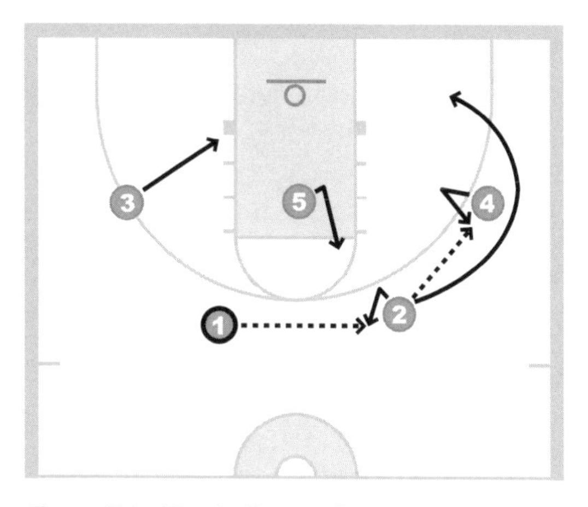

Figure 4.1 The ball goes from 1 to 2 to 4, and 2 goes around 4 to very near the low-post block.

Player 4 passes to 1, fakes a down screen for 2, and cuts over the top of 5, calling for the ball in the key (see figure 4.2). Player 3 remains fairly stationary, allowing his man to be distracted by 4's cut down the middle. Player 1 fakes a lob pass to 4 to help distract 3's defender even more.

Immediately after the fake, 5 heads down to the low block where he is met by 2 to set the double screen. Player 2 will be on the baseline side of the screen with his lowest foot on the block. Player 3 knows exactly where the screen will be set.

Figure 4.2 Player 4 passes to 1, then cuts over the top of 5, into the key.

Player 3 takes one step up the lane to make his man think he is flashing in the key and then makes a hard cut toward the block and the double screen. If the timing is perfect, he should arrive moments after the screen is formed. Because he faked toward the ball and because the play appeared to involve a lob for 4, 3 should be open when he comes off the screen if his defender is distracted. Without telegraphing the direction of the pass, 1 passes to 3 for the shot (see figure 4.3).

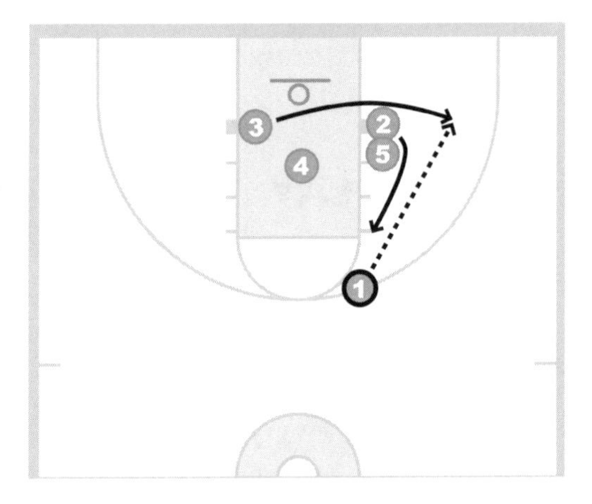

Figure 4.3 Player 3 deceives his defender and gets over to the other side past the double screen to receive the ball from 1.

If 3's defender gets wind of the play and follows 3 to the double screen, 3 makes the appropriate move to create as much space between himself and his man as possible. In other words, if 3's man goes over the top of the screen, 3 will flatten to the baseline. If the defender goes under the screen, 3 will move more toward the wing or even curl around the screen into the lane. When 3 passes the screen, 2 comes around 5 (in front) and comes to the ball-side high post, creating a strong-side triangle. But he must "pop the stack" at the appropriate time. Too soon and 3 won't be able to pass into the post (5). Too late and the offense is stagnated. After 3's shot, 4, 5, and 2 take inside rebounding assignments; 3, the shooter, becomes the long rebounder; and 1 is the protector.

ADDITIONAL OPTIONS

The flexibility of the high-post offense allows for several additional options, including a post-up opportunity for a forward and for a guard, a side-post game, an outside shot for a guard, and a backdoor. Some of the following options are available after the forward has come off the double screen. However, some occur before. Defenses bent on stopping the main play may find themselves vulnerable to these options.

Weak-Side Forward Inside Flash

If 3 is aware that 4 is a good post-up player, he may opt to pass up his shot if he thinks his teammate has an inside advantage. When 3 comes off the screen and receives the ball, 2 comes around 5 to the high post. Player 3 passes to 2. When the ball is on the way to 2, 4 cuts away, faking a cut across the bottom of the key, then changes direction and cuts in front of his defender (see figure 4.4).

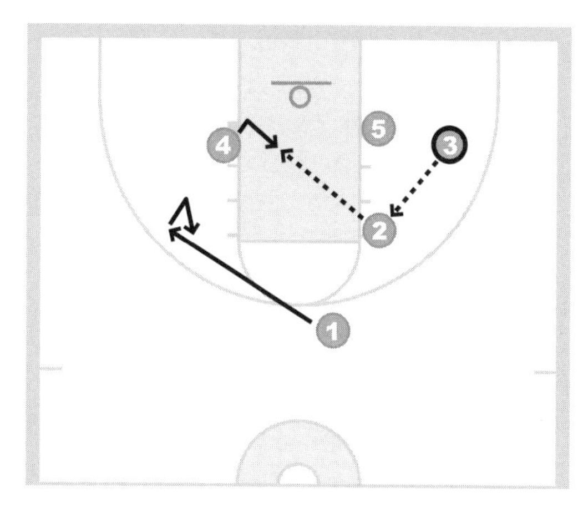

Figure 4.4 Player 4 gets a good inside advantage in the key, receiving the pass from 2 for the shot.

Simultaneous with 3's pass to 2, 1 moves to the weak side to form a triangle with 5 and 2. This is especially useful if 2 needs help getting the ball to 4. As 2 is looking for 4 inside, 1 prevents his defender from helping down on 4 by cutting in and then out, calling for the ball (see figure 4.4). Player 5 keeps his man occupied by flashing toward the ball on the strong side.

Side-Post Game

Player 3 passes the ball out to 1, who has faked toward the key and made a hard cut to the ball at about the free throw lane extended. Player 4 makes a fake cut toward the strong side, changes pace and direction, and comes hard to the weak-side elbow. Player 1 passes to 4, takes his defender directly at him, reads his man, and makes the appropriate cut to get open. It may be a cut down the lane or over the top for a handoff (see figure 4.5).

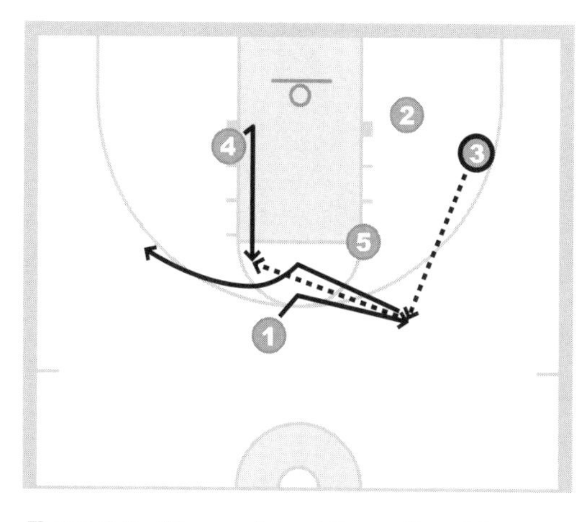

Figure 4.5 Players 3 and 1 run the side-post game, then 1 passes to 4 and gets open.

A skilled forward has many options at the side post. If he's overplayed when he catches the ball, he drops his inside leg and drives for the hoop. If his man anticipates a handoff and helps on 1, he drives. If 4 does not hand off to 1, and 1 flares out to the wing, 4 can pass the ball to 1 and cut for the basket—a "give-and-go." If none of the side-post options are used, 4 can pass the ball to 5, 2, or 3, who has come out as the protector.

Guard Post-Up

The play initiates as usual with 1 passing to 2, who passes to 4 and goes around 4. However, because he is a strong inside player, 2 continues to the low post. The play is for 2 to receive the ball at the block and score. Player 2's movement to the low post is a signal for 3 that he will not be coming off a double screen on that side, although he won't give that away. To prevent his man—and 3's man—from helping, 5 creates good weak-side action by making a cut toward the weak-side block, calling for the ball and screening for 3, who comes to the strong-side high post. Player 4 passes to 2 at the low post (see figure 4.6).

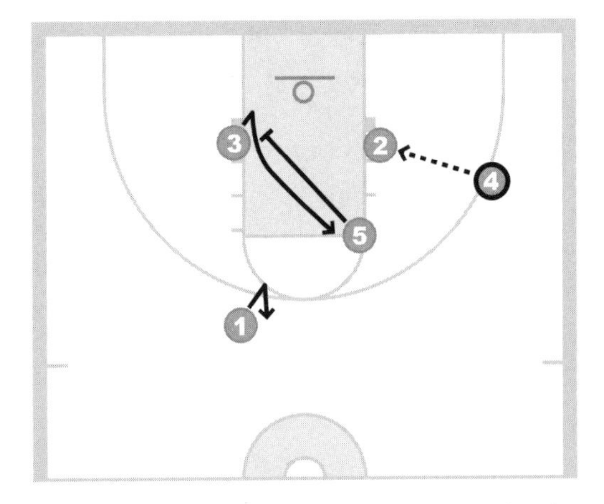

Figure 4.6 Players 5 and 3 distract defenders with cuts and a screen, allowing 2 to receive the pass at the block.

If, by chance, 2 is not open, 4 can pass to 3, who looks for 5 flashing into the key, or to 2 if he has sealed his man away from the basket.

Another method of getting the ball to 2 is via 1. Player 4 passes out to 1 and cuts over the top of 5 as in the main play. Player 2 heads toward the block as if to set the double screen with 5, but he turns and looks at 1. While 2 is moving to the block, 1 takes one quick dribble toward the wing and delivers a pass to 2 the moment he turns toward him (see figure 4.7). Player 5, instead of helping set the double screen, cuts away to set a screen for 3 on the weak-side block.

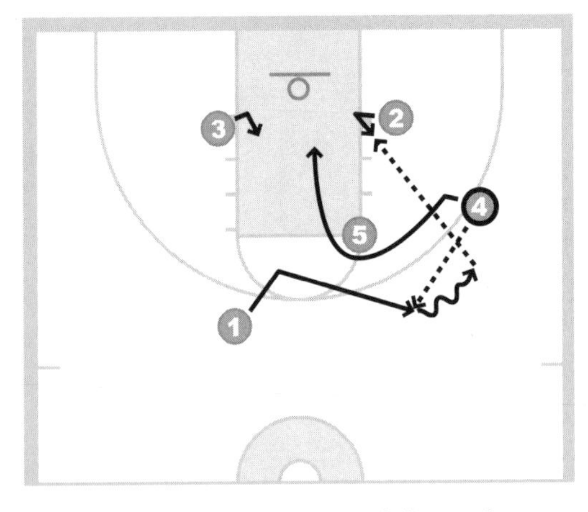

Figure 4.7 In this option, 4 delivers the ball to 2 via 1.

Down Screen for the Guard

Player 1 passes to 2, who passes to 4 and goes around him to the low-post area. Player 4 passes out to 1, who has cut away and come back. Player 4 fakes a cut over the top of 5, giving the appearance of the main play. Player 4 changes direction toward the strong-side block to screen for 2, who has gone into the key to set his man up for the screen. Player 1 passes to 2, who passes to 4 in the low post (see figure 4.8). Player 4 is careful to turn toward 2 when 2 has the ball, not before. As long as he is facing toward the weak side, his defender will play between him and the basket.

A cunning screener will sense when his defender drops toward the basket, leaving room for him to move into the key, and will "slip the screen," flashing toward the ball before the screen is set.

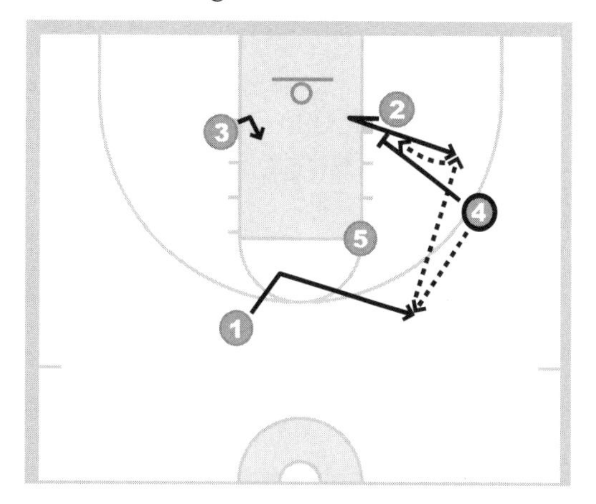

Figure 4.8 Player 4 down screens for 2, to allow him to receive the ball from 1.

Dribble Up

The execution of most of the previous additional options is dependent on the pass from 4 out to 1. Good defensive teams will, sooner or later, deny that pass. If so, and 1 is overplayed, 4 dribbles directly at him. Player 1 reverses to the basket, and a similar situation to the main play occurs. Players 5 and 2 set a double screen for 3 coming baseline from the weak side (see figure 4.9). As in the main play, 3 waits until his man is distracted by 1's reverse cut to head for the double screen.

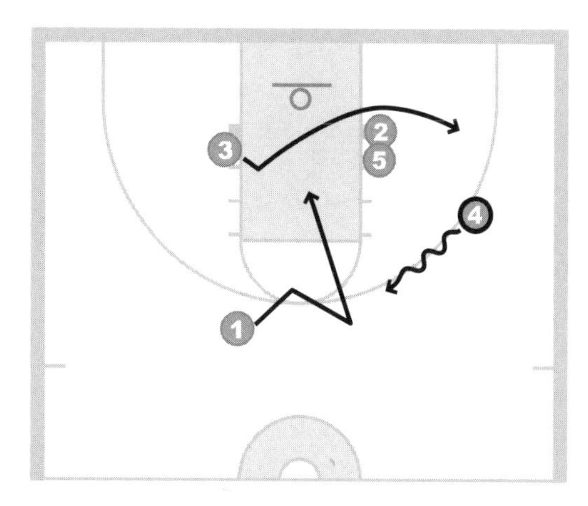

Figure 4.9 The pass from 4 to 1 was impossible because 1 was overplayed, so 1 reverses to the basket and 5 and 2 screen for 3.

Fred Slaughter, Pete Blackman, and Walt Hazzard joined Gary Cunningham and Johnny Green on the Bruin's roster for the 1961 to 1962 season. Although he was six-foot-five, Slaughter could move, pass, and set screens. Blackman was a cunning and creative forward who could read defenses and always seemed to make the quick, appropriate move. Hazzard was a tall guard with exceptional ballhandling, driving, and passing abilities. Cunningham was tall and a great outside shooter, while Green was a tall guard with outstanding and almost unstoppable low-post skills.

Although prospects for the season were promising with such talented players at each position, the challenge was to maximize those respective abilities while still emphasizing team play. The low-post scoring ability of Green and the outside shooting of Cunningham were definite priorities, but the other players' potential contributions could not be ignored. Driving and passing opportunities for Hazzard, one-on-one low-post opportunities for Blackman, and the incredible screening talent of Slaughter had to be incorporated into the offense as viable options.

When Cunningham passed up the jump shot off the double screen and sensed that Blackman had an advantage on the weak-side low post, he passed the ball to Hazzard, who had moved to the strong-side high post. Hazzard then delivered the ball to Blackman, who had flashed into the key.

Another effective and more-used option was Hazzard and Blackman running the side-post game. When Cunningham passed out to Hazzard after coming off the double screen, Hazzard passed to Blackman, who had come up to the weak-side elbow, and received a handoff when he cut over the top of him. Hazzard, a good passer, after receiving the handoff, often completed passes to Blackman when he rolled to the basket. If Blackman chose not to hand off to Hazzard, he was good at the one-on-one move. Blackman also read his own defensive man well, and if his defender was leaning when he received the pass at the high post, he dropped his foot (away from his man) and drove to the basket.

Johnny Green was very difficult for the opposition to defend when he had the ball in the low post. After he made the outside cut, he had the option to go inside and receive the pass from Blackman, aborting Cunningham's use of a double screen.

Blackman was good at the low post, and Green was a decent 15-foot shooter. After Blackman passed the ball out to Hazzard, instead of cutting over the top of Slaughter and setting up Cunningham's cut off the double screen, he sometimes elected to down screen for Green. Always watching the defense for a weakness, Blackman, once or twice a game, noticed his defender dropping toward the basket and "slipped the screen" into the key, receiving the pass from Hazzard for an easy one.

For the main play to work and get Cunningham the ball coming off the double screen, his defender was deceived. Blackman's cut over the top of Slaughter and down the key gave the impression that the Bruins were looking for a play there. Players are trained in team defense—and therefore help defense—and all it took for Cunningham to be open coming off the double screen was for his man to turn his head, for even a fraction of a second, to look at Blackman. The more aggressive Blackman was, the better decoy and distraction he became. Of course, good pass fakes by the guards helped set the play in motion.

Johnny Green had a knack for getting inside the defense from the low-post area. Here, he leaves his defender completely helpless.

CLOSING POINTS

For any play to work, it must have some element of surprise. In the previous example, that surprise was created by the play. But other means of making opponents think one thing while you are thinking something completely different are available. For example, individual initiative within the framework of the offense is crucial to long-term success. When players have freedom to read their defenders and explore opportunities, the offense graduates from robotic and methodical to unpredictable and diverse. Another means to creating surprise is faking, especially faking the pass. Defenders are trained to follow the basketball. When the ball is on the wing, weak-side defenders sag toward the strong side. A convincing pass fake from the top of the key to a wing, for example, will no doubt move the feet of defenders or at least make them turn their heads. Pass fakes are essential to deception, execution, and getting the shot where you want it. It was Hazzard's pass fake to Blackman that often froze Cunningham's man.

CHAPTER 5

GUARD TO GUARD TO FORWARD: UCLA CUT

The 1968 to 1969 season ended with a fifth NCAA championship flag being raised to the rafters of Pauley Pavilion. And the next year began with the daunting task of trying to fill the shoes of three departed starters from that title-winning team: Lewis Alcindor, Lynn Shackelford, and Kenny Heitz.

Without a dominant inside center, we shelved the high-low offense and returned to the high-post offense in preparing for the 1969 to 1970 season. Given the team's talents, we decided to make low-post play the priority and to let outside shooting come as a result of outside defenders dropping down to help. Many plays and options were suited to this group, but we needed to select a main play within the offense's structure. That play was the pass from guard to guard to forward, followed by the UCLA cut.

BASE PLAY

As with most plays, the UCLA cut can be run to either side, though we slightly favored the right because post players are generally right handed and, therefore, more experienced and effective on the left block. It is best to assign each forward—and the guards for that matter—a primary side of the floor (the side where they are most effective). Although the offense is designed to direct the ball to a specific side, in the course of reading the defense and using options, that may change. But, for the main play, players should be positioned in the areas where they operate best.

The play is initiated by 1 bringing the ball into the frontcourt aggressively and driving directly at his defender. Player 2 fakes in and comes back out two to three feet farther from the basket than 1. Without hesitation, unless 2 is overplayed, 1 passes to 2. Player 4 has faked a cut to the basket and comes out to the wing. Player 2 passes to 4. Player 5, who has faked away and come back before the pass, prepares to screen by turning his back to 2. Player 2 uses 5's screen to get open in the key or at the low post. This is the signature move of the UCLA cut. Player 3 quickly moves down to the weak-side post, keeping his defender busy so he can't help on 2 (see figure 5.1).

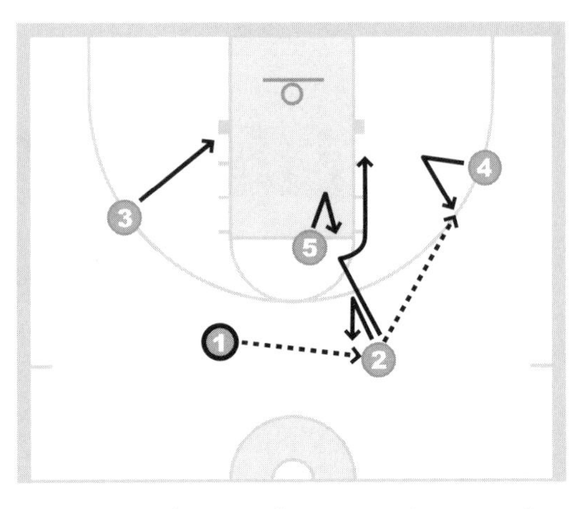

Figure 5.1 The pass from guard to guard to forward happens, and then 2 makes the UCLA cut by using 5's screen to get open at the low post.

Player 2 using 5's screen is a very important component of the play for two reasons. First, it is a good opportunity for the guard to get open for an easy shot. More important, it is the initial vertical penetrating move by the offense, and if done correctly, it will cause the defense to drop toward the basket, allowing a pass to the high post. Coaches must emphasize that each time the UCLA cut is run, the guard should be doing his very best to get open for a score; at no time should it be reduced to a move where the guard is simply going through the motions. Haphazard UCLA cuts hinder the ball from moving to the high post because the center's defender is not tempted to help prevent the layup.

Because of its importance, the UCLA cut must be perfected. As mentioned, the entire responsibility for getting open rests on the shoulders of the guard. The center has turned his back, and to prevent picking up an offensive foul, he is stationary. Above anything, the guard is looking for a layup. He looks for the pass from the forward. The forward never holds the ball over his head; he fakes down and usually makes the two-handed overhead pass to the cutting guard.

But a layup for the guard will not happen often. Most coaches teach their defenders to jump to the basketball and go to the ball side of a high-post screen, staying between the ball and their assignment. The guard takes his man directly toward the center (5) to the point where he almost touches him. At that point, he reads the defense and makes his move. If his man leans toward the key, he fakes that way and cuts over the top, along the side of the lane, looking for the pass for the layup. If his man plays toward the ball, he fakes that way and cuts behind the center, into the key, looking for the lob. If his man jumps behind the screen, the guard pops out looking for the jump shot.

If 4 does not pass to 2, he looks for 5 at the high post. Immediately after 2 uses his screen, 5 follows 2 for one step and then comes back out hard, no farther than 17 feet from the basket. He must time his cut so that he will be open after 4 has given 2 a good look. He receives the basketball, reverse pivots to maintain vision of the key area, and immediately looks for 3. Player 3 has set his man up by faking a cut across the bottom of the key and has changed direction to move into the middle of the key in front of his man (see figure 5.2). Player 5 executes one of two passes: the one-handed push pass or the overhead pass. If using the one-handed push pass, he may use an air or bounce pass. Regardless of which pass he employs, he pass fakes to set it up.

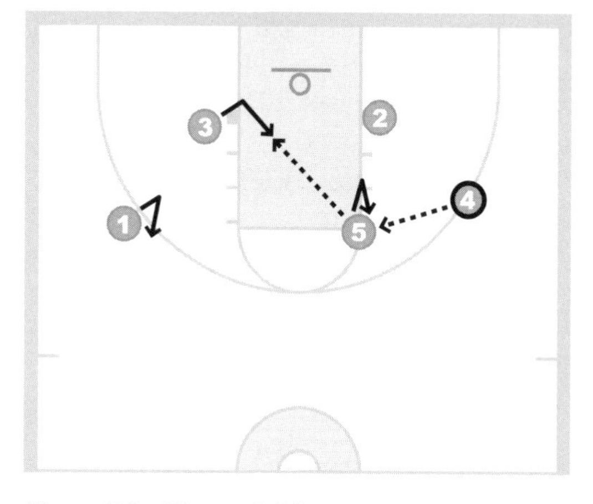

Figure 5.2 Player 5 fakes in and cuts out, just in time to receive 4's pass. Then 3 gets into the middle of the key for the pass from 5.

After passing to 5, 4 takes one step toward 5 and then changes direction toward the block, where he screens for 2 by turning with his backside toward the basket. Because both players know the screen will be set on the block, 2 can set his man up accordingly by faking into the key and cutting to the perimeter on a line crossing the bottom of the block (see figure 5.3). Player 5 passes to 2 for the jump shot and makes a cut toward the basket.

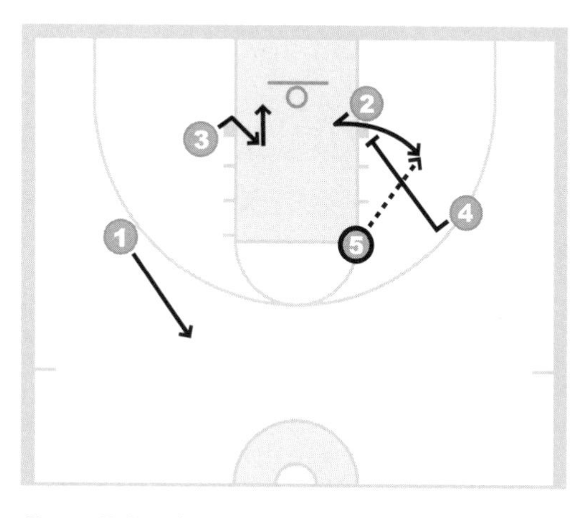

Figure 5.3 Player 2 cuts to the perimeter for the pass and a jump shot.

The weak-side low-post player can do a lot to make the pass to 2 successful. Not only will his flash into the key draw attention, but a cut up the side of the lane will also. And, if 2 receives the ball for the shot, the weak-side forward can quickly reverse and obtain excellent offensive rebounding position.

When looking for 3 in the deep post, 5 may see a defensive overplay. Against prepared defenses, this will happen. Player 1 has moved over to the left side to create a triangle and has faked in and come out to be an outside shooting threat, occupying his man so he can't help on 3. Player 3 seals his man toward 5, and 5 passes to 1, who looks for 3 inside.

Player 4's first passing option is to 2 using 5's screen, and his second option is to 5 at the high post. His third option is to 1, who fakes in and comes out to the strong-side free throw lane extended. Player 4 passes to 1. Player 3 fakes across the bottom of the key and comes to the side post. Player 1 passes to 3. Player 1 cuts directly toward 3, and if his defender plays toward the key, 1 comes over the top and looks for a handoff pass from 3. Meanwhile, 4 and 5 move to the weak-side block to set a double screen for 2 (see figure 5.4). This screen must be timed perfectly; 2 must be open when 3 is ready to pass. If 3 is still occupied in the side-post game, the double screen is useless. It is 2's responsibility to make his move at the correct time. Of course, if 3 hands off to 1, there will be no pass to 2. Nevertheless, 2 comes off the screen to the weak-side wing and is now the protector if a shot is taken from the strong side.

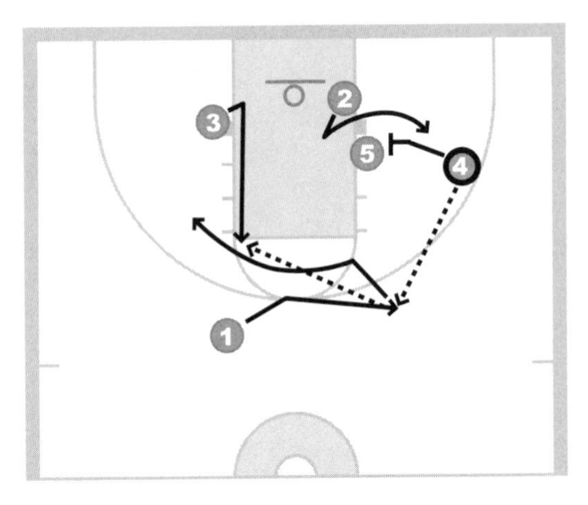

Figure 5.4 The ball gets to 3 via 1, and 1 comes over the top looking for a handoff from 3.

ADDITIONAL OPTIONS

As with every primary play in the offense, we have several options off the UCLA cut. All are viable alternatives depending on the defense's coverage and the offense's personnel at any point in the contest.

Guard Post-Up

A strong post-up guard may require a longer look into the post after he has used the center's screen. Whether he cuts in front of the center or behind (for the lob), the guard (2) enters the low-post area facing the baseline but turns toward the ball while making contact with his defender. Player 4 passes to 2. Player 5 cuts down the lane, looking for a backdoor pass from 2, and then down screens for 3, who comes to the high post (see figure 5.5). This action will occupy weak-side defenders, preventing them from assisting the posting guard's defender.

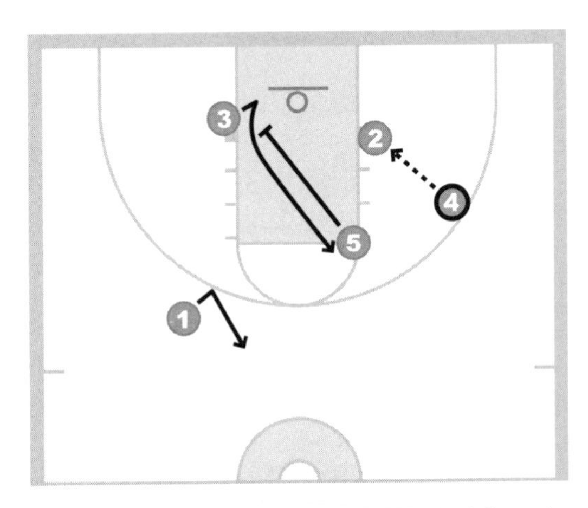

Figure 5.5 Player 4 passes to 2, and 5 and 3 switch places to distract defenders.

Guard Pop-Out

Reading his defensive man, the cutting guard has more than one option on the UCLA cut; instead of going to the low post, he can pop out for the jump shot if his defensive man goes behind the high-post screen. If he does, the strong-side forward can cut to the basket, and the center remains as a screener (see figure 5.6). The weak-side forward flashes into the key, and the weak-side guard cuts away and back to the ball in case he is needed to get the ball to the forward.

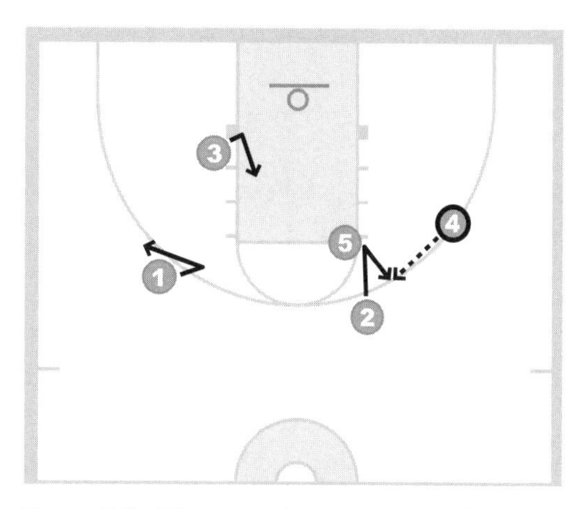

Figure 5.6 The guard pops out for the jump shot.

The guard pop-out is a defensive read. Coaches should emphasize that all players, especially without the basketball, must read and react at all times and in all plays and options. Players must be taught and encouraged to break the pattern when they see an extracurricular opportunity.

Ball Screen

When running the side-post game, the weak-side forward can elect to ball screen instead of receiving the ball at the high post. Player 3 continues out and sets a screen with his back to the middle of the floor (see figure 5.7). Player 1 reads the defense and has several options: driving down the middle if his defender anticipates him going off the screen, coming off the screen, and turning the corner to the basket, or coming off the screen and coming back if his man jumps toward the sideline. The double screen set by 5 and 4 is set as before, but 2, who comes off that screen, must see the play and time his cut accordingly.

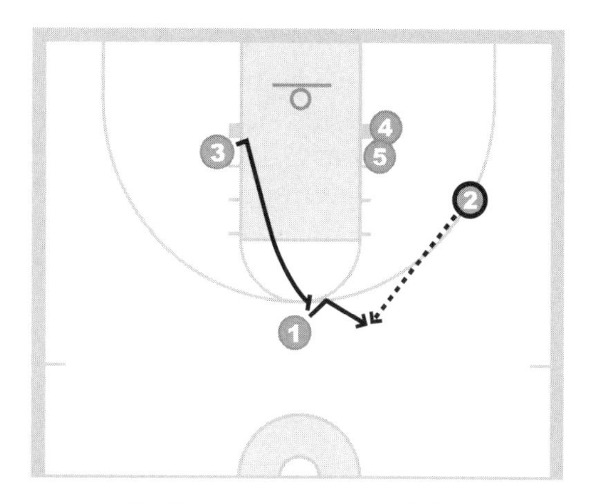

Figure 5.7 Player 3 screens, which gives 1 several options.

Center Post-Up

At the discretion of the center, he may cut to the strong-side block anytime after the guard-to-guard-to-forward pass has been made. He may do so because he senses that his man is cheating toward the inside and leaving a direct lane open to the low post, or because he believes he has a mismatch in size or talent. Player 4 passes to 5 at the low post; 4 and 2 may exchange, split the post, or remain where they are (see figure 5.8). No screening or interchanging is done by 1 and 3 because we want to keep the shooting guard on the perimeter and the forward on the weak-side block.

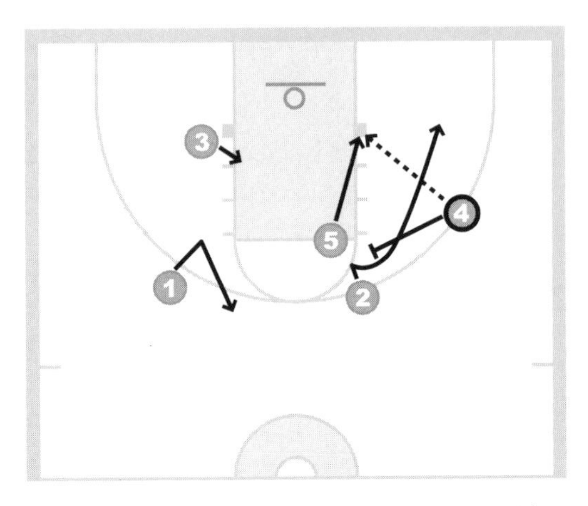

Figure 5.8 Player 5 cuts to the strong-side block and receives the pass from 4.

Side-Post Game

After the UCLA cut, when 4 passes the ball out to 1, 3 comes to the side post to help 1 run the side-post game (see figure 5.9). Player 1 passes to 3 and takes his defender directly toward him, forcing the defender to choose whether he will play to the inside or outside. The defensive man will most often play the inside, protecting against the handoff for the direct drive to the basket. Player 1 will cut over the top to receive the handoff and will have either a jump shot or a drive. Player 3 can roll to the basket or pop out for a return pass and jump shot.

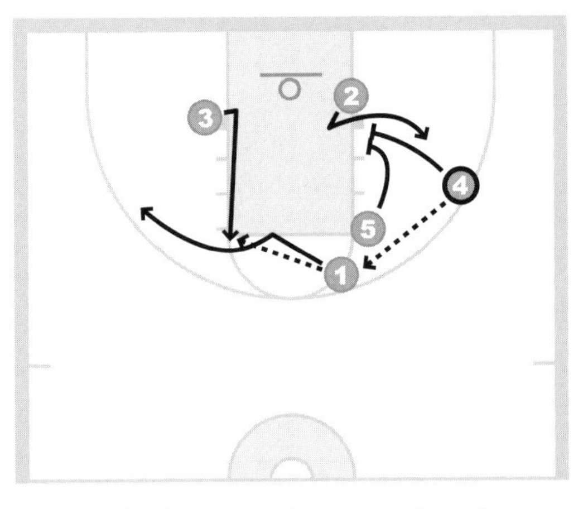

Figure 5.9 After the UCLA cut, 3 and 1 run the side-post game.

One-on-One for the Forward

For a quick forward who can also finish a drive, the side-post game is ideal. Player 1 passes to 3, who has faked away and come to the side post on the weak side. If his defender is overplaying the pass he just received, 3 immediately drops his leg, turns, and drives. Because the other three players are executing a double screen on the other side, weak-side defenders should not be able to help on 3's drive. If 1 does not receive the handoff pass, 3 reverse turns, faces his opponent, and makes the appropriate fake or shot (see figure 5.10). As 1 is passing him, 3 can also fake the handoff, turn, and drive down the lane. This play can be effective as a sideline out-of-bounds play or a play used at the end of the first half or the end of a game if enough seconds remain on the game clock.

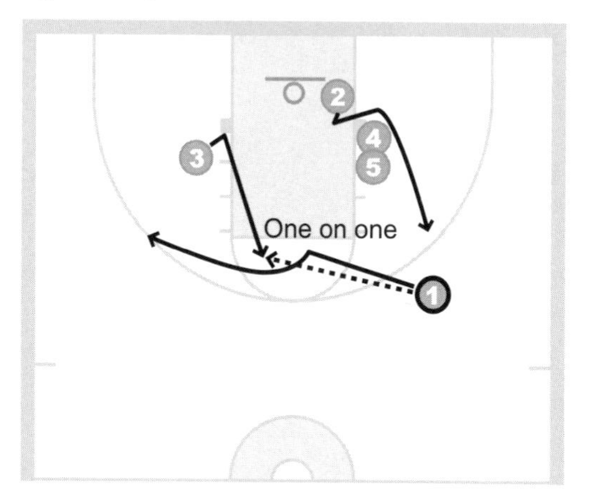

Figure 5.10 Players 2, 4, and 5 execute the double screen, drawing weak-side defenders away from 3's drive.

Inside-Out One-on-One for the Forward

This play provides the weak-side forward with a one-on-one situation and an opportunity to drive to his right.

Player 2 begins the play by passing to 1, who passes to 3 on the left wing. Player 1 makes the UCLA cut. Player 5 slides down the lane to the low-post block (see figure 5.11). Player 1 moves toward the weak side. Player 4 cuts down to the weak-side low post. Player 2 moves to the strong side, making the defense think the ball will be passed back out.

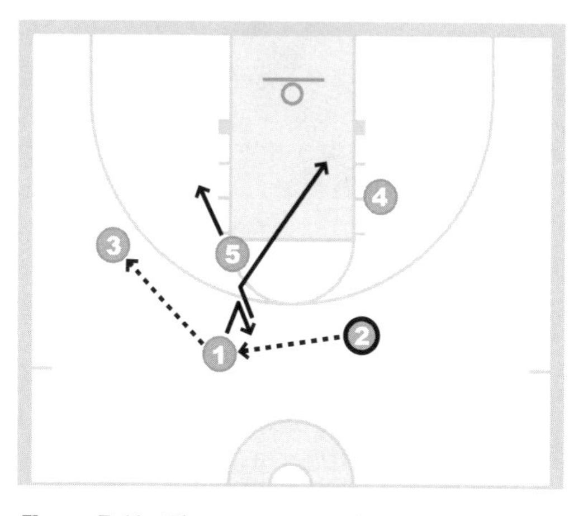

Figure 5.11 The pass goes from 2 to 1 to 3, then 1 makes the UCLA cut.

Player 3 passes to 5. The entire defense will drop toward the basket. Player 1 comes back to the ball, cutting below 5 and looking for a handoff pass. At that moment, 2 cuts in and comes out, receiving the inside-out pass from 5. Player 4 immediately comes to the high post, receives the ball, and has the entire right side of the key to work. Player 2 moves toward the right-side three-point line as a receiver in case his man helps on 4 (see figure 5.12).

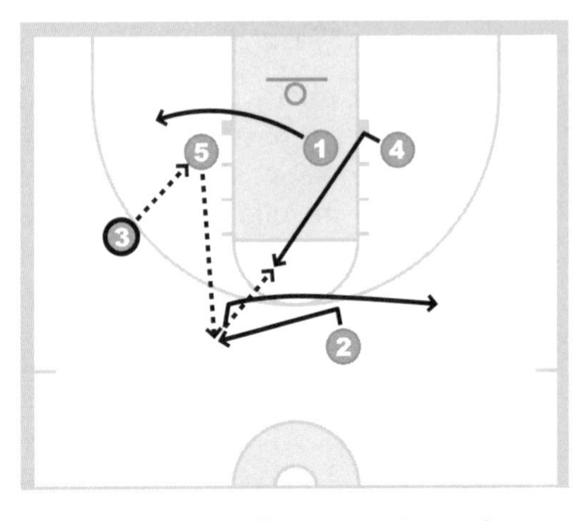

Figure 5.12 The ball goes inside out from 5 to 2.

CLOSING POINTS

Most coaches will admit that it's not so much the offense you run but how well you run the offense you have. That is true as long as the offense is founded on sound principles. Success is realized not in Xs and Os alone, but in the players' recognition of the defensive weaknesses and attention to detail in executing plays such as the UCLA cut. The key is to start with a sound offense—complete with vertical cuts, proper spacing, good weak-side action, and rebounding and defensive balance—and to run the plays that get the ball into the hands of scorers where they have high-percentage shots and one-on-one situations. The UCLA cut play was perfect for the 1969 to 1970 Bruins. It was a play designed to get the ball inside to Wicks and Rowe, with Bibby and our other capable perimeter shooters taking the outside shots when the defense dropped. The additional options that emerged during practice sessions completed a system that was ready for anything opponents may throw at it.

As famous as the UCLA cut was, and still is, we didn't score as much off it as some may think. However, the fact that it occasionally produced such a high-percentage shot apparently caused great concern among opponents. That worked to our advantage. The more urgency they had about stopping it, the more effective the next option—the forward-to-center pass—became, because the defensive center often dropped to help. For that reason, our guards were highly trained to do what they could to get open, even if it meant popping back out when defenders dropped below the screen. Incidentally, highly developing one option in order to help the next was not limited to the UCLA cut. The concept is valid for all options of all plays.

We witnessed several methods for attempting to derail the UCLA cut. At times, after the guard passed the ball to the forward, the guard's

A TREMENDOUS TANDEM

Sidney Wicks and Henry Bibby were virtually unstoppable when running the UCLA cut. Wicks was the most versatile offensive player on the 1969 to 1970 team. He was quick, had good shooting range, was excellent one on one, and could finish a drive with a variety of short jump shots or layups. Therefore, he was effective with the ball in a variety of locations. However, he was best at the weak-side block, using the duck-in move when receiving the ball from the center, Steve Patterson. If the ball was passed to the out guard, Wicks came up to the side post and received the ball, usually from Henry Bibby, an excellent shooter and ball handler. Bibby's abilities, coupled with the one-on-one talent of Wicks, made for a virtually unstoppable side-post game.

When Wicks was positioned on the side of the UCLA cut, any defender who dared overplay him was left helpless because his backdoor cut was lightning quick and Bibby's passing ability was excellent.

© Rich Clarkson/NCAA Photos

Henry Bibby demonstrates perfect release on his jump shot. If the three-point shot had been in effect then, Henry would certainly have stretched defenses out even more than he did.

defender would bump him in order to retard his forward progress. Trained offensive guards avoided the bump and cut right by their men. The most effective method was to jump toward the basketball after the guard-to-forward pass was made and to continue a front position all the way to the block. Cunning offensive players momentarily played a "cat and mouse" game, faking back up, drawing their men back toward half court, and cutting to the basket. However, for the most part, jumping to the ball was used most effectively.

Through the years, many offensive systems have included the UCLA cut. Some coaches have taught it extremely well, while others not so well. The difference is in persistent execution. If the importance of near-perfect execution, with the aim of scoring, is not continually taught for an entire season, generally speaking, the play will default to players going through the motions. The message must be sent that this option, if executed correctly each time, is the key to successful team play.

Part III

HIGH-LOW OFFENSE

The temptation for any successful team and coach is to stick with what has worked in the past. By 1966, UCLA had become one of the strongest college basketball programs in the country, one that had become synonymous with the high-post offense. Given that degree of success and the flexibility afforded by the offense—which enabled it to be tailored to the talent available each season—why opt for an alternate attack?

The answer is that we were fortunate to add to our program a very special player, Lewis Alcindor, whose offensive talents and height could only be fully used in something other than the high-post alignment. However, while we wanted to accentuate Lewis' assets, we also wanted to retain the principles underlying the high-post offense and ensure that the other players' passing, cutting, screening, and shooting skills could be incorporated into the attack. What emerged was an offense very similar to the high post, except it was to be initiated with the low-post player already in position on the block.

Our high-low offense typically started with Lewis on the left block and an excellent shooting forward, Lynn Shackelford, on that wing. After Lynn received the guard-to-forward pass, he either passed the ball into Lewis or took the shot. Because Lewis stayed close to the basket, the amount of cutting and ball movement was limited, but the results were very impressive.

We also employed the high-low offense when Bill Walton was at UCLA. Because Bill was a skilled passer, options were added to allow him to come to the high post, receive the ball, and pass to cutters and open perimeter players. A defensive player playing the passing lane to the forward on Bill's side would soon discover he was the victim of a backdoor cut and layup. When Walton was double-teamed in the low post, he almost always spotted and passed the ball to a teammate cutting down the lane or an open perimeter player.

The chapters in this section will illustrate the initial set of the high-low offense with a two-guard front, quickly morphing into a 1-3-1 set. However, because of Walton's ability to receive the ball at the high post and, therefore, being a primary passing option for the guards, that particular team often began the offense in the 1-3-1 set.

The conception and use of the high-low offense resulted from assessing the talent on hand and trying to maximize it. Its success, rather than suggesting inadequacies in the high-post attack, only confirmed that offense's virtues and its common features.

CHAPTER 6

HIGH-LOW: GUARD TO HIGH POST

One test of an offensive attack is how adaptable it is to allow you to maximize the talent available each season. Obviously, we were very pleased when Lewis Alcindor, out of Power Memorial Academy (New York), chose to attend UCLA. Lewis was seven-foot-two, extremely well coordinated for his height at such a young age, and skilled in many facets of the game. However, his arrival prompted us to rethink certain aspects of the offense.

Our opponents justifiably viewed Lewis as a great inside scoring threat, capable of creating a high-percentage shot whenever he received the ball. Adhering to the 10 principles was nonnegotiable, but adjustments had to be made. What concerned us was stereotyping our system by limiting the pass to Lewis from the strong-side forward. That predictability would have certainly resulted in double and triple teaming. We needed good ball movement—making use of every player on the floor—and several ways to get Lewis the ball while at the same time maintaining equal scoring opportunities for the other positions. We also needed extremely good weak-side action for three reasons: to keep defenders occupied, to create weak-side catch-and-score opportunities as Lewis passed the ball out of double teams, and to reverse the ball. Ball reversal was critical to getting the ball inside. After tapping into the experiences of great centers such as Wilt Chamberlain and George Mikan, gaining the knowledge of coaches who had coached very tall centers, and manipulating Xs and Os for many hours, a potential offense emerged. The new scheme made full use of Lewis' scoring ability by involving all other players in plays that allowed for a quick pass to him at any time in a variety of locations. Surprisingly, the result greatly resembled the high-post offense.

BASE PLAYS

To be able to initiate the offense to either wing, the offense must begin with two guards about 15 feet apart above the key (called a two-guard front), with one guard initiating the play, either with a pass to the other guard or to any of the other three players. As in the high-post set, the two forwards are on the wings at the free throw line extended. Indeed, the initial set of the high-low offense looks identical to the high-post offense except that the center is positioned low instead of high (see figure 6.1).

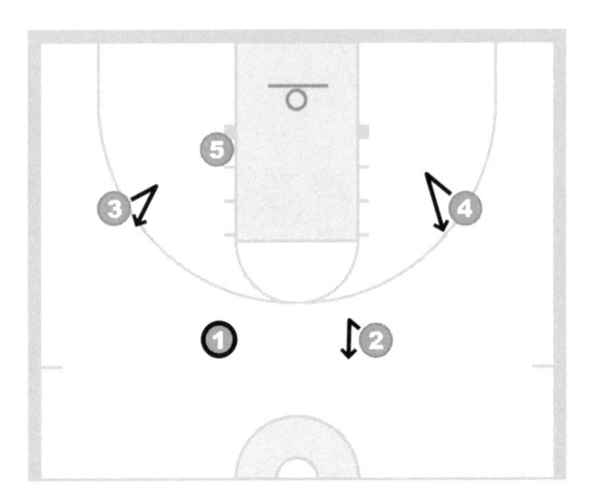

Figure 6.1 In the initial set of the high-low offense, the only difference from the high-post offense is the position of 5 at the low post.

For the high-post offense, the guard-to-guard pass moves the ball in order to make the entry pass to the weak-side forward. For the high-low offense, rather than receive the pass on the wing, the forward is reversed and then brought up to the high post, realigning the offense into a 1-3-1 set. The main play is focused on getting the ball from the guard to the forward breaking to the high post, and then to the center on the low post, if possible.

Guard to High Post

To bring 4 to the high post, 1 passes to 2, who dribbles hard and directly at 4, whether he is overplayed or not. Player 4 makes a hard backdoor cut, causing his defender to drop toward the basket. If 4 is open, 2 delivers the pass. Whether or not the pass is made, the hard backdoor cut and threat of the pass should cause 5's man to take a step toward the ball side. At this time, 5 may step into an open area within the key, and 2 has the option to pass to him in the key. If the backdoor pass is not made, 4 makes a 90-degree change of direction, heading to the high post (see figure 6.2).

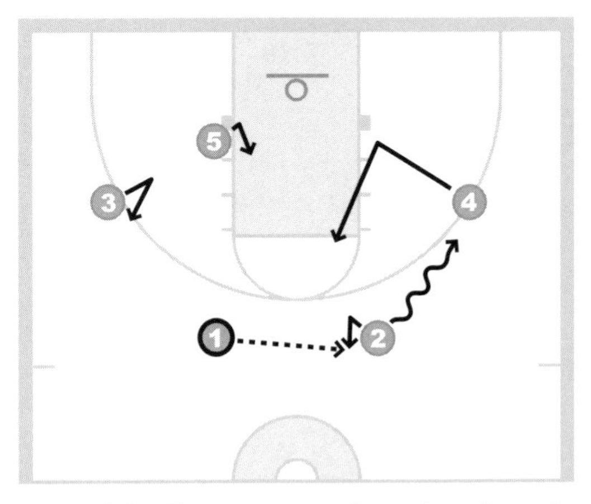

Figure 6.2 The pass goes from 1 to 2, and 4 makes a 90-degree turn toward the high post if 2 doesn't pass to him.

Player 2 passes back to 1, who has faked away and come back out. The offense is now in a 1-3-1 set (see figure 6.3 and figure 6.4).

Figure 6.3 Alignment for the 1-3-1 set.

With perfect timing so the pass is made when 4 is open at the high post, 1 fakes down, delivers a quick overhead pass to 4, and then moves to either side of the key, calling for the ball to keep his defender occupied. Player 4 immediately turns and looks for 5. Player 5 has faked a baseline cut to the ball side, dropping his defender closer to the baseline, and has stepped in front of his man just when 4 has turned and is ready to pass. Player 3 has already faked a basket cut and has come out to complete the 4, 5, 3 triangle. Player 2 stays busy to get open, and 1 is the protector if a shot is taken (see figure 6.5).

Well before 5 moves into the key, 3 must be aware of how 5's defender is playing. Once a game has commenced, it should not take long for all players to see if the center's man is playing behind, waiting for a double team, or actively denying the pass into the post. If 5 is not open because of high-side defense, 5, 4, and 3 work together to get him the ball from the wing area of the triangle. Player 4 fakes the pass to 5, 3

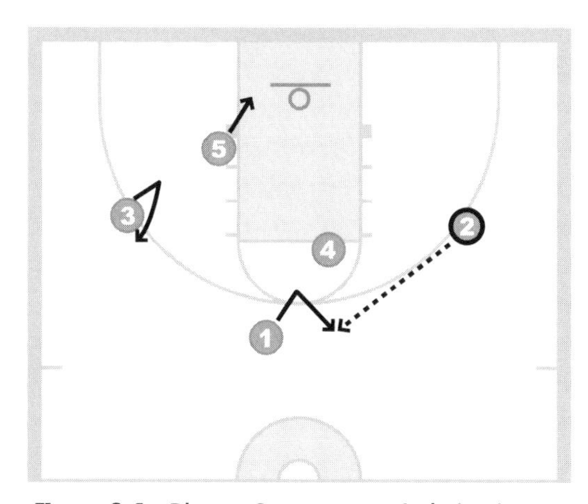

Figure 6.4 Player 2 passes to 1, bringing the players into 1-3-1 alignment.

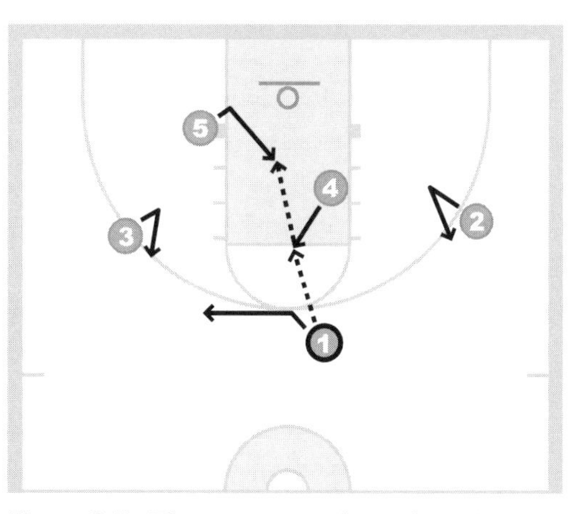

Figure 6.5 The pass goes from 1 to 4 at the high post, then to 5 who's dropped his defender at the baseline to get open.

fakes in and comes out to receive the pass from 4, and 5 seals his defender toward the high post and holds him there until the pass from 3 can be made. Player 3 leads 5 with a pass toward the block, all the while remaining conscious of any weak-side defender who is sagging in an attempt to steal the pass in (see figure 6.6).

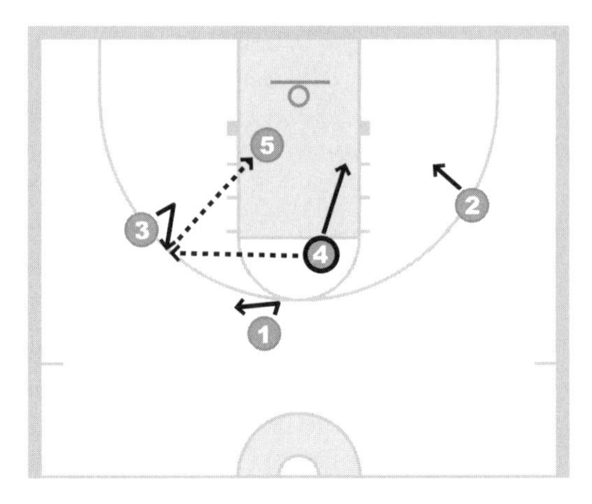

Figure 6.6 If 5 is pressured and cannot receive the pass from 4, 4 gets the ball to him via 3.

After the pass to 3, 4 takes one step toward him and cuts down the lane, calling for the ball. This gives his man something to do other than help on 5. This cut also places him in good rebound position if 3 passes to 5 for the catch and score.

If not open, and if 5 does not attempt to score, 4 continues to the opposite block and sets a screen for 2, who then comes to the high-post area on the strong side. It is critical that 4 gets to the block because 2 is to use that point of reference to set up the defender for the screen. If 2 knows exactly where the screen will be set, timing will be improved, and offensive screening fouls will be reduced. This is especially important in road games, when officials may be more inclined to call the visiting players for moving screens.

If, after the pass to 3, 5's defender fronts 5, a pass must be made back to the high post and then into 5 as he seals his man away from the key. Player 4 may choose to fake down the lane and come back out to catch the ball and deliver the pass to 5, or 2 may deliver the pass if 4 cuts down the lane and sets the screen on the weak-side block.

When 5 is fronted, his hip should be in contact with his defender's backside, and he should be facing the baseline. The elbow of the arm closest to his man should be above the defender's shoulders, helping prevent a push-off foul if the ball is lobbed. However, if he senses that the lob will not be thrown, he should turn toward the closest sideline by shooting his inside arm along his defender's back and toward the high post.

This pivot is contrary to how most post players are taught. However, in this instance, there are at least two reasons why it is better. One, it keeps the center's vision toward the ball, whereas the back pivot does not. This can mean the difference between a successful lob to the pivoting player and a turnover. Two, the front pivot toward the baseline allows the center to maintain contact with the defender, whereas the back pivot temporarily relieves that pressure, allowing the fronting defender to recover.

If 4 chooses not to explore that option, 5 continues across the lane to the opposite low-post area, calling for the ball. Player 4 passes to 2, who has kept his defender busy by faking toward the basket and coming out, and 2 looks for 5. After the pass, 4 takes one step toward 2 and cuts down the lane, calling for the ball. This keeps his defender occupied so he can't help on 5. Player 4 may receive the pass from 2, but if he doesn't, he continues to the opposite block and sets a screen for 3, with his backside facing toward the baseline. Player 3 has faked a baseline cut and changes direction at the block to come to the high post to create the 2, 5, 3 triangle (see figure 6.7). With 3 at the high post, the offense is now positioned in the four-options set.

Figure 6.7 Player 4 passes to 2, who passes to 5. Then 4 cuts down the lane to screen for 3 at the opposite block. Player 3 comes to the high post to create a triangle with 5 and 2.

Guard to Wing

Player 1 passes to 2, who dribbles hard toward 4 and reverses him, bringing him to the high post as before. Instead of passing to 4, 2 hits 1, who has faked a cut toward the key and come out. Player 1 quickly fakes a pass to 4, sucking the defense in, and hits 3 on the left wing. Player 3 has faked a cut toward the basket and come out. Player 3 looks for 5 at the block. Player 4 makes a one-step fake for the lob and comes to the strong-side high post to create the 3, 5, 4 triangle. Player 2 is on the weak-side wing, ready to be the protector. Player 1 is up top, faking to keep his man from helping on 4 if the pass goes there (see figure 6.8).

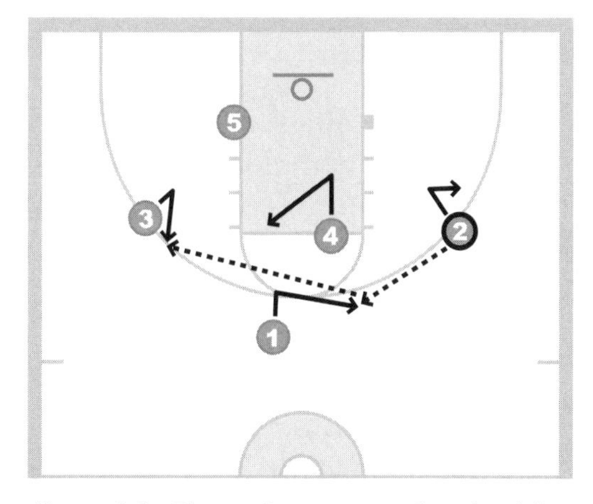

Figure 6.8 Player 2 passes to 1, who fakes a pass to 4 and sends the ball to 3 on the wing.

For 5 to be open when 3 is ready to pass, he must execute the following. First, he must face the key (not the wing) until 3 has caught the ball. This will keep his defender between him and the basket. As long as he is facing the key, the possibility of him cutting into or across the key is in his defender's mind. As soon as he turns toward the wing, that possibility no longer exists, and his defender can begin to deny the pass into him. Second, while turning toward 3, it is beneficial if he makes contact with his opponent, especially legs to legs or backside to legs. It is only the defender's legs that can move him into the passing lane between 3 and 5. When contact is made below the waist, movement is hindered, if not halted.

Player 5 presents a good target for 3. The hand away from defensive pressure should be up with the fingers completely extended, and the elbow should be completely straight. The upper arm of the other arm should be parallel to the floor with the forearm 90 degrees to the floor, providing a barrier for the defense. In most cases, when catching the basketball, he should make a slight jump forward, landing on both feet at the same time. This provides the possibility of using either foot for pivoting. Immediately after catching the ball, his back should be straight, the ball tucked under the chin, the elbows slightly out, and the head turned over the shoulder that is away from the baseline. He is now in position to make a move, because he can see where his defender is located and he is in position to see what is happening on the rest of the court.

If 3 passes to 5, 4 reads his own defender and either cuts down the lane for a pass and score or fakes in and comes back out for the jump shot. This action will hinder his defender from helping on 5. If his man shows any sign of creating a double team on 5, 4 cuts to the basket and should be open (see figure 6.9). Player 2 replaces 4 if 5 has not made his move.

If 5 is fronted, 4 fakes the cut down the lane, comes back to the strong-side high post, receives the pass from 3, and passes to 5, who has sealed his man. Player 5 must seal his man with a front pivot, brushing his inside arm against his man's back and stepping through toward the high post. This will maintain contact and seal his man out of the key while allowing 5 to maintain vision of the basketball. A bounce pass is not as effective as the straight pass because it takes longer to reach the post player and it is a lower pass. Player 4 fakes down and delivers a two-handed overhead pass, leading 5 slightly toward the basket (see figure 6.10). Player 5 should score without a dribble, using either a jump hook, running hook, or jump shot.

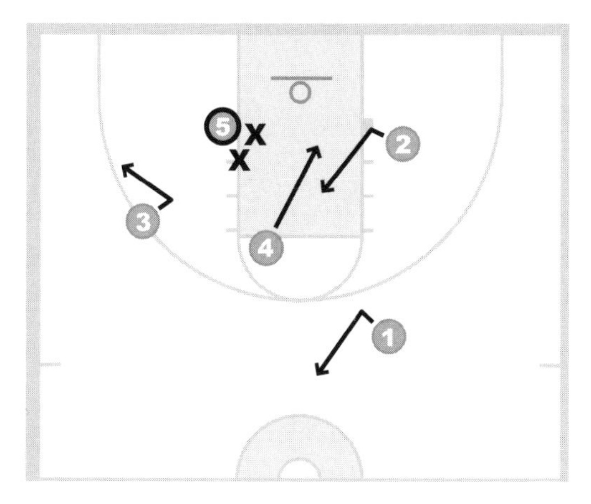

Figure 6.9 Player 5 is double teamed, so 4 cuts to the basket to get open.

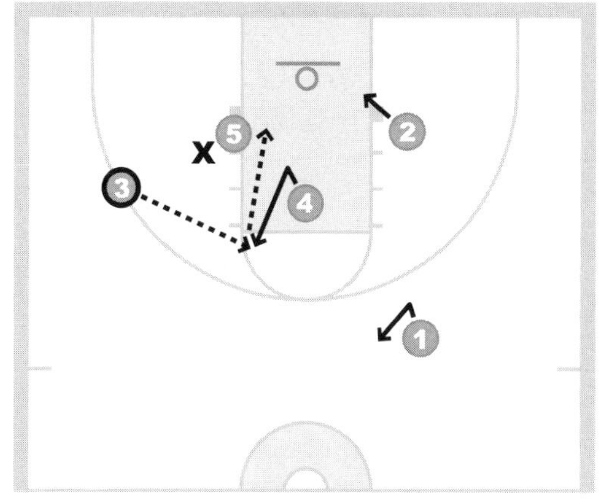

Figure 6.10 After 5 has sealed his man, 4 delivers a two-handed overhead pass, leading 5 slightly toward the basket.

ADDITIONAL OPTIONS

Depending on the abilities of the personnel, additional options are available as players are constantly engaged in reading the defense and taking what it provides. Players should continually be reminded that spacing, ball movement, cutting, and the constant changing of positions are a means to creating defensive errors and, therefore, openings and opportunities. Because some players are more gifted at reading defenses and in physical ability, the coach should be careful to give license only to those individuals who are capable of execution. For example, if you're going to have players play away from their weaknesses and to their strengths, it is probably not a good idea to have a nonshooter handle the ball at the high post.

One-on-One for the High-Post Forward

Each player, when he receives the ball, should be a scoring threat from the spot where he is operating. If not, some players are not placed in the correct positions. For example, if 4 is not a scoring threat when he receives the ball at the high post, his defender will definitely drop down to help on the center. When 4 receives the ball at the high post, he must be able to make the 15-foot jump shot, and preferably, he should be able to take one dribble for a short shot or one or two dribbles for the layup. A pass fake to 5 may cause his man to drop, opening up an opportunity to shoot. A pass fake to the wing often causes his man to lean, or relax, opening up the lane for a drive.

Forward Reverse (4 Has the Ball)

With 4 in possession of the ball at the high post looking for 5 inside or 3 on the wing, the defense may overplay both 5 and 3 so that 4 cannot make the pass to either player. When this occurs, 5 has the option to come up the side of the lane, receive the pass from 4, and reverse 3 for a backdoor situation (see figure 6.11). The pass from 4 to 5 is shorter in distance than a normal pass. Therefore, it is imperative that 4 is lined up well to the strong side along the free throw line. After 5 receives the ball, 4 cuts down the lane to take good rebounding position.

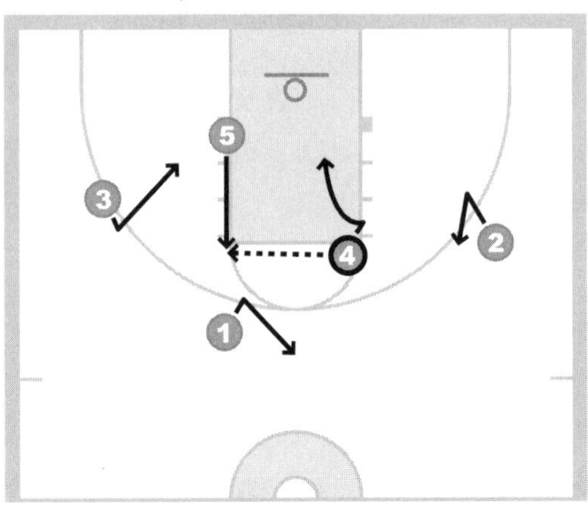

Figure 6.11 Player 4 can't get the pass to 5 or 3, so 5 comes up the side of the lane for the pass, and 3 reverses for a backdoor situation.

Forward Reverse (1 Has the Ball)

A mobile center with good passing skills makes for more possibilities. With the same method of initiating the play into the 1-3-1 set, 2 passes out to 1. Instead of passing to 4 at the high post, 1 fakes there and looks for 3. If the passing lane to 3 is pressured, 5 is alert to fake across the key and come to the strong side of the high post to receive the pass from 1, who makes the appropriate pass depending on the initial position of his defender's hands (see figure 6.12). Player 5 should time his move so he is approaching the high post when 1 receives the pass from 2. Player 3 takes his defender out and makes the backdoor cut. Player 4 moves down the lane and gets open should his man help on 3's backdoor cut.

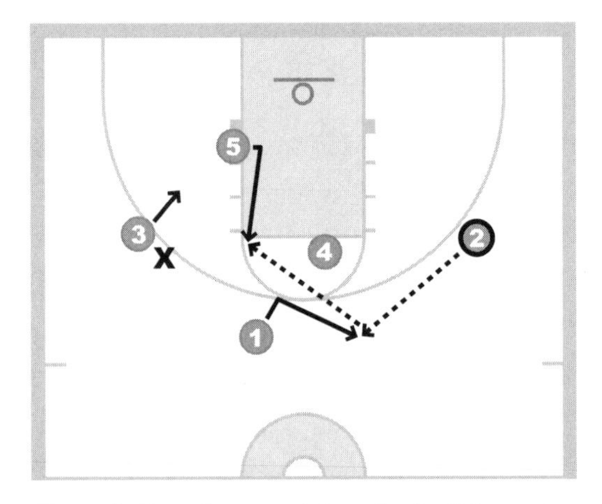

Figure 6.12 After receiving the ball from 2, 1 looks for 3, but he's pressured, so 5 fakes across the key to the high post for the pass.

Timing is never more important than on backdoor cuts; the basketball should move from 1 to 5 to 3 in a fluent, but not hurried, manner. Therefore, 3 must be well on his way to the basket when 5 receives the ball. It would seem helpful if some point of reference could be given, such as exactly where 3 should be, in relation to 5, when 5 is ready to pass. That cannot, and should not, be done because much of timing is dependent on the physical abilities of the players (such as quickness) and the position of the defense at any given moment in the play. However, suffice it to say that 3 should be well on his way to the basket.

Center Back Screen

Another option for 5 is to set a back screen for 3. Player 4 fakes the pass to 3, drawing 3's defender even farther from the basket, while 5 sprints to the wing, turns toward the baseline to avoid a moving screen violation, and sets the back screen (see figure 6.13). Player 3 uses the screen to cut to the basket for a pass from 4 and a layup or short jump shot. Player 4's and 2's defenders are the only players that can provide help. If 4's man helps, 4 has a jump shot. If 2's man helps, he gets to an open spot for the layup. If 2 is positioned near the three-point line, he may have that shot. Player 5 can roll to the basket or stay for a short jump shot.

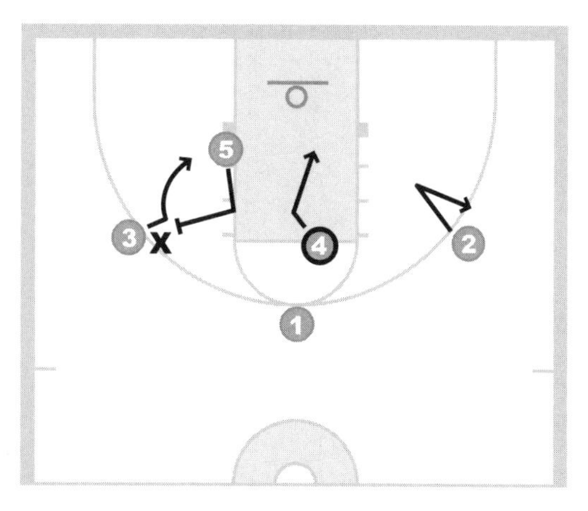

Figure 6.13 Player 5 sets the back screen for 3, who cuts toward the basket for a pass from 4.

4 and 2 Give-and-Go

When 4 receives the pass from 2, his first look is for 5, who has flashed into the key. If he thinks he has a quickness advantage over his defender, or a height advantage to post up, he may elect to pass to 2 on the wing and cut to the basket. When he does, he will receive the return pass for the layup, or if the pass is not there, he will post his man up, receive the ball, and make a move inside (see figure 6.14).

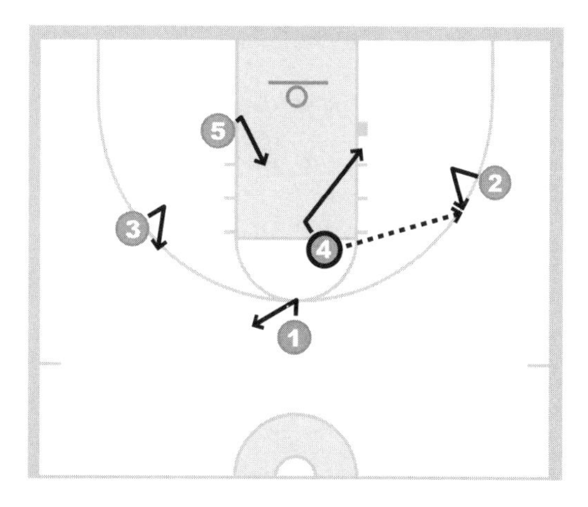

Figure 6.14 Player 4 passes to 2, then cuts to the basket to be available for the return pass and shot.

Guard Reverse

If 1 cannot complete the pass to 2 because 2's defender is playing the passing lane, 4 comes from the weak side to the high post and receives a pass from 1. This option is explained and diagrammed in the section on pressure release (see chapter 8).

1-3-1 Alignment

The 1-3-1 alignment can be very effective if the team has a dominant offensive center. The point guard initiates the play to either the left wing, the center, or the forward who begins at the low post and comes to the side post (see figure 6.15).

UCLA often used this method for initiating the offense when we had Bill Walton at center. Bill (5) would come as high as needed to receive the ball. Keith Wilkes (4), positioned at the high post, would read the collapsing defense on Walton and make the move to get open. Most often, because the defense collapsed and a cut toward the basket would result in running into a crowd, Keith stayed at the high post. Bill had the option to pass there, pass to his strong-side wing man (2), who was always a good shooter, or pass back out to 1 (see figure 6.16).

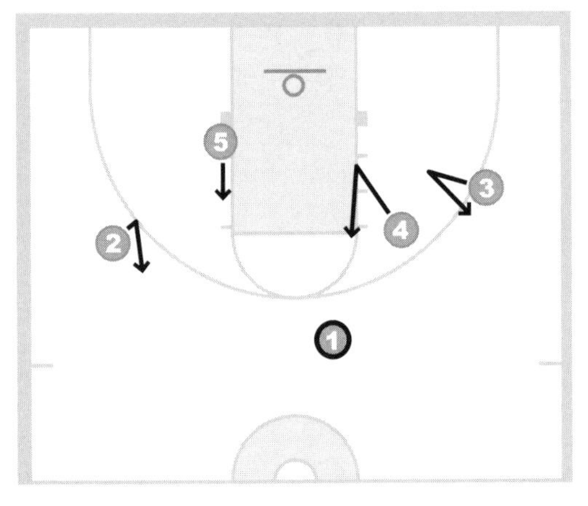

Figure 6.15 In 1-3-1 alignment, 1 can start with a pass to 2, 5, or 4.

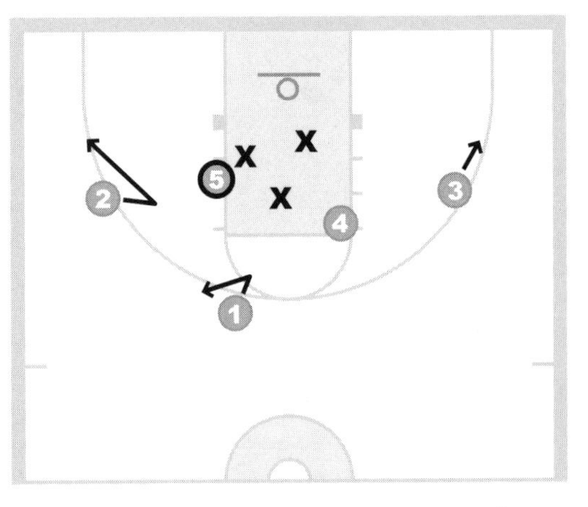

Figure 6.16 In this option, 5 receives the pass from 1, then has the option to pass to 4, 2, or 1.

Against Walton's teams, many opponents played man-to-man defense, but once Bill received the ball—or even before—the defense often changed to a zone, with at least three players surrounding him. For that reason, the UCLA cut was rarely used, because spacing became more important than cutting. Out of the 1-3-1 initial alignment, a very effective play was 1 to 4 to 5. Without the UCLA cut, Walton was free to roam the entire inside area. After cutting across the key, he often came back a step toward the free throw line, received the pass from Wilkes, and made the spin to the weak side for a one-dribble move and layup (see figure 6.17).

Occasionally, 1 may have trouble making the entry pass. That's when 4 can set the ball screen to initiate the offense. For some reason, when the screen is set, all defenders abort overplay, and the guard-to-forward pass is open. Therefore, the UCLA cut can be made out of the ball screen (see figure 6.18).

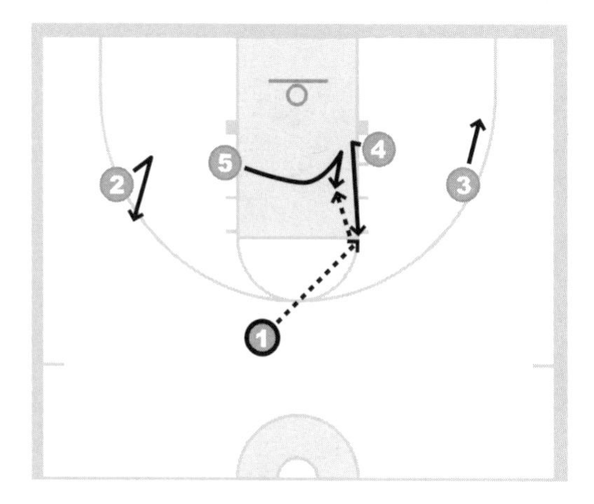

Figure 6.17 The 1-to-4-to-5 pass worked well for Walton's teams.

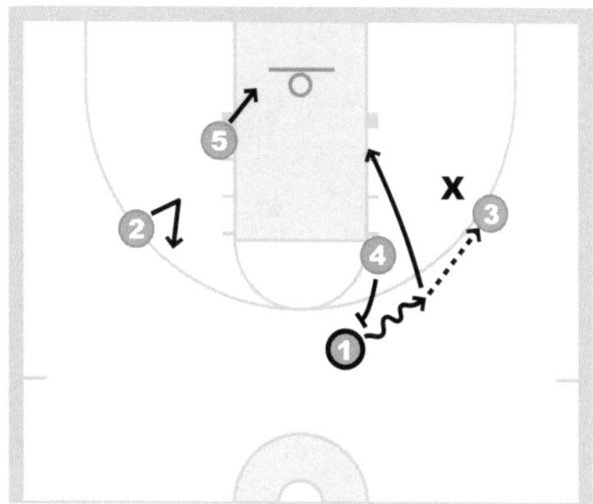

Figure 6.18 If 1 can't make the pass inside, 4 can set a screen allowing 1 to pass to the forward on the wing.

DOUBLE TROUBLE

The 1967 squad was especially well suited to run the high-low offense. In addition to Lewis Alcindor at the center position, the team featured Mike Warren, one of the most valuable point guards in Bruin basketball history, at one guard spot. Lucius Allen, a good driver and mid-range shooter, was Mike's running mate at guard. Lynn Shackelford, six-foot-five and a deadly shooter from what is now the three-point line, took the wing on Lewis' side. And Kenny Heitz, a good mid-range shooter and passer, took the wing opposite Lynn. Lewis was licensed to position himself on either side of the lane to start the play but usually began on the left.

Because we needed Lewis to play close to the basket, player movement in the offense was less than desired, but the results were nevertheless pleasing. Because of his dominant inside play and the effectiveness of the offense in getting him the basketball in scoring position, most of our opponents chose to play zone defense.

Zone defenses were very similar to a double- or triple-teaming man-to-man; everyone, other than the players around Lewis, played an area. Whether facing zone defense or a trapping man-to-man, all screening ceased and each of the other four players dashed into openings, either by slashing down the key or moving to an open perimeter position. It really was not more complicated than that. Once Lewis passed the ball out, our team was very good at passing back in to him as he repositioned himself. He was open because, once he did pass the ball out, the players who were teaming up on him ran to cover perimeter players.

No matter how high Elvin Hayes jumped, it was not high enough to reach Lewis Alcindor's unstoppable jump shot. Here, Lewis scores over the great Hayes in the 1967 NCAA semifinals.

Additional attention for Lewis played into the hands of deadeye shooter Lynn Shackelford, who was positioned at the wing on Lewis' side of the floor and rarely left that area. Lynn had a quick release and was taller than most perimeter players at that time, so he could easily launch his shots if an opposing defense tried to sag inside to cover Lewis.

Of course, when the defense extended the zone, Lynn would get the ball to Lewis in a position to score. And, even at that time, Lewis had what came to be known as the "sky hook"—perhaps as near to an indefensible shot as the game has ever seen. The Alcindor and Shackelford combination was virtually unstoppable.

CLOSING POINTS

We created and opted to run the high-low offense for six seasons to maximize the special qualities of two exceptional centers. We lost only six games during the Lewis Alcindor and Bill Walton years, and much of the credit belonged to the team spirit of those two men and the willingness of their teammates to sacrifice personal glory for the welfare of the team. However, we also believe that the offensive adjustments made to suit their unique size and talent contributed to our success.

This chapter focused mostly on the initial conception and execution of the high-low offense during Alcindor's UCLA career. But two years after Lewis' graduation, when Walton arrived on campus, we made some creative additions to the post player's role in the high-low offense. You will learn more about those modifications in chapter 7.

CHAPTER 7

HIGH-LOW: GUARD TO WING

After the Alcindor years, UCLA returned to the high-post attack with Lewis' backup, Steve Patterson, at the center position. Although Steve was very capable of playing in the high-low set, we opted for the high-post offense to make full use of our talented forward tandem, Sidney Wicks and Curtis Rowe. The result was two more NCAA championships, bringing the total to five in a row.

At that point, Bill Walton, Keith Wilkes, and Greg Lee had just completed their freshman year and were ready to step up to varsity competition. Larry Farmer, a junior, and Henry Bibby, a senior, completed the starting five for that 1971 to 1972 season.

Had Walton been effective only at the low post, the choice of offense would have been rather simple. We would have run the high-low offense as we did with Alcindor. But Bill had a different set of skills; he was effective as both a passer and a shooter anywhere in the high post along the free throw lane. So we allowed him a bit more freedom to create scoring opportunities farther away from the basket than had been the case with Alcindor.

Also, the talents of forward Keith Wilkes afforded even more opportunities for flexibility and extensions. Both cunning and quick in the high-post area, Wilkes allowed those Bruin teams to run options on the side away from the low-post player. Yes, the guard to high post was still the main play, but it was complemented by an attack away from Walton's side of the court, which created additional opportunities to get Bill the ball.

BASE PLAY

Player 1 passes to 2, who dribbles hard at 4, looking for the backdoor pass. After taking his defender one step farther away from the basket and then reversing hard toward the block, 4 makes a change of pace and change of direction, cutting to the high post (see figure 7.1). Player 1 can immediately cut off 4, who has turned to face the basket to set the screen, or receive a pass from 2, pass it back, and then make the

UCLA cut. Either way is acceptable, although the first option is the quickest.

When 1 cuts to the basket, 4 follows him for one step and comes out to receive the ball from 2. Player 5 has faked a baseline cut and moves in front of his man to flash into the key. Player 3 cuts toward the basket and comes back out to keep his man busy and unable to help on 5 (see figure 7.2).

If 5's defender plays between 5 and the ball, 4 hits 3, who has faked in and come out, and 3 passes to 5, who has sealed his man away from the block to create space for the pass (see figure 7.3). To deliver the pass, 3 fakes down and delivers the quick two-handed overhead pass if his defender's hands are down. If they are up, he fakes up and makes the one-handed bounce pass so that 5 can catch it on the move to the basket. Player 3 must be aware of sagging weak-side defenders who are trained to anticipate the pass and make the steal.

After passing to 3, 4 cuts down the lane, calling for the ball. If his defender stops to help on 5, he could be open for a pass from 3. Player 4 continues toward the block, where he turns his backside toward the baseline and sets a screen for 1 (see figure 7.4). Player 1 has set up his man by faking into the key and coming around the block to the high post. In these down screening situations, players must avoid offensive screening fouls. Timing is critical and is chiefly the responsibility of the player for whom the screen is being set. Player 2 takes the weak side but is conscious of being the protector if a shot is taken.

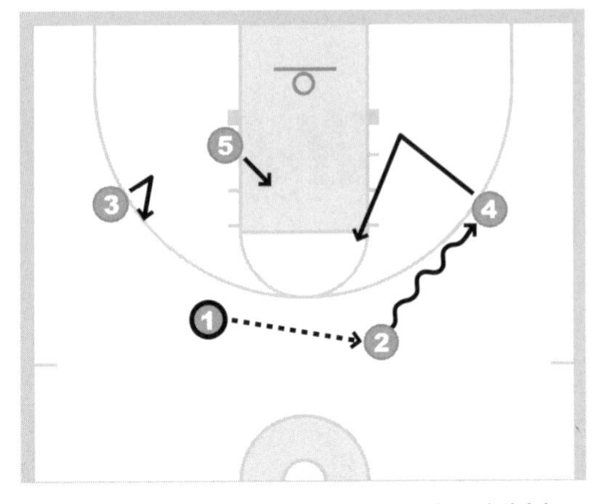

Figure 7.1 Player 1 passes to 2, who dribbles at 4. Player 4 cuts toward the block then changes direction and cuts to the high post.

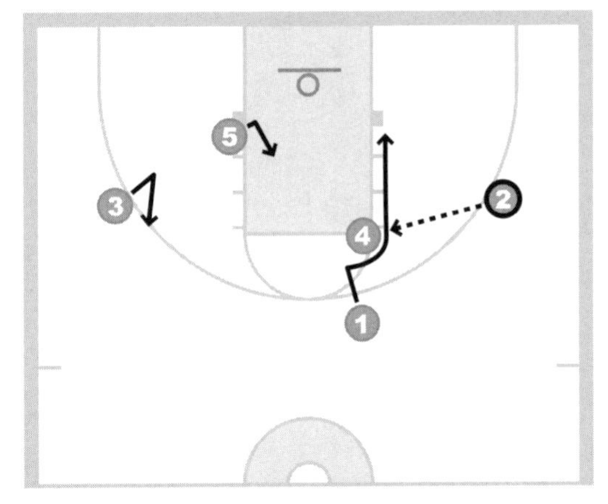

Figure 7.2 Player 1 cuts to the basket while 4 receives the pass from 2.

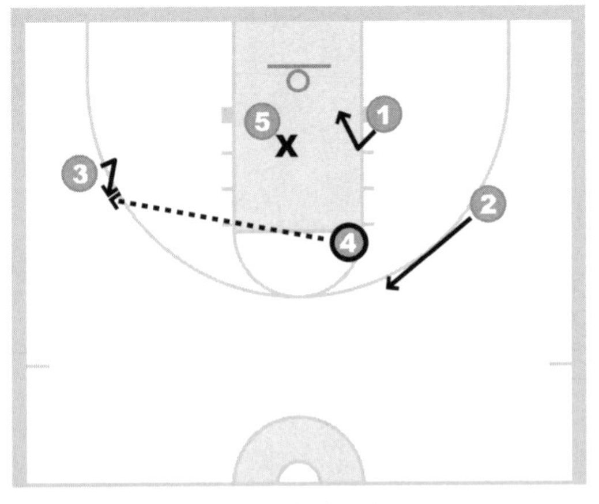

Figure 7.3 Player 5's defender prevents a pass from 4 to 5, so 4 passes to 3. Player 5 seals his man away from the block to become open for the pass from 3.

After the UCLA cut and the pass to 4, 4 looks for 5 on the flash move in the key. Player 2 cuts to the block, turns his back to the basket, and sets a screen for 1 to come out to the wing for the jump shot. After passing to 1, 4 takes one step toward the sideline and cuts down the lane, calling for the ball. Player 4 then screens for 5, who replaces him at the strong-side elbow (see figure 7.5). If 1 takes the shot, 5, 4, and 1 are inside rebounders, 2 is the long rebounder, and 3 is the protector.

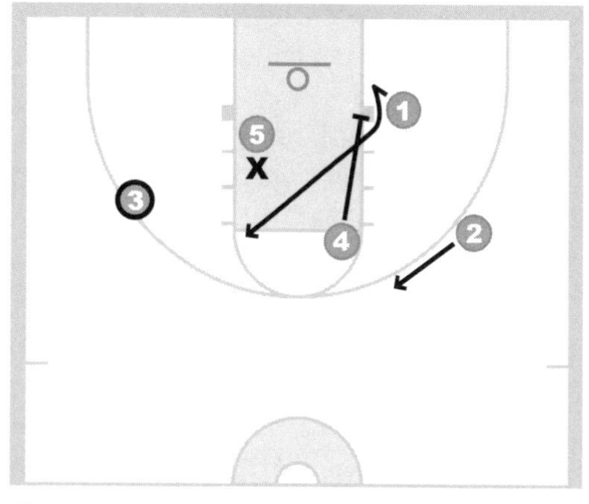

Figure 7.4 Player 4 cuts down the lane, possibly becoming open for the pass, and then sets a screen for 1 at the block.

ADDITIONAL OPTIONS

The skills and savvy of players will dictate the diversity of choices off the guard-to-wing pass in the high-low offense. If the team is sharp and capable of taking advantage of defensive lapses, several more options of attack can be unleashed from this offense.

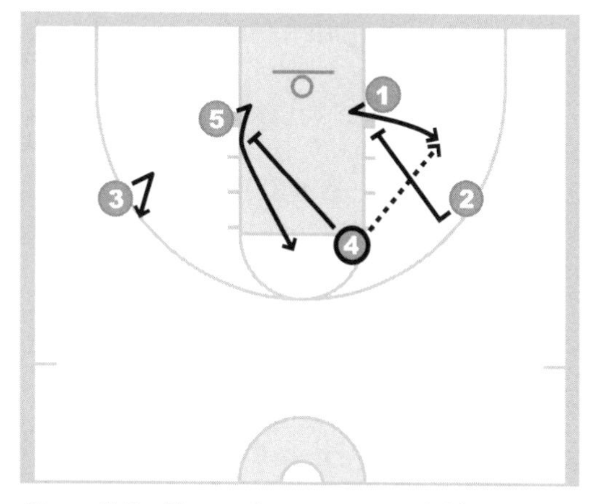

Figure 7.5 Player 1 goes around 2's screen to receive the pass from 4 on the wing.

Forward Reverse

After 2 dribbles hard at 4, looking for the backdoor pass or for 4 to move to the high post, 2 passes back out to 1. Player 1 is attempting to get the ball to 3, who will explore passing to 5 on the block. However, 3 is being played tightly, so 5, without faking to the baseline as usual, sprints to the free throw line area on the weak side to receive the pass. Player 5 then looks for 3 reversing to the basket (see figure 7.6). In almost every case, he will be open. When 2 and 4 see 5 heading for the free throw line, they set a weak-side double screen for 3, with 2 on the baseline side with

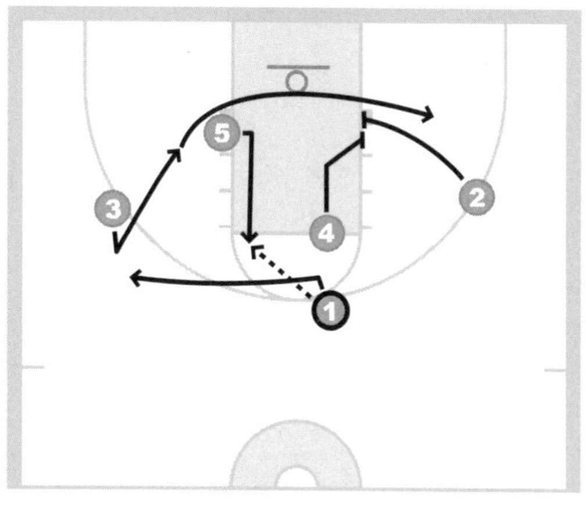

Figure 7.6 Player 1 passes to 5 at the free throw line. Player 3 reverses to the basket as 5 receives the ball and then goes around the screen set by 2 and 4.

his lower foot on the block. Player 1 replaces 3 on the wing to balance the floor.

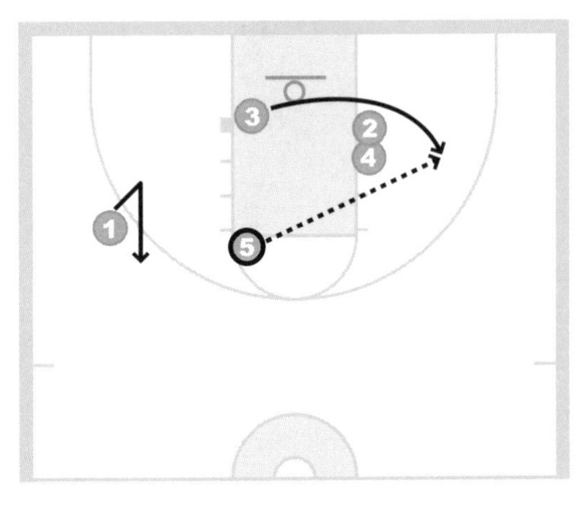

Figure 7.7 Player 3 receives the pass from 5.

For this option to work, 3 must recognize the overplay and set his man up by taking him one step farther away from the basket. However, he should not take too much time because he should be well on his way to the basket when 5 receives the ball. To get an idea of the timing of the play, 5 should not have the ball in his hands much longer than one second before delivering a pass that leads 3 toward the block. Quick execution not only gets 3 open for a catch and layup, but it also prevents weak-side defenders from reacting in time to help.

If 3 does not receive the backdoor pass, he continues through the lane and uses the double screen to get open for a jump shot or three-point shot if he has the range. Player 5 passes to 3 and cuts hard down the lane, calling for the lob pass (see figure 7.7). Player 2 comes around the ball side of 4 to the high post to create the 4, 3, 2 triangle. The offense is now in the four-options set.

Guard Post-Up

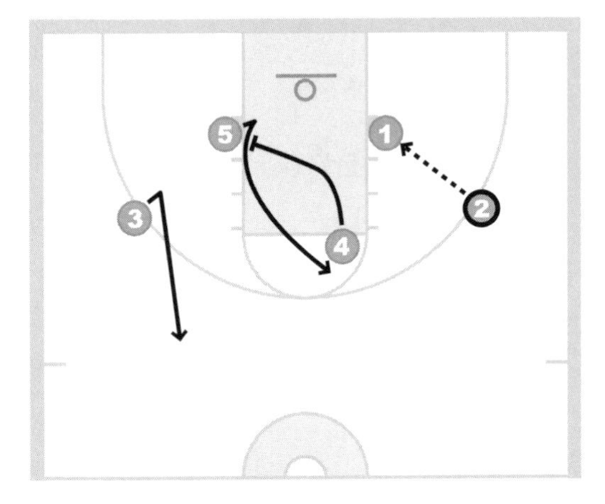

Figure 7.8 During 2's pass to 1, 4 down screens for 5, who comes to the high post.

If the team has a guard who is skilled at the low post, this option becomes appealing. After 1 passes to 2 and 2 dribbles at 4 (sending him backdoor and then to the high post), 1 makes the UCLA cut and establishes position on the block. Player 2 uses his head, his feet, or the ball to fake in the direction his defender's hands are and delivers the appropriate pass to 1. While that pass is made, 4 cuts down the lane, calling for the ball and occupying his defender, and sets a down screen with his back to the baseline. Player 5, after faking in, comes around the block to the high post (see figure 7.8). Player 2 reestablishes position at the three-point line or perimeter in the event his man double-teams 1. Player 3 is the protector.

Forward Post-Up

After the UCLA cut, 4 passes back to 2 on the wing, takes one step toward that side of the floor, and cuts down the lane, calling for the ball while 2 is looking for 1 on the block. Player 4 sets a down screen for 5, who has faked away. Player 5 comes to the strong-side high post. Player 4 steps out of the lane, which causes his defender to drop in the key, toward the strong side, as a helper. Player 2 passes to 5 as 4 flashes into the key to receive the pass from 5 (see figure 7.9). Player 4, 5, and 1 are inside rebounders, 3 is the long rebounder, and 2 is the protector.

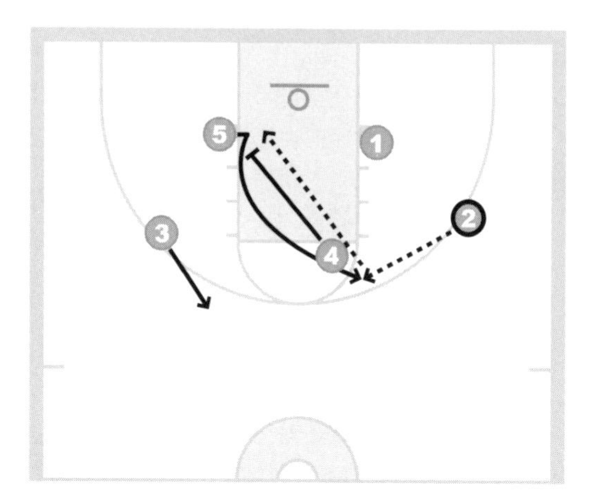

Figure 7.9 Player 4's screen allows 5 to come to the high post for the pass from 2. Then 4 is available in the key for 5's pass.

Side-Post Game

The side-post game is most effective if the guard is a strong ball handler who is capable of driving to the basket, and if the player coming to the side post is a good shooter and driver. Equally as important to the success of this play is the ability of both players to read their defensive men and react quickly and effectively.

After 4 passes to 3, who is looking for 5 at the low post, 4 cuts down the lane, calling for the ball, and sets a screen for 1 on the block. Player 1 comes to the strong-side high post. Player 2 starts on the weak side, fakes a cut toward the key, and comes to the strong-side free throw lane extended to receive the pass from 3 (see figure 7.10). He must time his cut so he is open immediately after 3 has given 1 a good look at the high post.

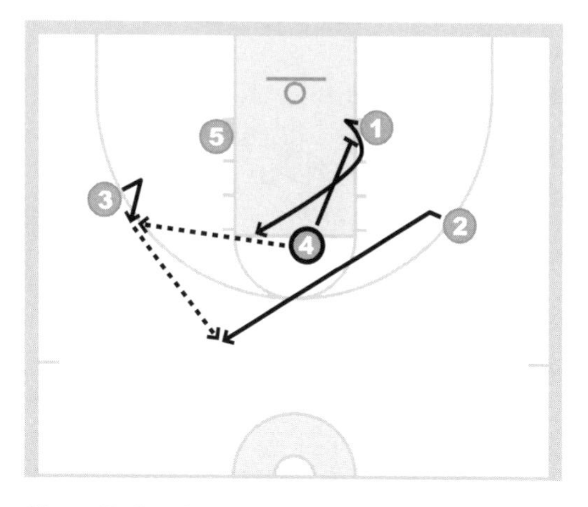

Figure 7.10 Player 1 comes to the high post off 4's screen, but 3 passes to 2, who has come from the weak side.

Player 4 changes direction and comes back to the side post where he receives a pass from 2, who will usually fake down and deliver the two-handed overhead pass. Players 5 and 1 head to the block and form a double screen with 1 on the baseline side (his foot closest to the baseline is on the block). Player 2 makes a cut just to the inside of 4, reads his defender, and makes the move to get open. Against good defenders, he will cut over the top and receive a handoff pass. Player 4 can roll to the basket or pop out to the three-point line, if he has the range. Players 1 and 5 set a double screen for 3, who pops out when 4 has explored the options with 2 (see figure 7.11). Whether 4 passes to 3 or not, 1 moves over the top of 5 and comes to the high post.

Figure 7.11 Player 4's options here include handing off to 2, shooting, or passing to 3.

Of all the plays in basketball, the side-post game is arguably the most difficult to defend. It involves a two-player screening game away from the basket, with the path between the players and the basket being virtually unimpeded, and good weak-side action. With practice, the guard and high-post player should learn to read the defense and collect a repertoire of maneuvers based on what the defense gives them.

If his defender plays the passing lane, the high-post player may choose to slip to the basket rather than the standard move to the high post. Or, the high-post player might opt to continue out and set a ball screen. After receiving a handoff from the high-post player, the guard may flare out for the outside jump shot or continue around the high-post player and drive to the basket. Finally, the high-post player may not hand the ball off but instead pass it to the guard after he has cut for the basket—a give-and-go. All of these options and more are available in the two-player side-post game. Ability will determine viable moves, and that ability can only be discovered in practice sessions.

The combination of Walton and Wilkes proved to be virtually unstoppable. Wilkes was skilled at passing to Walton on the flash move, and Bill was good at passing to Keith if Keith's man helped on Bill and he cut down the lane. Both players were gifted at reading each other's defenders, getting open, and making the right pass. Though Wilkes was fundamentally sound and extremely economical in his movements, there was nothing robotic or mechanical about his play. When passing to the wing on Bill's side and cutting down the lane, he would often come back out, receive a return pass, and shoot the jump shot from the free throw line.

Walton used a play he may have learned from Alcindor—when receiving the ball in the low post, he often passed back out to the wing, causing his defender to relax and give up position. Walton then repositioned himself closer to the basket and received a return pass for the score.

Bill loved to come to the high post and reverse the forward on his side. Opponents were well aware of this play and made it a point to try to deny the pass to Walton. With Henry Bibby passing to Greg Lee (guard to guard), and Lee dribbling toward Wilkes, looking for the backdoor and bringing Keith to the high post, Walton started up the lane, anticipating the pass from Lee out to Bibby. But Greg faked the pass to Henry, and with Walton's defender going with him to the high post, Greg made the lob pass to Walton, who reversed to the basket.

Again, these are the kinds of opportunities that the high-low set permitted, given the great skills of the center. Perhaps your team can come up with additional options that work particularly well for you.

A SPECIAL PERFORMANCE

Quick player and ball movement made double-teaming Bill Walton difficult, although not impossible. Most teams managed to put another defender on him at least some of the time. However, one opposing team decided to play Walton one on one for an entire game.

In the 1973 NCAA championship game, Memphis State believed that if they stopped all of our other players, Bill could not beat them by himself. That is typically a sound philosophy, because basketball is a team game, and five players should always beat one. However, in this

© UCLA Photography

Here, Bill Walton scores two of his 44 points in the 1973 NCAA championship game against Memphis State University. UCLA won its seventh straight NCAA championship.

continued »

» continued

case, Bill's teammates made the most of the opportunity to get the ball to him with only one defender assigned to stop him.

The result was not what Memphis State had hoped for. Bill had what most observers consider to be the most amazing performance in NCAA tournament history. He made 21 out of 22 shot attempts and played a nearly flawless overall game. But the assistance from his teammates cannot be overlooked, because time and again they presented him the ball in a position to score against the lone defender.

CLOSING POINTS

The guard to high post was the main option for Bill Walton to receive the ball inside. However, if any offense limits itself to one option for a good scorer, opponents will soon find a way to stop it. Bill was so talented and versatile that he found additional ways to get his hands on the ball. The "forward reverse" is an option he invented. Not only was Walton able to deliver the backdoor pass to Bibby or Larry Hollyfield, but when that pass was not available, he would often pass out to the guard who replaced them and cut to the basket for a return pass and layup.

Encouraging the most talented players to explore options of getting to the basketball makes the offense more flexible. The more flexibility, the more difficult it becomes to defend, even in the postseason.

Part IV

SOLUTIONS TO PRESSURE DEFENSE

The institution of the 10-second rule encouraged many teams to apply full-court pressure. The rule meant that a pressing defense might not only force a steal or a ballhandling miscue, it could also cause the offensive team to commit a backcourt time violation.

But aggressive and quick teams have been applying as much pressure as the rules would allow throughout the game's history. And that will continue to be the case as long as the results of those efforts are beneficial. From an offensive standpoint, the challenge of pressing teams is not merely the increased probability of a turnover or violation but also the disruption of the offense's flow.

Teams must be fully prepared to deal with defensive pressure, whether applied full, three-quarter, or half court, and whether in the form of a man-to-man or some type of zone alignment. The key is to emphasize sound offensive principles such as proper spacing, quick cutting, deceptive passing, getting the ball to the middle of the court, and looking to score. Any press offense that adheres to those precepts will either neutralize or conquer any pressure defense.

The press offense must be organized to supply at least two or three passing options, in succession, to all ball handlers. Also, the system should feature plays and options that closely resemble the movement patterns of the standard half-court attack.

The UCLA offense has all the elements needed to handle pressure if players are prepared to execute it as intended. And a well-schooled squad won't be satisfied with simply surviving a possession against a press; the goal should be to make the defense regret that they attempted to apply pressure by slicing through the opposing team for an easy score.

CHAPTER 8

HALF-COURT PRESSURE RELEASE

You've seen how the high-post and high-low offenses *should* work. Of course, Xs and Os always work so nicely on paper and dry-erase or magnetic boards.

Things change a bit when you step onto the court. Not only is the potential for error in offensive execution ever present with young athletes of various skill levels, but the defense is also likely to do everything within its power to disrupt the plays and options that you've so neatly drawn up. The result is this: Errors will be made.

For example, pressure defense is designed to take the offense out of its normal pattern. The ball handler is played very closely, forcing a low-percentage pass, a dribble, or a three-second call. Players one pass away are pressured to receive the ball farther away from the basket, extending the offense and eliminating quick penetration. The defense is looking for a perimeter pass that can be intercepted or, in the least, trying to take the offense to the brink of a shot clock violation, forcing a turnover or an unnatural, low-percentage shot.

But you can reduce the degree to which the offense is disrupted by effectively teaching and preparing players to run the offense against all likely situations you will encounter throughout the season, providing the players are fundamentally sound at high speed. Conversely, failing to prepare is preparing to fail.

The UCLA offense will work against any defense if players are schooled to react quickly and properly to whatever situation they might encounter on each possession. It makes no difference what defensive strategies are used—zone or man-to-man; half-court, three-quarter-court, or full-court pressure; switching or nonswitching; trapping or run-and-jump—all can be conquered with the poised and precise execution developed through intensive practices, instruction, and competition.

In no area of offensive basketball is the principle of preparation more true than in the execution of releasing defensive pressure. The pressure release options presented in the UCLA offense are custom made to counter-attack an aggressive defense that tries to force the action.

In fact, assertiveness and aggression will work against them. The defense's attempt to force a turnover on a perimeter or penetrating pass and to stifle penetration will be countered by an organized system of piercing passes and intelligent player movement. The defense's attempt to control the offense will backfire and result in just the opposite—the offense will control the defense and make it react. The following strategies can be applied to both the high-post and high-low offenses. We will illustrate the high-post offense only.

BASE PLAY

For the high-post and high-low offenses to function optimally, all players except the ball handler must shift their focus and alter their movements before crossing the half-court line. They need to diagnose the defense quickly and determine how best to set up their defenders to receive the ball in their designated positions. So, before even establishing the initial offensive set, all five players are mentally and physically engaged in analyzing the defense and determining counterstrategies, as shown in figure 8.1.

Figure 8.1 The five players getting into half-court position.

Continuing into the frontcourt, the center (5) and the two forwards (3 and 4) should be well ahead of the basketball, while the off-guard (2) stays slightly behind in case defensive pressure is administered on 1 and a cross-court pass is needed. If not, 1 dribbles hard toward his defender. This sets the tone for aggressive offense and signals the start of an offensive play.

The forwards set up their men to get open by faking a backdoor cut and then reversing direction to move back out. The center begins somewhere under the basket and times his cut according to what play the guard initiates.

The off-guard also makes a shallow but quick cut toward the basket and then comes back out to a position slightly farther away from the basket than 1. The guard-to-guard pass is the preferred method for initiating the offense, and a slightly backward lateral pass creates more space to complete that pass.

But this play is not always available. At times, 2's defender is playing the passing lane, hoping for a steal. In that case, the defense has called the guard reverse play.

As any high-post or high-low play designates, the weak-side wing player moves to the low-post area on the weak side. Positioned there and recognizing passing-lane pressure on 2, he immediately sprints from the low block to the free throw line area to receive the pass from 1.

When 2 sees the play coming, he lures his defender out just a little farther, calling for the ball to deceive his man into thinking he wants it. What he is actually doing is luring him into a backdoor situation. Player 2 begins his backdoor cut to the basket before 1 makes his pass to 4. If 2's defender sees the pass and gets wind of the play, he will immediately drop toward the basket, aborting the reverse. Player 2 must time his reverse cut so he is well on his way to the basket when 4 receives the pass from 1 (see figure 8.2). Player 4, whose back remains to the basket, gives 2 the pass if he is open.

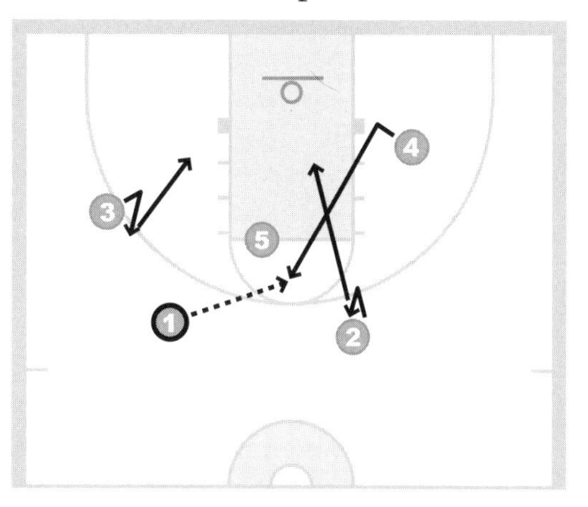

Figure 8.2 Player 2 must be well on his way to the basket when 1 makes the pass to 4.

Simultaneous with the backdoor cut is the immediate movement of 5 and 3 to the opposite low-post area, anticipating the setting of a double screen for 2, who is coming around if he does not receive the backdoor pass. Players 5 and 3 set the double screen by facing in toward the basket with 3 on the baseline side (his foot closest to the baseline is on the block). Player 1, after passing to 4, cuts off 4 and moves to the side that 2 has vacated to balance the floor (see figure 8.3). Player 2 comes around the double screen set by 5 and 3. The other players are in position.

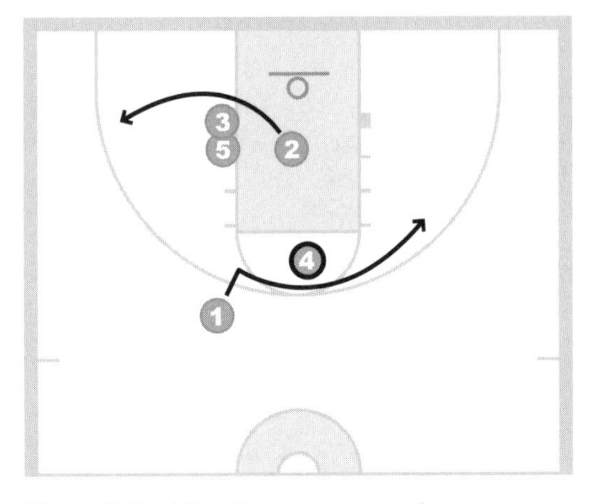

Figure 8.3 After 2 moves past the screen set by 3 and 5, 1 goes to the other side to balance the floor.

If 4 passes to 2, 4 cuts hard to the opposite low-post area, calling for the ball. Player 3, who is on the low side of the double screen, cuts over the top of 5 and moves to the side of the high-post area, called the elbow, on the strong side (see figure 8.4). Player 3 times his move to the elbow so he arrives immediately after 2 has had a good look at getting the ball to 5.

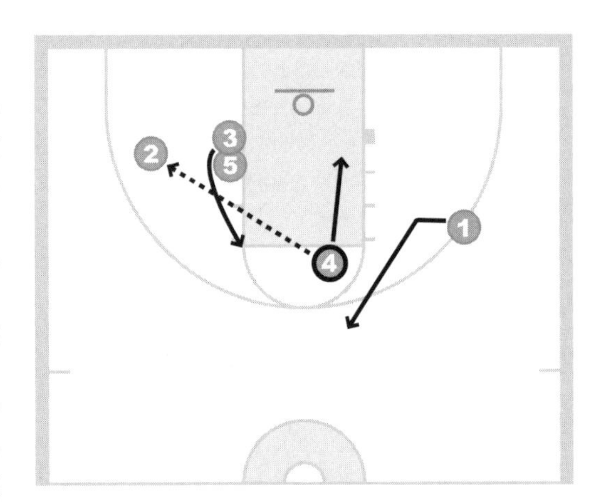

Figure 8.4 Player 4 passes to 2, then moves to the low-post area. Player 3 cuts in front of 5 toward the strong-side elbow.

The strategy behind 3's cut in front of 5 is that it clears that area for a split second, allowing room for a pass from 2 to 5, as shown in figure 8.5. Because 3 has passed in front of 5, the only possible way 5's defender can pressure the pass is from the baseline side—sure suicide; a pass from 2 to 5's left side will result in a one-step hook shot and a score. Player 5's job is to make the 180-degree turn into his man, initiating and maintaining contact. Contact is in the favor of the offensive player because it freezes defenders. When 5 times his turn perfectly, he could have a quick drop step to the baseline or, as mentioned, a hook shot across the key with no dribble needed. The defense will not have time to double-team the center because of the quick pass, catch, and shoot action.

Figure 8.5 Player 3's cut in front of 5 clears the way for a pass from 2 to 5.

If 2 chooses not to shoot when coming off the double screen, the offense is in the four-options set. The very thing the defense was attempting to divert—half-court execution to attack the inside—has occurred.

Player 2's first option is a pass to 5. If he cannot hit 5, option two is to pass to 3 at the elbow of the lane. There are two reasons he would do so: because 5 is being fronted, and the triangle is being used to get him the ball as he seals his defender away from the basket (see figure 8.6); or because 4, who is now at the weak-side low post, is a good post-up player and has an advantage. In that case, 3, 4, and 1 use their triangle to get a high-percentage shot.

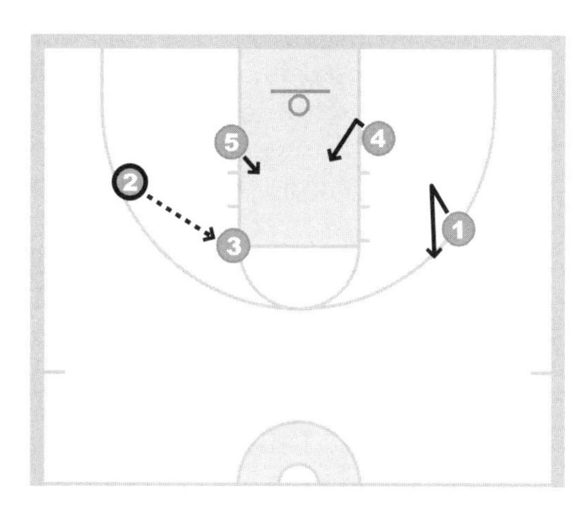

Figure 8.6 If 5 is not open, 2 can pass to 3 at the elbow.

A third option for 2 is to pass the basketball out to 1, who has come back to the strong side. Player 1 must fake in and time his cut so he receives the ball 15 to 20 feet away from the basket and slightly to the strong side. This will provide a good angle for the next pass.

The pass from 2 to 1 signals the play for the side-post game, which is a play that all players enjoy (see figure 8.7).

Player 4, on seeing the ball being passed out to 1, makes his cut to the weak-side high-post elbow. Player 1 passes him the ball and cuts off him, looking for the handoff (notice the angle of his cut). At the same time, 3 moves to the low post to help 5 set another double screen for 2, who moves behind the screen, almost under the basket (see figure 8.8).

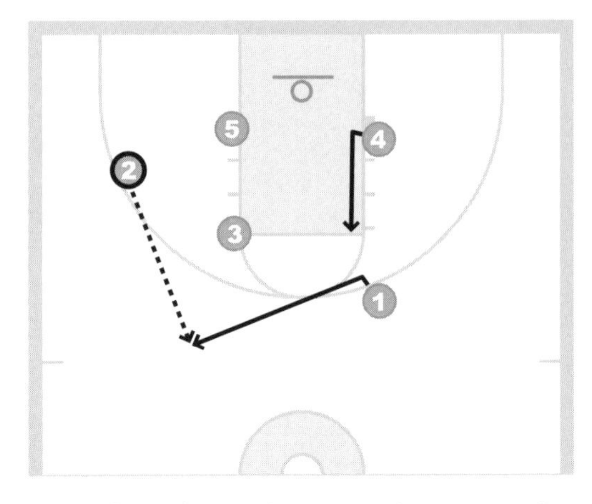

Figure 8.7 Alternative to passing to 5 or 3, 2 can pass to 1, who has cut over toward the strong side.

Figure 8.8 Player 4 has cut to the high-post elbow on the weak side to receive the pass from 1, who then cuts past 4 for the handoff.

Players 4 and 1 have a plethora of options depending on their abilities. Player 1 can take the handoff from 4 and drive to the basket or flare out to the perimeter if his defender gets caught behind the screen. He may receive the handoff and, if his man recovers, take him one on one. Player 4 may keep the ball for a one-on-one play if he has a quickness or talent advantage. If 4 catches 1's pass and finds that his defender extended himself, he can drop his foot away from the defender and drive to the basket. A few UCLA forwards were extremely skilled at this move.

Player 5 should be ready to flash into the key at any time in case his defender moves toward the baseline or moves out to switch on 2. Though not likely, if the player is alert, the opportunity will occasionally present itself, especially against switching defenses and unsuspecting defenders. The timing of these options must be mastered and become second nature. For example, 2 should not make his move to come off the double screen until 1 has cut off 4 and 4 has turned to face the basket.

When the play was initiated with the pass from 1 to 4, 2 made the backdoor cut and 1 followed behind him, coming off 4 and looking for a possible handoff. Player 4 had the option to pass to 2 or 1. Had he passed to 2, another world of possibilities would have opened up.

A skilled forward, after receiving the ball from 1, can at times fake the handoff to 1. The fake may shift his own defender toward 1's cut, allowing him to drop a leg toward the basket and drive for the score, as shown in figure 8.9. If executed in the early part of a game, this move often keeps the defender honest for the remainder of the game, allowing the handoff to be more effective.

Figure 8.9 At the high post, the forward fakes the handoff to the guard and is beginning his spin to the basket the opposite way.

A play that has been part of basketball since its inception, the give-and-go, can also be used because the entire right side of the floor is available (see figure 8.10). If 4 hands off to 1 or passes the ball to him on the wing, and then rolls to the low-post area, 3 should come to the strong-side elbow to form the 4, 1, 3 triangle and offer help if 4 is fronted. Although a team will rarely take any play this far, the four-options set has been formed once again, but this time on the opposite side of the floor (see figure 8.11).

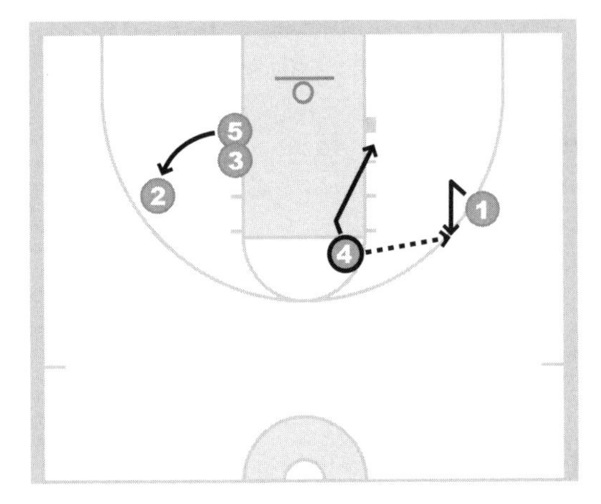

Figure 8.10 Players 4 and 1 use the give-and-go.

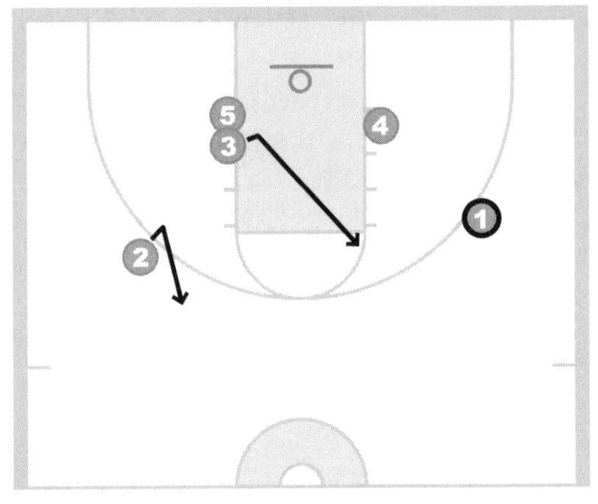

Figure 8.11 The 4, 1, 3 triangle is formed and the players are now in the four-options set.

ADDITIONAL OPTIONS

When executed properly, the guard-to-guard pressure release and the primary options off it will not only solve any press applied by the defense but will also result in a high-percentage scoring opportunity. However, in certain circumstances, alternate pressure-defeating plays might be preferable. We found it beneficial to have the following options in our arsenal.

Reverse for the Reverser

Although the quick movement of 4 coming to the high post from the weak-side low post is difficult to prevent, that might be the case if 4's defender plays between him and the ball, anticipating his cut. Coaches who teach pressure defense and have scouted the play may begin the game pressuring the off-guard and the off-forward.

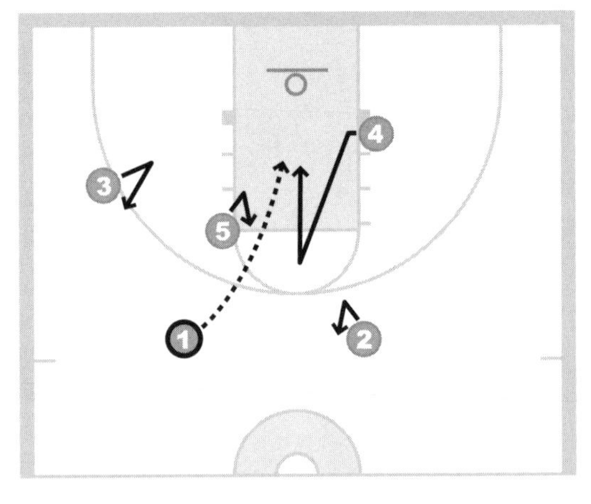

Figure 8.12 Player 1's pass fake and 4's cut must be convincing for this play to work.

Since the high-post offense begins in a high set (all five men at the free throw line or higher), 1 can execute a lob if 4 fakes up and reverses his cut to the basket (see figure 8.12). To be successful, 4 must make a convincing cut to the ball, and 1 must make an equally convincing pass fake to him. If 5 times his cut to the high post so he arrives after 4, he will keep his defender busy so he can't help on 4's backdoor cut.

But that lob pass requires a large degree of accuracy and has an equal margin for error. The best way to get 4 the ball is for the center (5) to be involved. Player 5 recognizes the overplay on 4 and arrives at the high post. He comes out to receive the pass at the strong-side elbow area or a little higher. Player 4 times his backdoor cut so he has begun his route to the basket just before 5 has received the ball. Player 5 delivers a two-handed overhead pass or a hook pass while turning (see figure 8.13). There is no time to pivot. The entire basket area should be empty of defenders. It will only take one success to exploit the defensive weakness and cause doubt in the mind of the opponent.

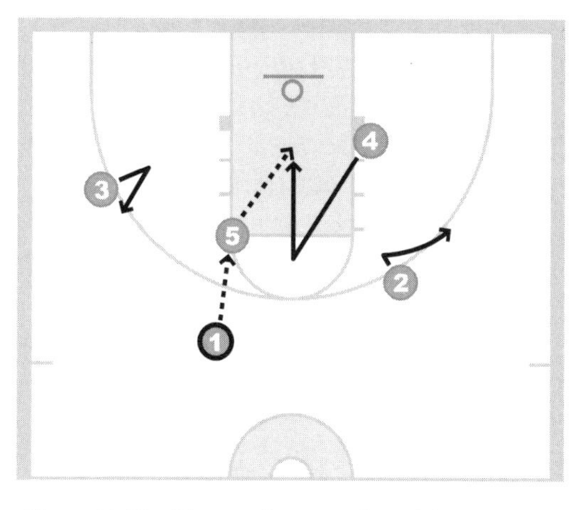

Figure 8.13 Player 4 must time his cut so that he's on his way to the basket as 5 receives the ball from 1.

Forward One-on-One

The guard reverse is an excellent play to give a skilled forward a one-on-one opportunity. When 4 comes to the high post to reverse 2, 2 clears the area by cutting through and coming off the double screen. Player 1 comes off 4, looking for the handoff. Player 4 makes the one-on-one move and has passing options to 2 for the three-point shot, 5 inside, 3 at the high post, and 1 on the opposite wing (see figure 8.14).

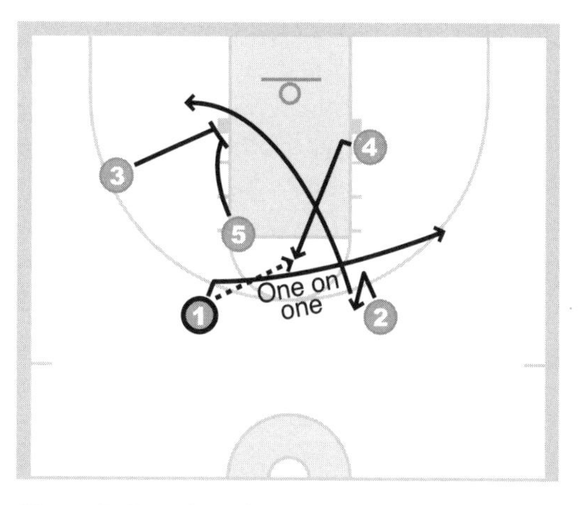

Figure 8.14 After the one-on-one, 4 can pass to any of the other players.

Guard to Center, Forward Reverse

When entering the frontcourt, the ballhandling guard may see two pressure release plays simultaneously: pressure on the opposite guard and pressure on the ball-side forward. The weak-side forward will always come to the high post when he sees pressure on the guard on his side.

But the ballhandling guard is not obligated to pass him the basketball. He may see an even better situation on the strong side—a backdoor play for the ball-side forward.

His decision to run this option is influenced by whether the team has the correct personnel for the series. A good passing center, as well as a quick forward who can also shoot the outside shot after coming off a weak-side double screen, are two criteria needed for a decision to explore the forward reverse.

On the strong side, three players are involved: the guard (1), the center (5), and the forward (3). Player 3 takes his defender toward the basket and makes his cut out to the wing. His defender is trained to float toward the ball and pressure the passing lane, not allowing 3 to receive a pass. Even before the initial set, 5, knowing it's his responsibility, has kept an eye on how his teammate, 3, is being played. He recognizes pressure and is eager to help. Player 1 has brought the ball up the floor and also recognizes overplay on the forward (see figure 8.15). Player 1 has two options to reverse 3: He can pass to 5 or dribble hard toward 3.

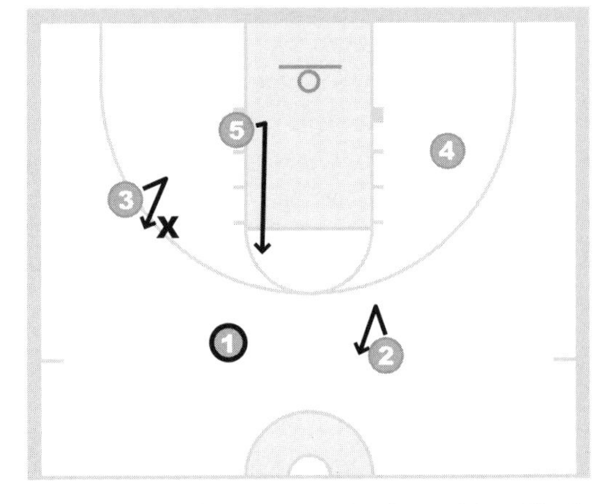

Figure 8.15 Players 1 and 5 have identified 3 being overplayed and weigh the options.

Player 1 takes a good look at 3. Simultaneously, 5, who has cut toward the basket, makes a hard cut to the area just above the free throw line (but not outside the free throw lane extended). Too far out and he will not have a good backdoor passing angle to 3. Player 1 passes to 5. When 3 sees that 1 is about to pass to 5, he takes his man one more step out and quickly reverses to the basket. He times his cut so he is on his way to the basket when 5 catches the ball (see figure 8.16).

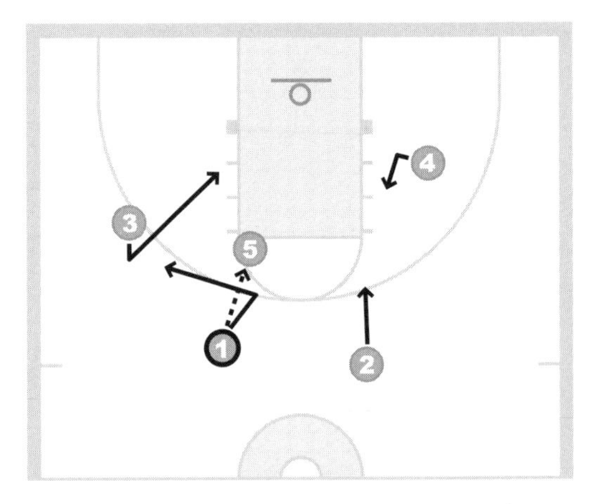

Figure 8.16 Player 1 passes to 5 near the free throw line, reversing 3 to the basket.

Near-perfect timing is the key. Again, if 3 reverses too quickly, there is no passing angle for 5. If he reverses too late, his defensive man may recover.

The first option for 5 is to give 3 a backdoor pass. He drops his right foot toward the baseline and delivers a right-handed bounce pass that leads his receiver. If 3 receives the basketball and drives for the layup, the other players take their rebounding assignments. If 3 receives the basketball and help arrives (from defenders guarding 5 and 4), 5 or 4 may be open for a pass and score underneath.

If 5 decides not to give 3 the backdoor pass, 4 and 2 set a weak-side double screen with 2 on the baseline side (his foot closest to the baseline is on the block). When 4 recognizes the play, he should immediately head toward the low-post area on the weak side. Player 1 has already taken the wing area that 3 has vacated (see figure 8.17).

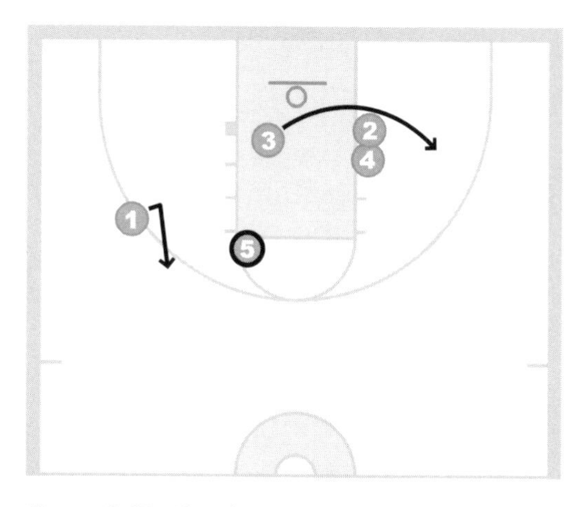

Figure 8.17 If 5 doesn't pass to 3, 4 and 2 set a screen for 3, and 1 takes 3's place on the wing.

Player 3 continues through the lane and comes off the double screen, reading his defender to get him caught in the screen. If 5 passes 3 the basketball, 2 comes over the front of 4 and assumes a position at the strong-side elbow, creating a triangle and two passing options for 3. Player 5 cuts down the lane, calling for the ball and keeping his defender from providing weak-side help. Player 1 moves along the perimeter toward the top of the key, but not to the ball side until he is needed (see figure 8.18).

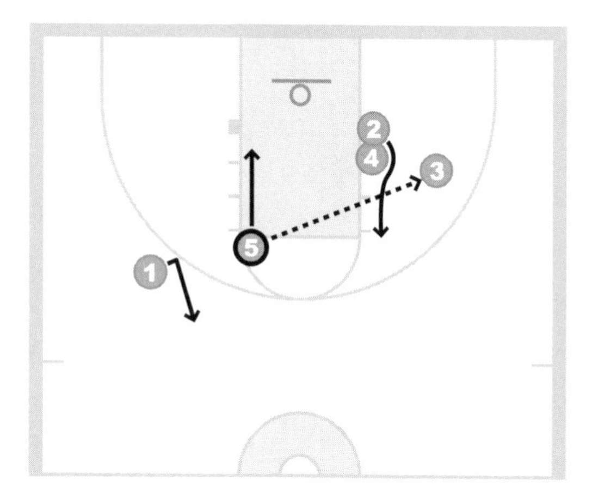

Figure 8.18 Player 5 passes to 3, 2 comes to the elbow to create a triangle, and 5 cuts down the lane, distracting his defender.

The team is now in the four-options set. Player 3 may pass to 4 at the low post, pass to 2 at the elbow, pass out to 1 (who comes over to the strong side), or dribble directly at 1. To make a good decision, he must recognize where the high-percentage play is. Who is guarding 4 at the low post and is 4 a skilled low-post player? Does 2 have a good high-post situation? Does 5 have a high-percentage "flash" situation (stepping in the key to receive a pass from 2)? Do 5 and 1 have a good "side-post game" on the weak side?

Guard to Wing, Dribble Reverse

Player 1's second option to reverse 3 is to dribble directly at him, forcing a backdoor cut. When he sees 1 coming, 3 takes one quick step out away from the basket, luring his man to the perimeter, and quickly reverses to the basket (see figure 8.19). Player 1 may deliver the backdoor pass. It will most likely be a one-handed bounce pass, as shown in figure 8.20*a-b*.

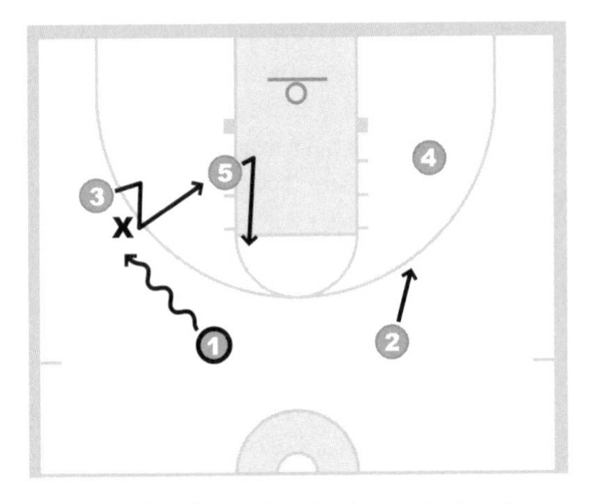

Figure 8.19 Player 1 dribbles at 3, forcing 3 to do a backdoor cut.

Figure 8.20 The backdoor one-handed bounce pass from 1 to 3.

If no backdoor pass is made, 1 passes quickly to 5, who has stepped out. Player 5 will most likely be open, especially if his defender helped on 3's cut. However, he does have the option to reverse if he is overplayed. Player 4 and 2 form a weak-side double screen, with 2 on the lower side, and 3 comes off the screen. Player 1 moves slightly toward the middle of the court. Player 5 may hit 3, who has come around the double screen (see figure 8.21).

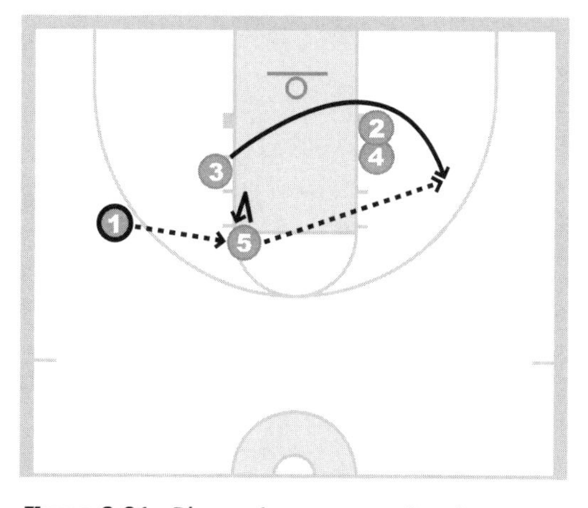

Figure 8.21 Player 1 passes to 5, who passes to 3 after 3 comes off the double screen.

Player 2 cuts in front of 4 to the strong-side elbow to form a triangle. Player 5 makes a hard cut, looking for the pass, to the weak-side low post (see figure 8.22). Player 1 waits. Again, the alignment is the four-options set. Player 3 may have a quick pass to 4 on the block. His second option is a pass to 2 at the high post. If 5 is good inside, 2 may pass to him at the weak-side low post, as 5 flashes into the key. His third option is a pass back out to 1 who runs the side-post game with 5. The last option is for 3 to dribble directly at 1 who reverses to the basket. Player 5 then comes off the double screen set by 3 and 4.

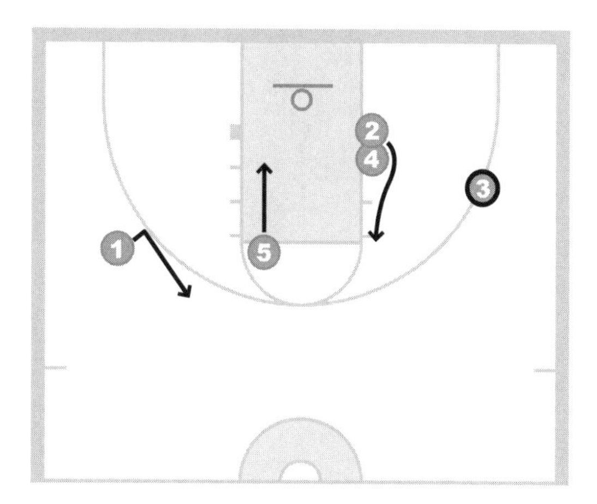

Figure 8.22 After player 2 cuts to the strong-side elbow and 5 moves to the low post on the weak side, the players are in the four-options set.

ANDRE'S VALUABLE SKILL

The 1974 to 1975 Bruins were tested at every turn. Without Bill Walton and Keith Wilkes, opponents often pressured the offense in the front-court. The keen ballhandling of guard Andre McCarter proved invaluable. It was foolish for any defender to play him closely and try to force him to make an errant pass. Andre would drive right by him and create an offensive advantage.

McCarter's dribbling ability reached its pinnacle in the final seconds of the NCAA championship game against the University of Kentucky. As defenders attempted to catch him, he put on a most incredible dribbling exhibition. The clock ran out and UCLA had won its 10th national championship in 12 years.

Andre McCarter was a tremendous dribbler. Rarely was any defender able to take the ball away from him.

CLOSING POINTS

Whether executing the guard-to-guard or guard-to-forward pressure release, continuous and safe ball movement is essential, which requires crisp passing, safe receiving, proper pivoting, and quick and timely cutting, all at high speed. Players must be in constant motion, faking away and moving toward their positions to receive those passes at exactly the right time. Poor timing, standing, or making halfhearted efforts to get open will close off passing lanes and result in limited ball movement—in other words, play right into a pressure defense's hands.

However, maintaining composure, making strong moves, and penetrating against a very active and aggressive defense will turn the tables because the defense will begin to react to the offensive attack. When that occurs, the defense typically responds with added intensity and tends to gamble more, which should result in a high-percentage shot. The key for the offense is to be proactive, yet patient, and to be prepared to take advantage when those defensive breakdowns arise.

CHAPTER 9

THREE-QUARTER-COURT PRESS ATTACK

Breaking a backcourt press can also break the back of a defense if the offense stays poised and takes advantage of opportunities. At no other time is it more imperative for ball handlers to combine their mental and physical skills than when encountering extended defensive pressure.

Conquering a press can be especially challenging against very quick, athletic, long-armed players who move their feet and anticipate passes well. Against such teams, offenses are sometimes relieved just to make it over the half-court line without a 10-second violation or turnover. And, the safe option after crossing midcourt against a press is to set up and run a half-court offense. That's often the choice when a coach or lead guard does not believe the team has the personnel to attack a press aggressively. They may lack the ballhandling and decision-making skills to convert those opportunities consistently. Or they might fear getting into an up-tempo running game with the opponent, which could happen if they shorten the length of their possessions. But what often occurs when players are caught in a "keep-away" mind-set is that the offense loses sight of the purpose of ball possession—to score. The other danger of this tactic is that it eliminates the defense's risk in pressing; if defenders are assured that their tight ball pressure and steal attempts won't result in an easy basket for the offense, why not keep it up or even ratchet it up a bit? A press offense that abandons the option to score quickly simply encourages and enhances the defensive pressure against it.

Although it certainly is reasonable for teams to adopt a somewhat conservative offensive strategy against presses, the threat of a quick score must always be present. And, a funny thing happens to defenses after they've been beaten a few times for easy baskets: They retreat. Or, at minimum, they are less aggressive and more hesitant to intensify and extend their pressure.

Whether pushing the ball aggressively up the court to score against the press or more selectively choosing when to take the ball to the bucket or set up the half-court attack, an offense's success against three-quarter-court pressure will be determined by the ability of the players to automatically execute the fundamentals at high speed, and by how well the offense adheres to the 10 principles presented in chapter 2. Four of those principles, in fact, warrant special emphasis against backcourt presses:

1. Penetration—This becomes more important than ever because penetration will collapse an extended defense and put the fear of the vulnerability of their own basket in their hearts. Extended defense is designed to stop the penetrating dribble and pass. When it repeatedly fails, no matter what the coach says, the confidence of the players is diminished.

2. Passing—Whether against a man-to-man or zone press, the ball should be moved primarily by the pass. The ball can be moved more quickly through the air than on the ground, and dribbling cannot fake a defense out of position, something that is essential to creating openings. A pressing defense is taught to anticipate the pass and to steal it. A convincing pass fake to one side or to the middle will shift any extended defense and open cutting and passing lanes in other areas. Both passer and receiver are responsible for the success of the fake; the passer fakes the pass, and the receiver fakes the reception, or at least he moves in the direction of the ball. Pass fakes will disrupt defensive timing and teamwork.

3. Timing—Attacking extended defenses will sometimes require longer cuts, sprints, and passes. When this is the case, timing will differ. It must be worked on in practice. More than ever, it is important for cutters to be open at the right time—when it is their turn in the passer's sequence of options.

4. Equal opportunity—Because there is little chance for the immediate score, and more passing may be required than in the half-court attack, the involvement of all five players becomes even more important when attacking a defense far away from the goal.

Rebounding is also important, with the preferred alignment of three inside rebounders, a long rebounder, and a protector. Because the defense is retreating when penetrated, it is often in poor position to match up, player to player. For that reason, offensive second shots are definite possibilities.

Finally, a reminder: When penetrating against an aggressive defense for a score, it is critical that the offense be protective of its rear flank. Whether a shot attempt is or isn't successful, many opponents will try to counter that quick shot with a fast break. Therefore, the offense must be trained, as in the half-court set, to finish the possession in proper alignment.

KEYS TO SUCCESS

Extended defense works best when all five players are focused on the basketball, working together to stop penetration by closing down passing and driving lanes. Therefore, a goal of the offense is to keep defenders occupied by and concerned about players moving to get open off the ball. The only way to do that is by making purposeful cuts, staying well spaced on the court, and keeping active throughout the possession. When defenders have to attend to offensive players moving without the ball in their area, it hinders their efforts to focus solely on the ball.

To get open, receivers who are down the floor (the center and the two forwards) must get behind their defenders (in their blind spots if possible), fake, and come to the ball from the back side. Defenders prefer to have their assignments in front so they can see them. Offensive men behind them will cause them to drop back, stretching the defense. This is good for the offense because it keeps defenders occupied away from the basketball.

Aggressive, coordinated, and penetrating cuts, combined with quick ball movement, will surely put the defense on the defensive. Such offensive assertiveness lets the opponent know who is in control of play.

Finally, good timing between passers and receivers is nearly impossible to defend. To gauge whether timing is optimal, answer this: Was the receiver slowing down when he received the pass? If the answer is yes, the timing needs work. Receivers must accelerate to the basketball because if they don't, their defenders will, and a steal is almost certain.

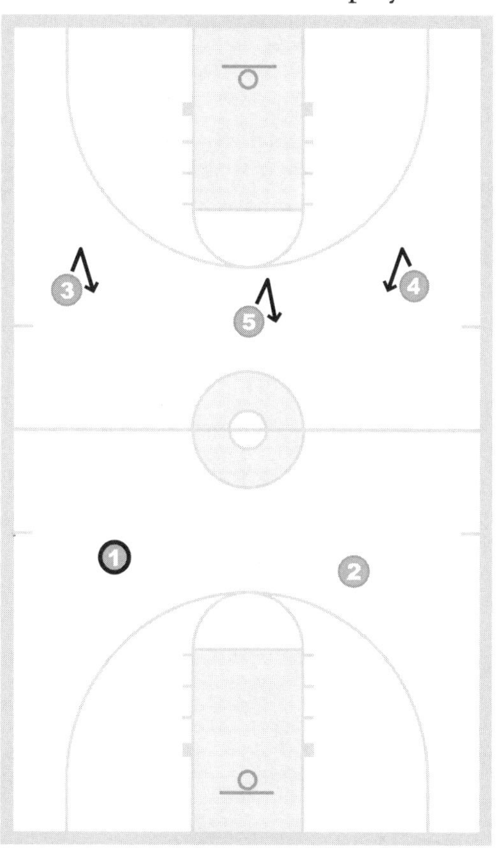

Figure 9.1 Initial alignment with two-guard front, center in middle, and forwards on the wings.

INITIAL ALIGNMENT

If there is one key to breaking pressure beyond half court, it is getting the basketball to the middle of the floor. That's also important in a half-court attack, but in that case, the focal point is the high post rather than the half-court area.

Therefore, as in half-court offense, the initial alignment should include a two-guard front, the center in the middle, and the forwards on the wings (see figure 9.1). The two-guard front provides two points from which the ball can be passed into the middle. The center is stationed in the middle of the floor, though he is not necessarily the primary receiver in that area. That will be determined by the coach. Either forward, positioned on the respective wings, could pop into the center-court area as well, displacing the center at any time.

BASE PLAYS

To start, the passing guard has three passing options to advance the ball: a pass to the weak-side forward, to the strong-side forward, or to the center. The reverse pass to guard 2 will be presented as an additional option. This section will show a possible passing sequence for each option that could lead to a score. However, as with any offensive play in a triangle-type system, each option offers several possibilities for players to read the defense and make adjustments. Players, through trial and error and with encouragement and guidance from their coach, will find ways to get the ball to the best players in the best positions.

Not only is this true within any particular play, but it is also true when 1 is deciding which of the three plays to use. Should he pass to the weak-side forward coming to the middle, to the center, or to the strong-side forward? This question is impossible to answer here because every team has unique strengths and weaknesses, defensive alignment varies, and, depending on player ability, one play may be wiser than another. What works and what doesn't will be determined through resourcefulness and editing. For example, a team may discover that a particular forward may be limited in passing and ballhandling ability. The center may lack receiving and passing ability but may be effective on the catch and score when the second line of defense is broken and a two-on-one or three-on-two situation emerges. Coaches should keep things simple by editing plays and options so the best players receive the ball in good positions, increasing the possibility of ball advancement without a turnover and the chance of a score.

Variety is a tool of the cunning. Occasionally choosing another play or another angle of attack maintains unpredictability and helps keep the defense off balance and less likely to anticipate the pass and cut.

Guard Reverse

This option is much like the guard reverse pressure release in the high-post and high-low offenses (see chapter 8). However, because the ball is in the backcourt and must be advanced past the centerline in 10 seconds, the guard-to-guard pass is not the first option.

The first objective is to get the ball safely into the middle of the floor as soon as possible. Advancing the ball to the middle of the court collapses the defense both vertically (as the defense retreats) and horizontally (as it squeezes in toward the middle to prevent another pass down the middle). When 4 senses an opening, he comes hard to the ball, either across half court or before, depending on how long the pass is and how safe it is. He must be careful not to leave the ground in the frontcourt, catch the ball in the air, and land in the backcourt. On seeing 4 come to the middle, 5 sprints down the middle, toward the basket, and positions himself about 20 feet from 4 as the next potential receiver. Player 3 sprints down the sideline and is ready to come back to the ball as well. Player 1 passes to 4 (see figure 9.2).

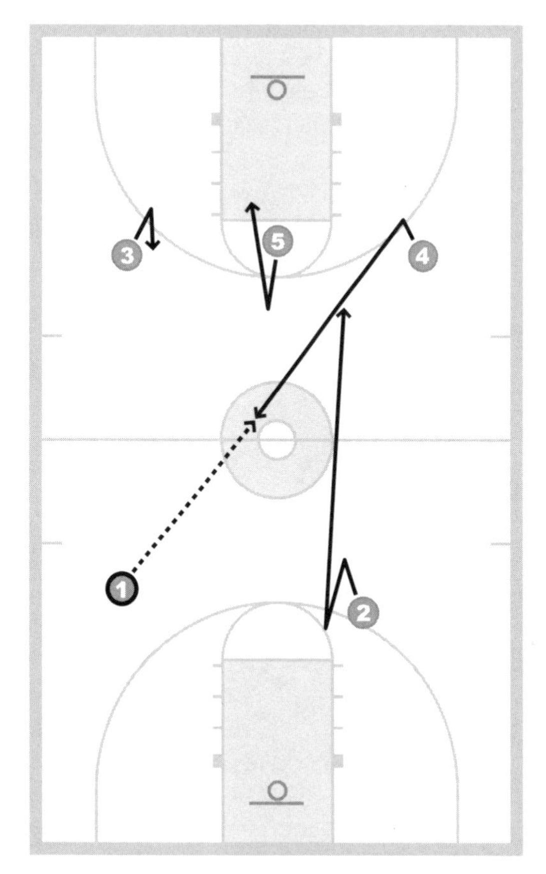

Figure 9.2 Player 4 makes himself available for the pass by coming to half court.

When 1 passes the ball to 4, 2 makes a hard backdoor cut toward the basket. Players 3 and 5 have made basket cuts and also come hard to the basketball. If all defensive players extend, 2 may have a layup. If the defense is playing zone, 2 may have a one-on-one move against one defender, resulting in a score or a pass for a score.

With the ball in 4's hands, 2 continues his backdoor cut, and, different from the half-court pressure release, 1 also cuts toward the basket. After faking away, 5 comes to the ball, ready to receive a pass from 4. Player 1 enters the frontcourt to prevent 4 from passing the ball back over the centerline if 4 has received the ball in the frontcourt.

Player 2 then makes a quick change of pace and change of direction, cutting out to the right wing to be a receiver for 4. Player 4 passes the ball to 2 and cuts hard backdoor for a give-and-go (see figure 9.3). Player 4 can use 5 as a screener if 5 is in position and the defense is playing man-to-man. Player 5 turns his back to 4.

If 4 does not receive the pass, he cuts to the wing. With 4 cutting through and 2 foregoing the pass to him, 2 can pass back to 1, and the offense needs no repositioning of players; it's ready for any play (see figure 9.4).

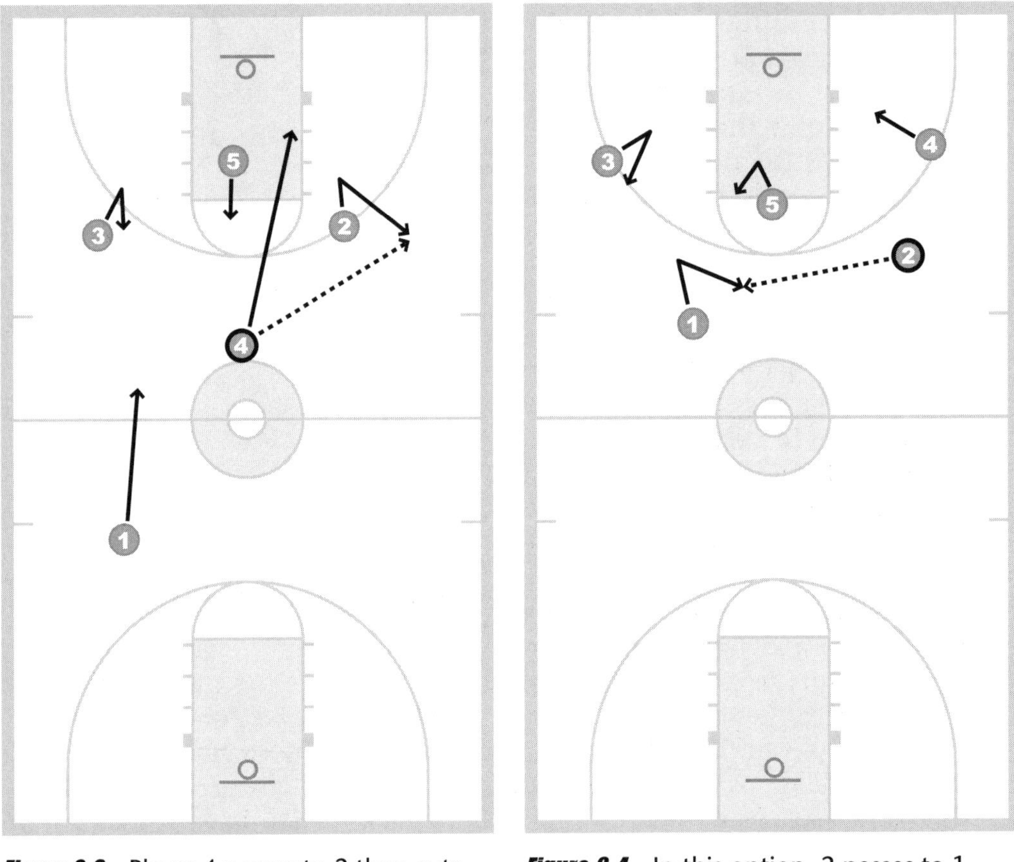

Figure 9.3 Player 4 passes to 2 then cuts backdoor for a give-and-go.

Figure 9.4 In this option, 2 passes to 1 instead of 4.

Guard to Ball-Side Forward

A second option starts with 1 passing to 3, who has freed himself by cutting away and coming back to the corner. Player 5 sets a screen for 1, who uses it to cut to the basket. Player 3 gives 1 the pass if that pass does not lead him into a waiting defender (see figure 9.5).

After setting the screen for 1, 5 will most likely be open because his man will drop to help. Player 3 passes to 5 and comes off a back screen set by 1, who has come back. Player 4 moves to the middle of the court, and 2 enters the frontcourt to prevent a pass into the backcourt (see figure 9.6).

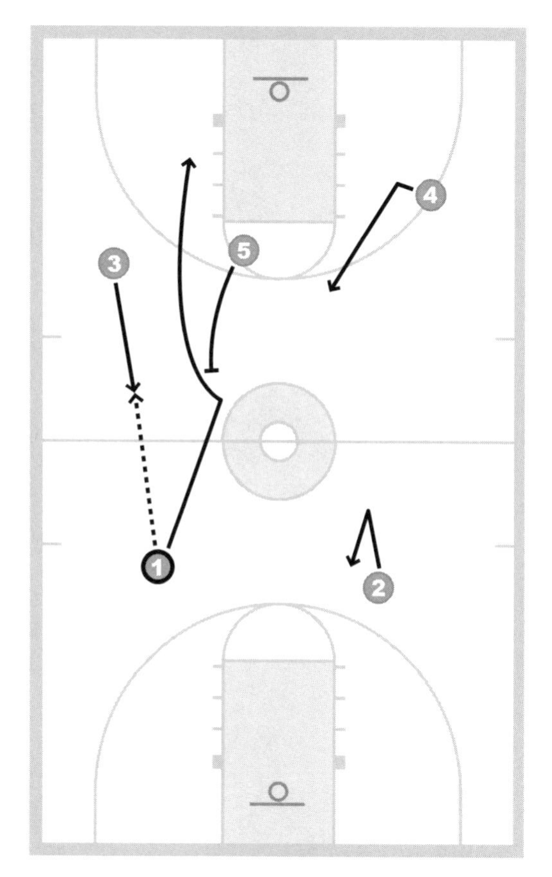

Figure 9.5 Player 1 passes to 3 and then cuts past 5's screen to the basket, becoming open for the pass from 3.

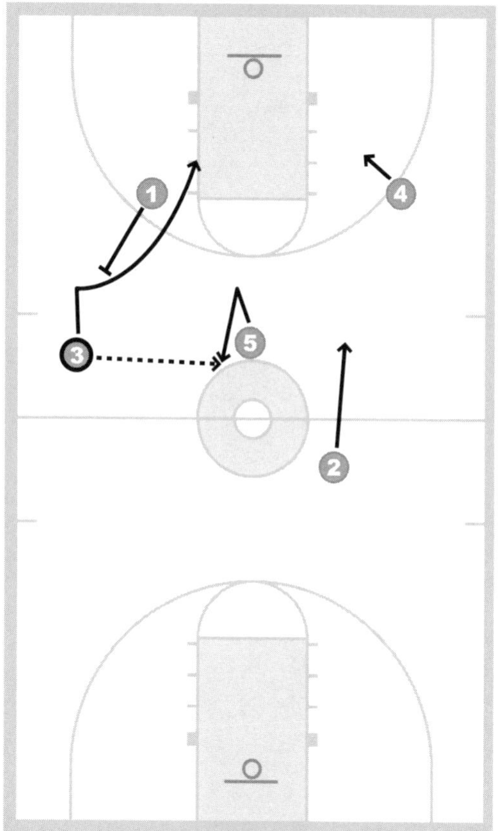

Figure 9.6 Player 3 passes to 5 and then moves toward the key past 1's back screen.

If 5 senses too much pressure to pass to 1, the next option is a pass to 4 at the high post. Player 2 should be alert and be well on his way to the basket when 5 makes the pass to the high post. If they can get into position in time, 3 and 5 set a double screen for 2 on the opposite low post. Player 1 fakes an inside cut and comes over the top of 4, looking for a handoff pass (see figure 9.7).

Another option for 5 is a pass to 2 on the right side. After the pass, 5 cuts hard toward the basket, and 4 clears the way by flaring out to the wing (see figure 9.8). If no pass is made, 2 can pass to 1, and the offense is in motion without a hitch.

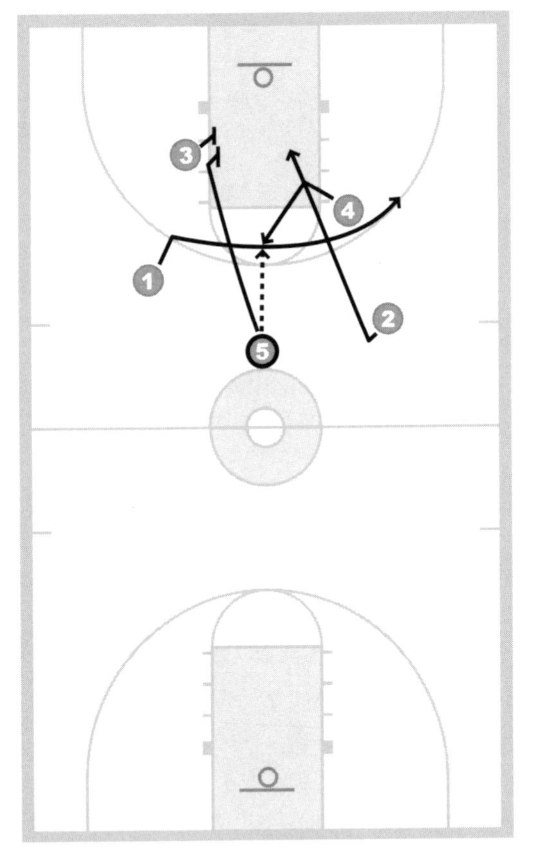

Figure 9.7 Player 2 times his cut so that he's on his way to the basket when 5 passes to 4.

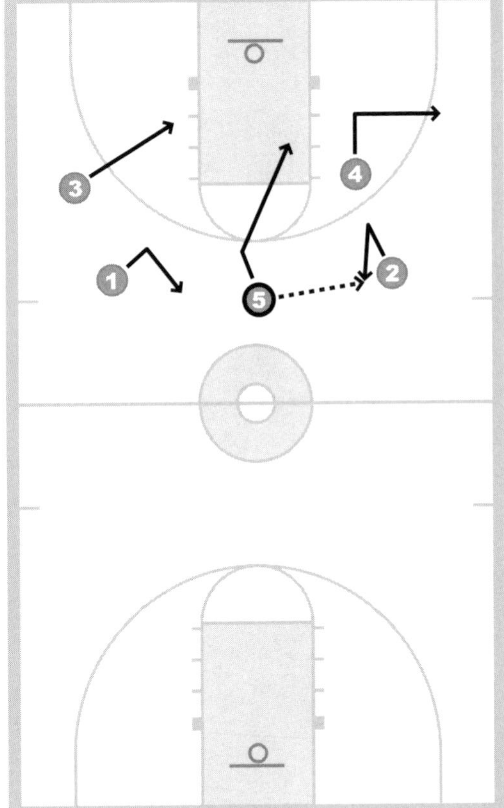

Figure 9.8 In this option, 5 passes to 2 and then cuts to the basket.

Guard to Center

The third option begins with a pass from 1 to 5, who has cut away and come to the ball. Players 3 and 4 reverse hard to the basket, looking for a backdoor pass (see figure 9.9).

Players 1 and 2 enter the frontcourt and cut down the two sides of the lane. As in the guard-to-center option in the half-court offense, both guards, one guard, or neither can cross over or cut down the lane based on their reading of the defense. Players 1 and 2 may screen for 3 and 4 to bring them to the wings, or they may reverse back out. Player 5 passes to 1 or 2, takes his position at the high post, and the offense is in motion (see figure 9.10).

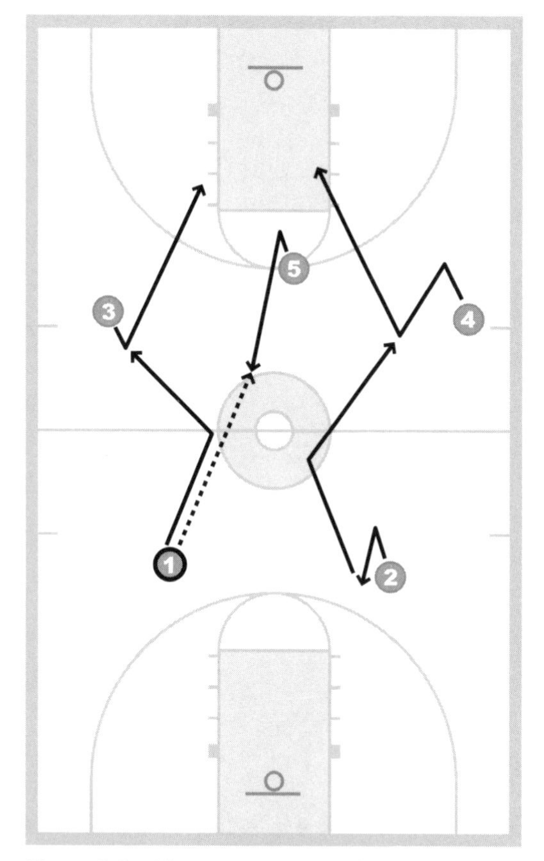

Figure 9.9 Player 5 receives the ball from 1, then 3 and 4 reverse to the basket for a possible backdoor pass.

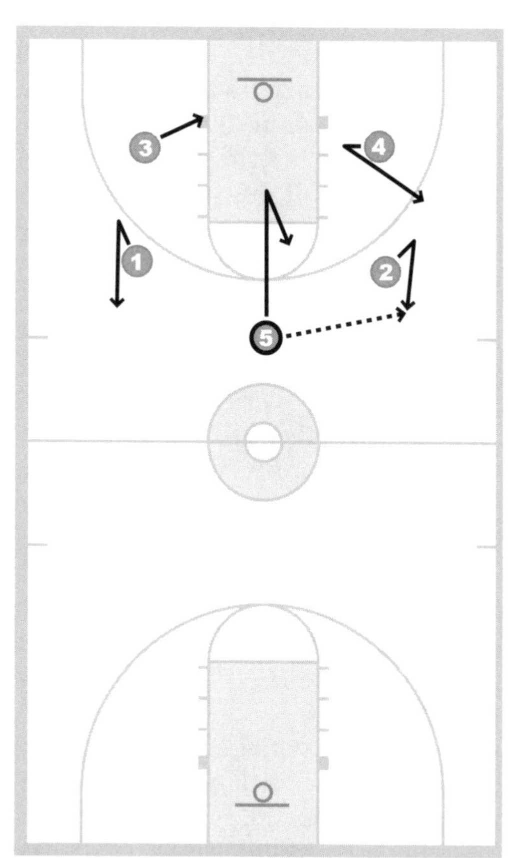

Figure 9.10 Player 5 passes to 2, who has come back out, and then moves to the high post.

ADDITIONAL OPTIONS

Diagrams are only that—diagrams. All coaches know that Xs and Os are helpful in developing a structure and illustrating player options. However, because the movements and ploys of the defense can have so many looks, an attacking offense must have an equal amount of plays to counteract. Following are a few additional options, but, mind you, your players will create many more as they continue to face various defensive alignments.

4 Horizontal Cut

Versus the man-to-man or zone press, the guard reverse may not be open because most man-to-man presses deny the middle pass and most zone defenses position a defender in the middle of the court. For all presses, keeping the ball out of the middle is key to maintaining ball and passing-lane pressure.

Beginning with the initial 2-1-2 set, 4 comes to the middle, and 5 retreats. If 4 is pressured, he makes a horizontal cut to the strong-side sideline. Against zone defenses, he will either take the middle man with him or be open. Against man-to-man, his defender will stay with him. In either case, the middle is open for 5 to come hard to the ball and receive the pass from 1 (see figure 9.11).

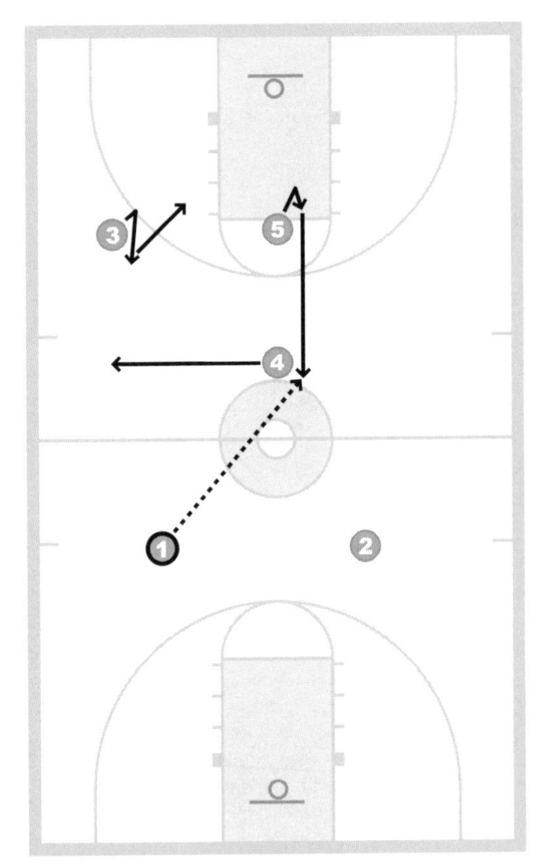

Figure 9.11 Player 4 cuts to the strong-side sideline, freeing up the middle for 5 to receive the pass from 1.

Player 3 replaces 5's position in the middle to balance the floor and provide a possible second consecutive pass up the middle. With the basketball in 5's possession, 2 makes a hard backdoor cut. The entire side is open. Player 4 cuts hard down the sideline and comes back as a potential receiver. Player 5 has three passing options: 2, 3, and 4 (see figure 9.12).

Player 2 is key to 5 receiving the ball and to the score, especially against a zone. When he sees the play develop and makes an early cut—before 5 makes his move to the ball—he will draw the attention of the defender responsible for preventing 5 from receiving. This defender is the last line of defense and cannot let 2 get below him.

As is often the case, 3 may be the team's best athlete and ball handler. The pass from 5 to 3 may prove to be a high-percentage situation.

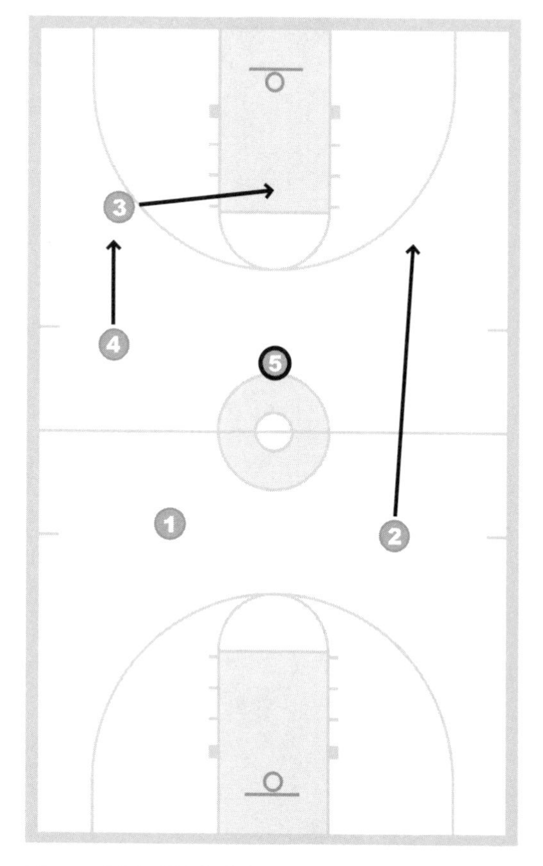

Figure 9.12 With 5 in possession of the ball, 3 moves to the middle, 4 goes down the sideline, and 2 makes a backdoor cut—all three are available for the pass.

Ball Reversal

Often, pressing defenses place partial responsibility for middle denial in the hands of the front-line defender (guard) who is not defending the ball. He will drop toward the center circle. In that case, the 2 guard is open. Player 1 passes to 2, who dribbles hard toward the frontcourt. With 4 down the sideline, the back defender cannot come up and guard 2. The middle man comes over, opening up the middle momentarily. Player 2 makes a quick pass to 5, who looks for 4 and 3 (see figure 9.13).

Possibly an even better situation is 5 cutting straight to the basket and 3 (the better athlete) coming to the middle to receive the pass from 2 (see figure 9.14).

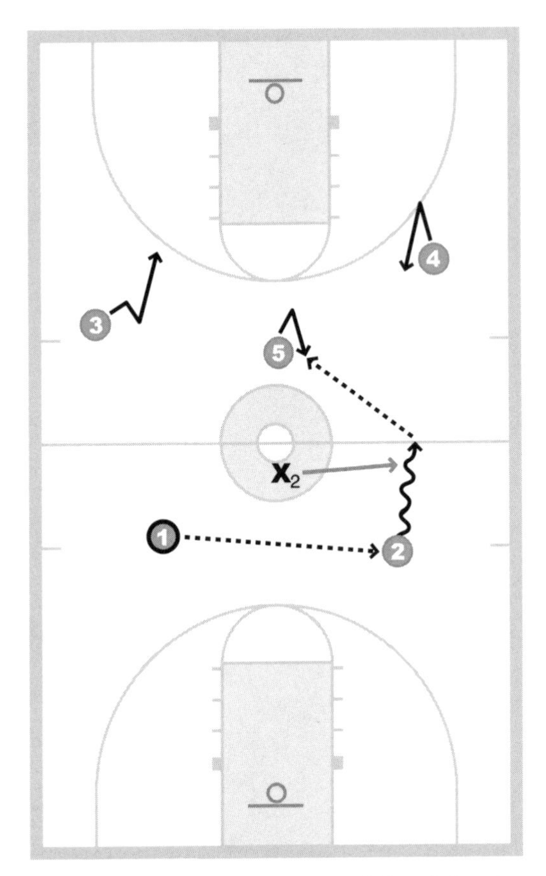

Figure 9.13 The movement of the defending guard first allows 2 to receive the pass from 1, and then allows 5 to be open for 2's pass.

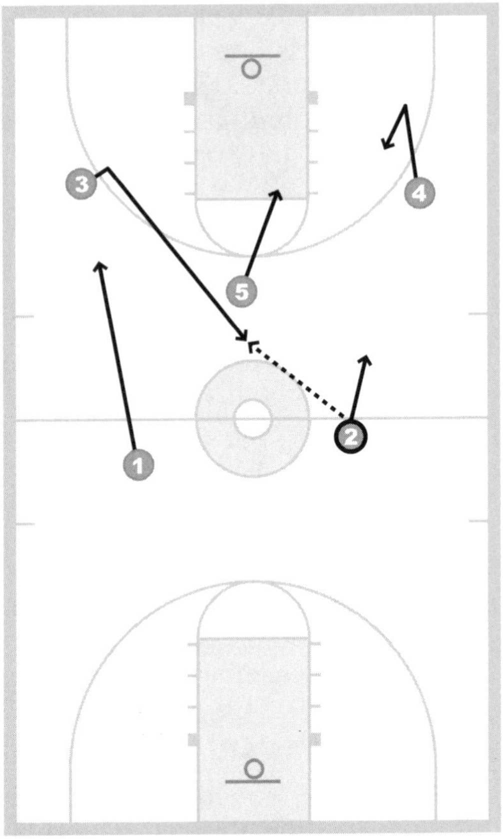

Figure 9.14 Another alternative is 3 coming to the middle to receive the pass.

CLOSING POINTS

A common reason for defensive pressure is to force the action and speed up the game. Opponents who are trailing often do this to increase the number of possessions—and thus generate more opportunities to score and to chip into that deficit.

The offense may have something different in mind—ball control. A common offensive error in these situations is to become less aggressive, reflected in fewer penetrating cuts and scoring threats. The objective changes from scoring to running time off the clock. This will certainly lead to increased defensive pressure and turnovers.

A press offense can continue to look for the score and still be more selective in its shot attempts. What is essential is that players are prepared to execute the fundamentals of passing, dribbling, receiving,

MIKE'S MAGIC

Because they generally handle the basketball more than the other positions, guards tend to have the most turnovers. That was not the case for Mike Warren, the starting point guard for the Lewis Alcindor teams in the late 1960s. In fact, an incredible statistic that may not be matched in NCAA history is when Mike went nine consecutive games without a single turnover. But he didn't do it with fancy, behind-the-back dribbling; he was fundamentally sound, keeping his head up at all times, and always ready to make the play. His signature move was a hard dribble followed by a stop, crossover, and go.

© UCLA Photography

Mike Warren is shown in perfect balance as he dribbles the basketball toward the basket. A mastery of the fundamentals was largely responsible for his extremely low turnover-to-assist ratio.

When he was pressured in the backcourt to pass or pick up his dribble, that "go" meant he penetrated the defense, finished his drive with a score, or, as he often did, made the pass to an open player. When he passed his defender, he was particularly adept at driving directly at the defender who was guarding a good shooter, making him commit, and then passing the ball to his teammate.

and cutting while under the duress they'll encounter in high-speed, high-pressure game conditions. In addition, players must be able to clearly identify what is and is not a high-percentage scoring situation, and they must practice their decision-making skills against gamelike, pressing defenses.

Two final points should be kept in mind. First, although the diagrams in this chapter show the three-quarter-court press offense initiated exclusively from one side, all of the plays presented can be run from the right or left side. Second, as players become more proficient in executing the designated plays, and more familiar with one another, those who are capable can be given more freedom and can exercise more creativity to make it even more difficult for the defense to apply pressure without adding to its risk of allowing an easy basket. Therefore, the Xs and Os presented in this chapter serve, at best, as an incomplete menu of possibilities. Many more are available, depending, of course, on the abilities of the players.

CHAPTER 10

FULL-COURT PRESS ATTACK

Why do teams use a pressing defense? At UCLA, we chose to use it for two primary reasons. One was to avoid getting stuck in a half-court game in which the opposition could dictate the pace and—even if outmanned—reduce the number of possessions to keep the score close. Two, we believed the press allowed us to exploit opponents who were not fundamentally sound in their spacing, cutting, passing, and dribbling.

To those two reasons, I might add a third rationale that applied to our teams in the early 1960s: Our players were too short to sit back and let taller opponents get the ball up the court unimpeded and shoot the ball over them. For example, our starting center from 1962 to 1964 was Fred Slaughter, who was a mere six-foot-five.

Those pressing Bruin teams were extremely quick, in superb physical condition, fundamentally sound, and most of all, determined not to permit opponents to get the ball near their basket. Indeed, there were often several stretches in games when the pressing defense made a steal or forced a turnover before the opposition could even get a shot attempt. And, because we tried to convert those take-aways into easy buckets on our end, it was not unheard of for those squads to score more than 100 points.

From an offensive perspective, it is essential to be prepared for full-court pressure. Players must be well drilled to make passes, pivots, cuts, and receptions without withering under a defensive onslaught. In addition, the offense must have a tactical plan for breaking the press, and the team must have absolute faith in that attack.

A successful half-court offense, such as the one we used for many years at UCLA, will encounter all kinds of defenses attempting to prevent it from getting the ball into the frontcourt and running its preferred play options. We prepared our teams for the pressure and disruptions by emphasizing the correct execution of fundamentals and the repeated rehearsal and refinement of the plays that follow.

INITIAL ALIGNMENT

The first priority is to identify the right inbounds passer. This player should be tall, poised, have full-court vision, and be capable of exercising good judgment in a short period of time (five seconds). He should be trained to keep the ball close to his body and just under his chin, allowing for quick overhead, left-handed, right-handed, or bounce passing. He should not pass "around" his defender but rather "by" him. If his defender crowds him and has both hands high in the air, attempting to discourage the pass over the top, the inbounder will most likely fake up and make the bounce pass. If the inbounder is also a good post defensive player, all the better. Then, if the ball is stolen, he will be in position to help the center protect the basket.

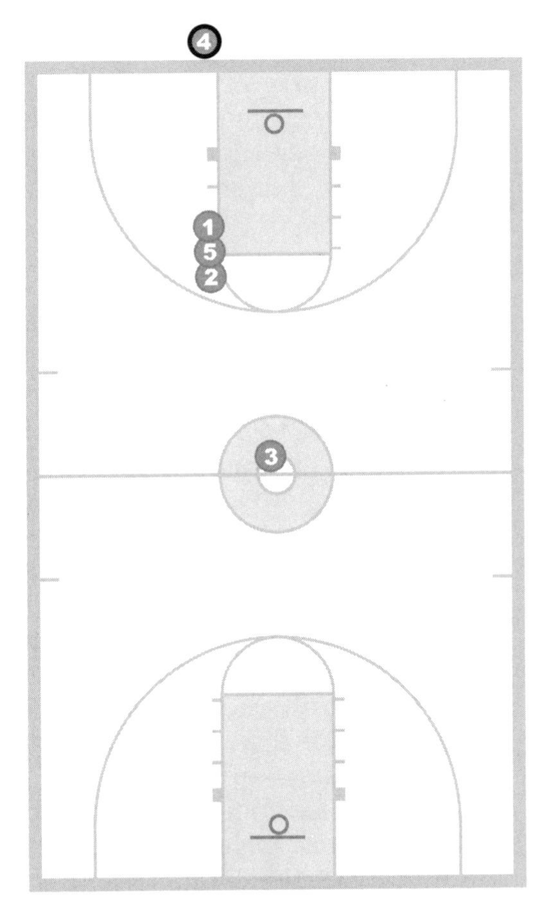

Figure 10.1 Initial alignment places 1, 5, and 2 in a vertical stack, with 3 at about half court.

Once selected, that player and one substitute will be the inbounders in all out-of-bounds situations. For our purposes here, we'll specify the power forward (4) as the inbounder.

At the strong-side elbow, both guards (1 and 2) and the center (5) are placed in a vertical stack. The point guard is located exactly on the elbow, the center directly behind him, and the two guard directly behind the center. The small forward (3) is located at about the half-court line near the jump ball circle (see figure 10.1).

Player 4 stands about three feet behind the baseline and avoids leaning or being out of balance. When the vertical stack forms and he is ready to pass, 4 signals to start the play. His signal can be raising the ball over his head, slapping the ball, or a verbal indicator.

BASE PLAYS

In the rare instances that 3 gets free downcourt, 4 can opt to hit him with a baseball pass. Otherwise, 4's two primary passing options are 1 and 5. Let's look at each of those options in succession.

Inbounds Pass to the Point Guard

Player 3 fakes a cut down the court, and 4 can fake the pass. Player 1 reads his defender and makes the first move. If the defender is playing to the inside, 1 fakes there and cuts to the strong-side corner, calling for the ball. If the defender is playing to the outside or "face guards" 1, he fakes that direction and cuts toward the basket and to the other corner, but not all the way.

To shift the defense, 4 fakes a pass in the same direction that 1 had faked his cut. Player 2 reads 1 and goes in the opposite direction. He times his cut so 4 has ample time to give 1 a good look. Player 5 steps toward the basket after 4 has looked at 2. Player 3 comes back to see if he is needed to get the ball inbounds.

Because the primary objective of breaking a full-court press is to get the ball inbounds, 4 hits the first open man. In this scenario, let's say that 1 receives the pass from 4 (see figure 10.2). (Please note that because the floor is balanced when the inbounder has possession of the ball, if the inbounds pass is made to 2 rather than 1, all options are the same, with 1 and 2 exchanging roles.) At that point, 1 has two passing options. He can pass to 2 making the diagonal cut, or he can hit 3 coming back to the ball.

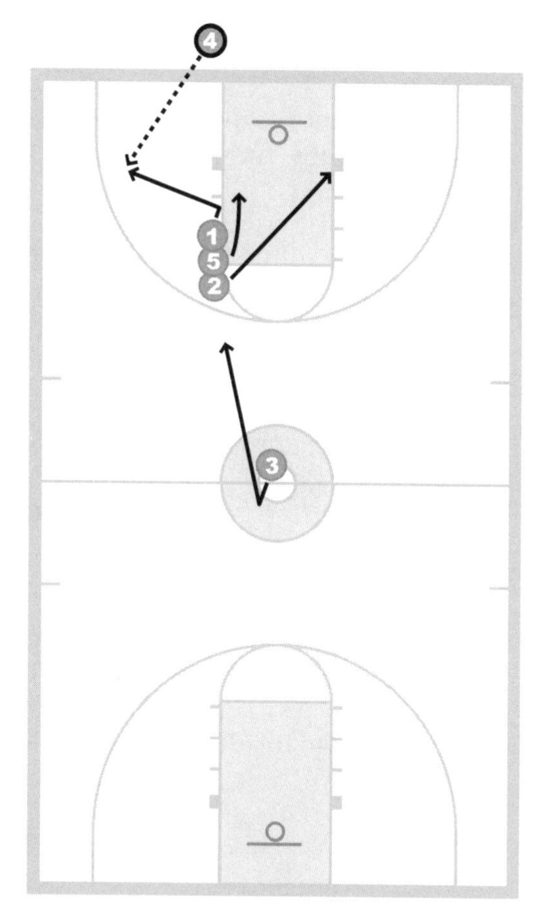

Figure 10.2 In this option, 4 passes to 1.

Point Guard to Two Guard

After receiving the pass from 4, 1 pivots to look down the court and fakes to 3, who is moving toward the strong-side sideline. Player 2 fakes in and makes a diagonal cut perpendicular to 1's pass if he were to throw it.

Player 2 should not be moving away from 1, because that can often lead to a turnover. Also, 1 must use good judgment when considering the pass to 2. Player 1 must be careful not to lead 2 into a coming defender.

Player 5 moves over to the weak side of the lane, turns away from 4, and sets a screen for 4, who comes from out of bounds. This screen will only be fully effective against a man-to-man defense. Player 5 remains in that area to be an outlet receiver for 1 and to balance the floor. We always want a two-guard front, even if that "guard" is not a guard. This allows for swinging the ball and attacking the defense from the other side. Player 1 passes to 2 (see figure 10.3).

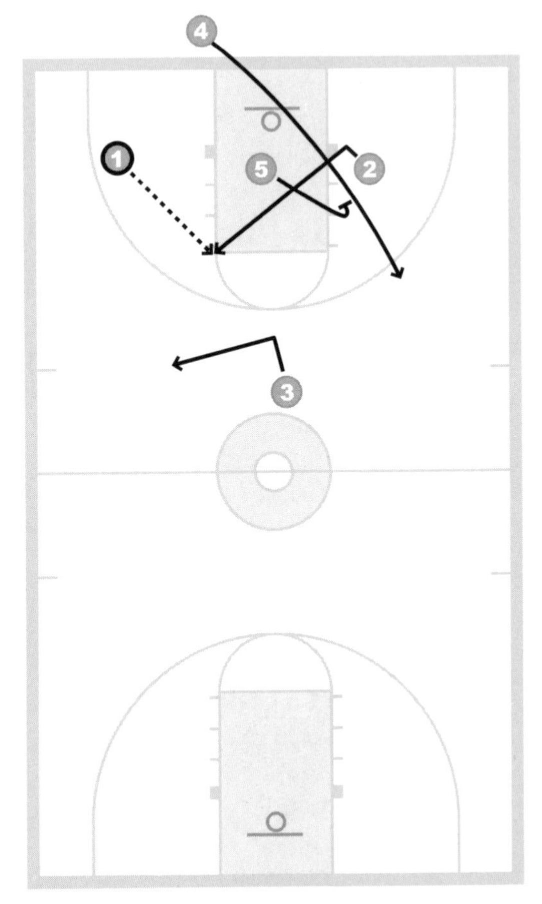

Figure 10.3 Player 1 passes to 2 if it's safe, and 5 screens for 4, which is effective only against man-to-man defense.

Player 2 has four passing options: a pass to 5 to swing the ball, to 4 coming back from the weak side, to 1 cutting down the sideline, and to 3 coming to the middle. His first look is to 3 because that will be the first pass available and will penetrate the inside of the defense. Player 2 passes to 3 and stays back with 5. Player 1 sprints down the sideline as does 4 on the other side (see figure 10.4).

Player 3 may take the ball on the dribble or, if defended, can pass to 4 or 1. When 4 and 1 recognize pressure on 3, they come back to the ball as potential receivers.

Point Guard to Small Forward

If 1 elects not to pass to 2, 2 continues his diagonal cut, calling for the ball, and heads toward the strong-side sideline. Player 1 pass fakes to 2. Player 3 cuts toward the other sideline, changes direction, and comes toward 1. Players 4 and 5 have the same roles as before. Player 1 passes to 3 (see figure 10.5). Player 3 pivots and looks up the floor. Player 3 may dribble if he has an advantage or pass to 2 or 4 to continue penetrating the defense. After a pass to 2 or 4, 3 cuts straight for the basket, calling for the ball.

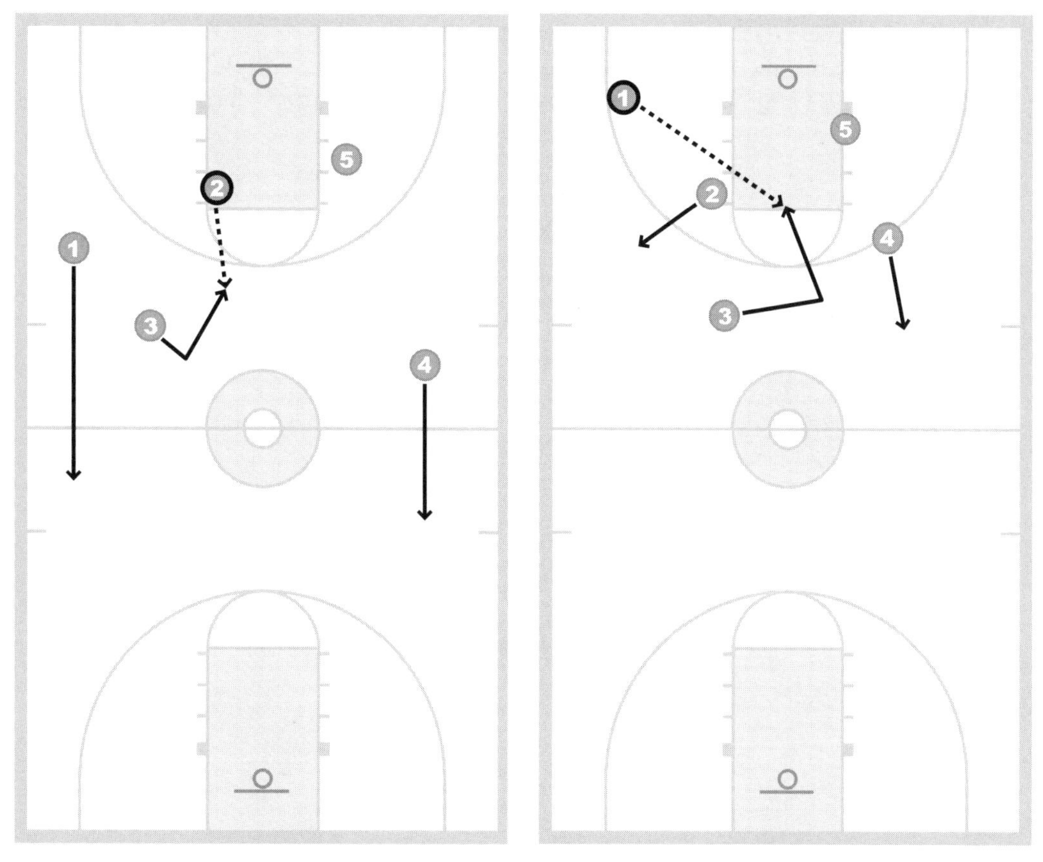

Figure 10.4 Player 2 passes to 3, to penetrate the inside of the defense.

Figure 10.5 If 1 doesn't pass to 2, he can pass to 3, who has cut toward the other side and changed direction.

Inbounds Pass to the Center

Player 3 makes his cut down the court and comes back toward the ball. Player 1 is covered, 2 cuts to the opposite side, and 5 comes to the ball. Player 4 delivers a quick, high pass to 5, who makes an inside pivot, swinging his nonpivot leg behind him so he has quick vision of the court (see figure 10.6). Player 4 steps inbounds to the weak side to balance the floor. Player 5 has three passing options: a pass to 2 on the diagonal cut, to 1 down the sideline, and to 3 down the middle.

Center to Two Guard

Player 2 makes his diagonal cut, calling for the ball. Player 1 heads down the sideline, and 3 cuts away and comes back toward the ball, leaving plenty of space for 2's cut. Player 4 sprints down the weak-side sideline. Player 5 passes to 2 (see figure 10.7). Player 2 may dribble or make additional penetrating passes to 1, 3, or 4 (as 4 cuts to the middle from the weak side).

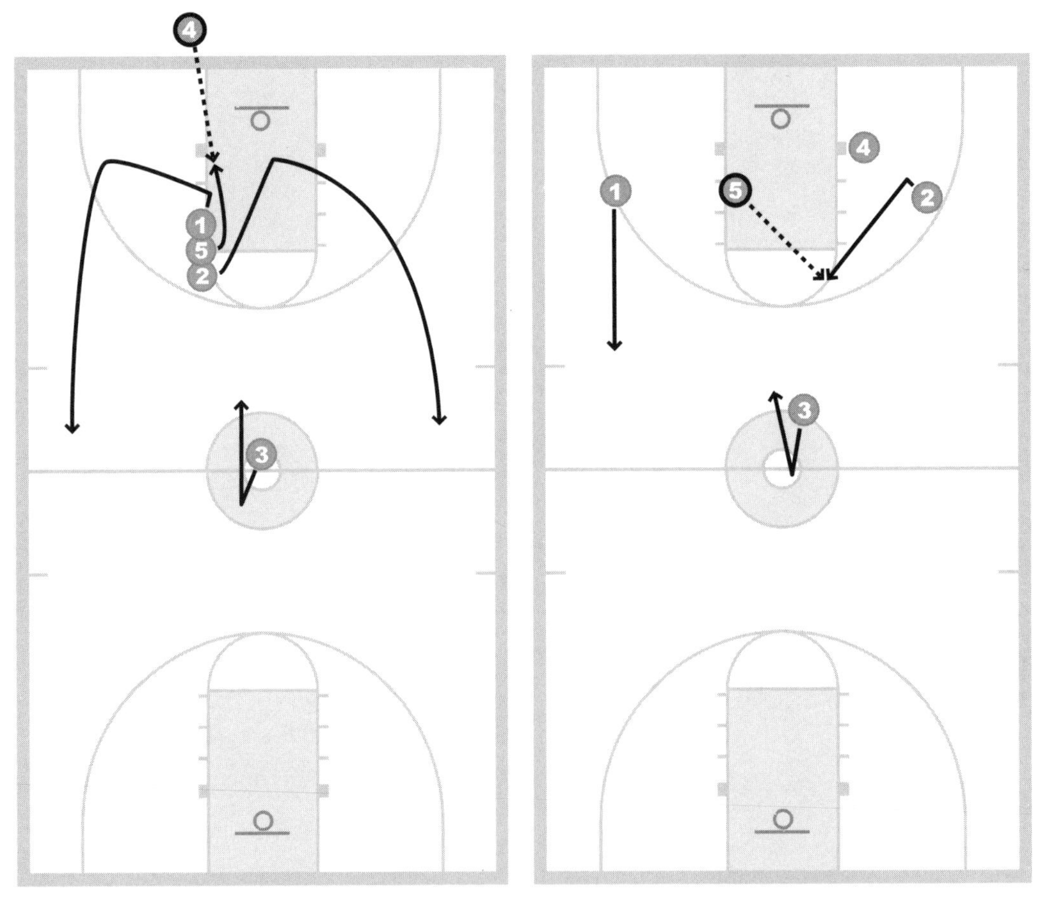

Figure 10.6 Players 1 and 2 cut out to the sides, while 5 receives the ball.

Figure 10.7 Player 2 cuts diagonally and receives the pass from 5.

Center to Point Guard

Player 5 passes to 1 while 2 is making his diagonal cut. Player 3 heads toward the strong-side sideline. Players 4 and 5 have the same roles as before. Player 1 passes to 2 (see figure 10.8). Player 2 decides whether to dribble and create a fast break with 3 and 4 on the wings, 1 trailing, and 5 as the safety. If not, he has 3 and 4 as options for additional penetrating passes. The pass from 5 to 1 is available often.

Center to Small Forward

Player 1 sprints down the strong-side sideline. Player 2 makes his diagonal cut, but 5 does not give him the ball. Player 3 fakes away and comes to the ball, arriving at a spot about 15 to 20 feet from 5 immediately after 2 has cut through. Players 4 and 5 have the same roles as before. Player 4, seeing 3 come to the ball, cuts to the middle of the floor to fill the spot 3 has vacated. Player 5 passes to 3 (see figure 10.9). Although rare, if 5 cannot pass to 3, 2, or 1, 4 comes back to balance the floor and take the other guard position.

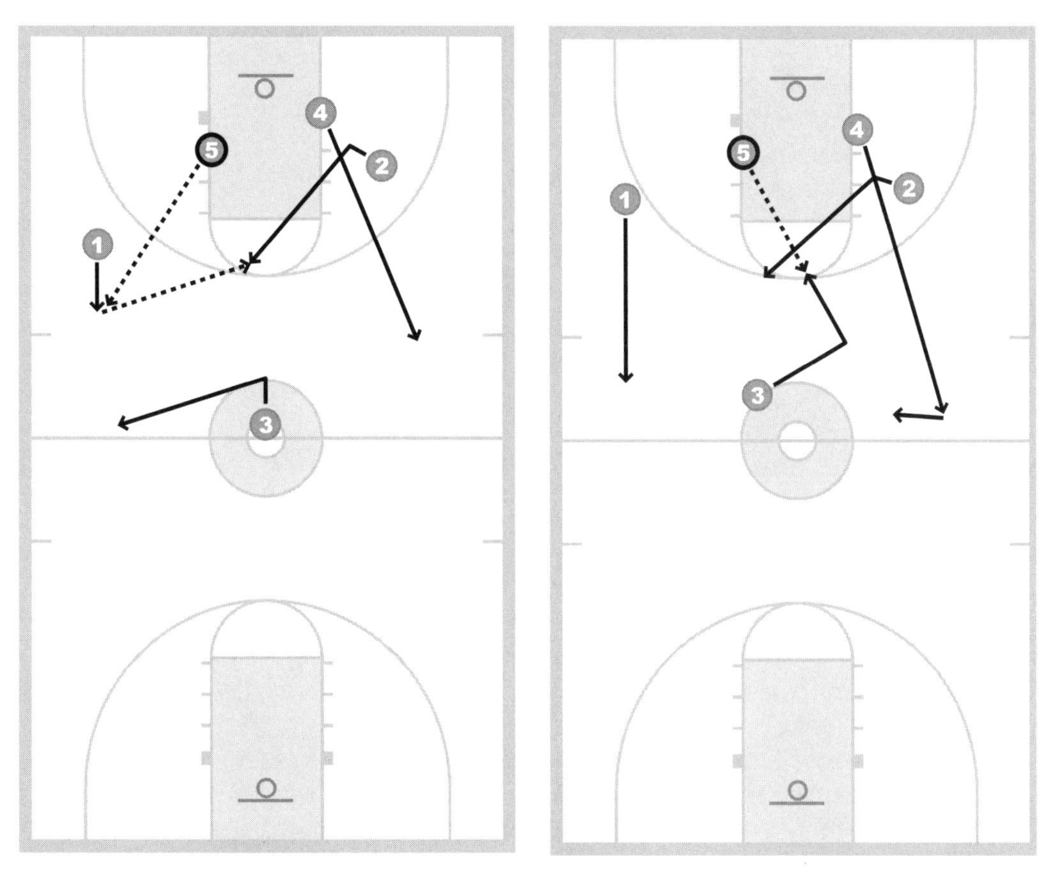

Figure 10.8 In this option, 2 makes the same cut, but 5 gets the ball to 1 first, who then passes to 2.

Figure 10.9 Player 3 comes toward the ball after 2 has cut, and 3 receives the pass from 5.

ADDITIONAL OPTIONS

If 4 makes the inbounds pass to the weak-side guard, toward the basket, the same options are available. The opposite guard makes the diagonal cut. After a guard receives the inbounds pass, he has the option to dribble to the middle after the other guard makes the diagonal cut.

Center to Point Guard Downcourt Pass

By far, the most successful play for UCLA was the center to point guard downcourt pass. Player 1 breaks out of the stack and does not receive the ball. Player 5 receives the pass while 1 fakes toward the ball, making his defender think he is a receiver.

Just before 5 catches the ball, 1 changes direction and sprints down the sideline, and 5 hits him with a two-handed overhead pass or a leading bounce pass. At this point, the coach may elect to have 1 dribble the ball, rather than pass to 2, who is making the diagonal cut (see figure 10.10). If 1 dribbles to the middle—which he should—2 becomes the trailer while 3 and 4 occupy the lanes. Player 5 is the protector.

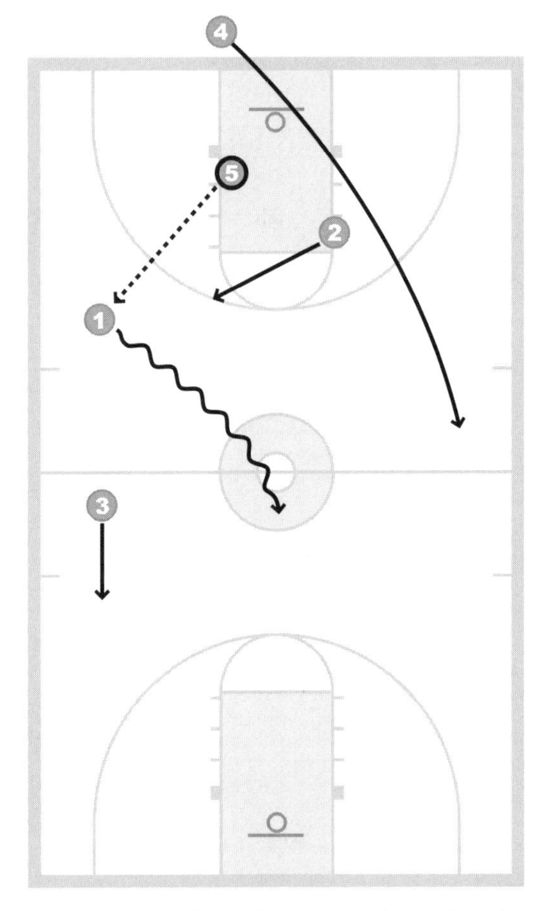

Figure 10.10 Player 1 receives the ball and then dribbles toward the middle.

Changing the Position of the Center

The previous diagrams show the center very involved in moving the ball. However, some teams have centers who are not yet ready for that job description, and coaches wisely choose to position them down the floor as a finisher.

In that case, 3 takes 5's position in the stack. Player 5 starts at half court. When the inbounds signal is made, he fakes toward the ball and sprints downcourt (see figure 10.11). He remains downcourt around the offensive basket and is used for a catch and score only. Player 4, after inbounding to 1, 2, or 3, cuts down the opposite sideline, as before, but changes direction toward the middle to be a receiver.

Inbounds Pass to the Strong Forward

This is a called play. Players 1 and 2 make their usual moves to the ball, cut to their respective sidelines, and sprint downcourt. Player 4 fakes a pass to both. Player 5 takes one step toward 4, calling for the ball and drawing one defender, and then makes a sharp left turn toward the sideline, taking the defender with him. Player 3 comes right behind him and receives the inbounds pass. He turns and looks up the floor. The team has their three quickest players down the floor (see figure 10.12).

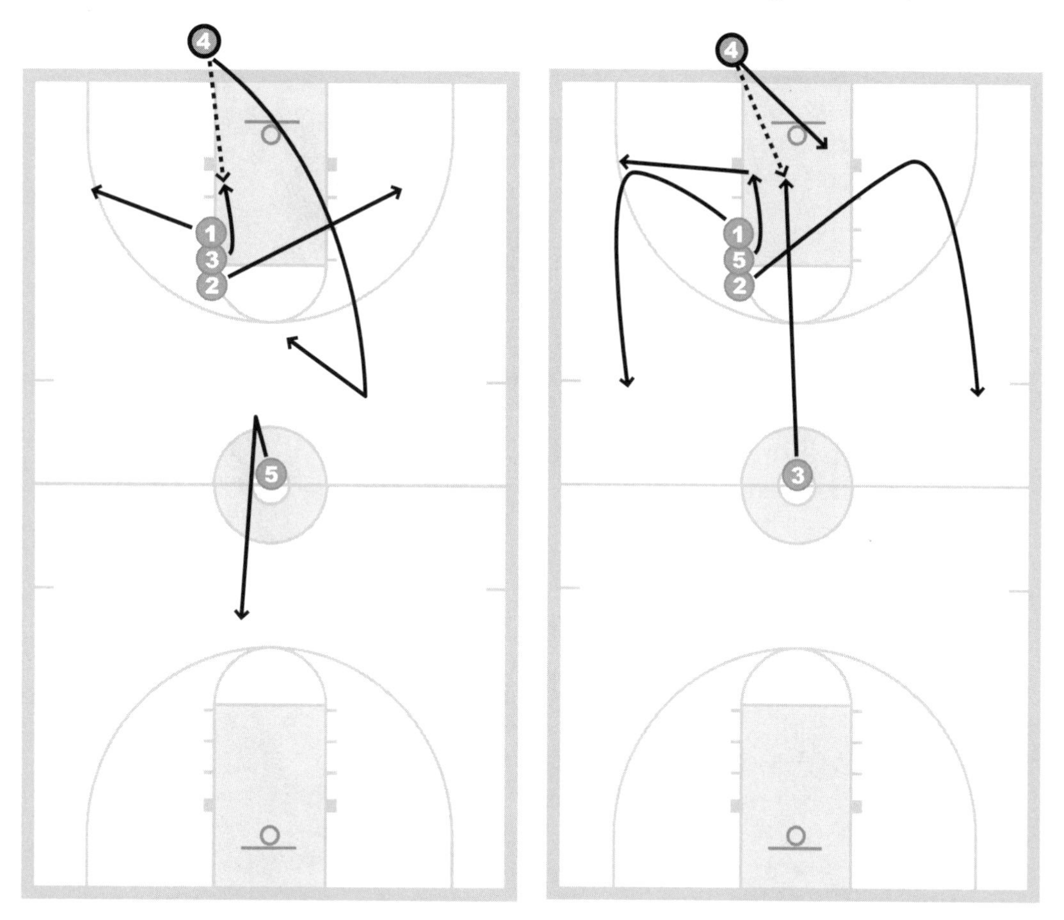

Figure 10.11 This option takes 5 out of the stack and places him in the middle and then downcourt; 3 takes 5's place in the stack.

Figure 10.12 Players 1, 2, and 5 move to the sides, while 3 comes down for the pass.

PRESS READY

The 1962 to 1963 UCLA team had all the ingredients to be an outstanding pressing team. So, that entire season, starters Walt Hazzard, Gail Goodrich, Fred Slaughter, Jack Hirsch, and Keith Erickson, as well as the reserves, pressed after every made basket, all game, every game. At times it seemed to backfire, allowing opponents to penetrate and score, but it worked far more often than not.

The next year, with all the starters returning and a year of experience under their belts, the Bruins, again committed to the full-court press, went undefeated and won our first national championship. The following year, opponents prepared for the press, but most fell prey to 40 minutes of pressure. UCLA won a second consecutive title.

Those UCLA teams were hardly the first to use a press so successfully. The University of California at Berkeley, under the direction of Pete Newell, won a national championship using various forms of pressing defenses. University of Kansas, led by coach Phog Allen, used an extended half-court press and almost won the title. Bill Russell, K.C. Jones, and the University of San Francisco won two national championships with a similar style press.

What is interesting about all of those teams is that they were very difficult to press when they had the ball. Because players were so accustomed to encountering pressure on the practice court, and were therefore required to develop successful ways of counteracting it when on offense, the turnover ratio between those teams and their opponents was very much to their advantage.

The ability of Gail Goodrich to create his own shot within the framework of the offense was a benefit to the Bruins. Being left-handed didn't hurt him either.

CLOSING POINTS

No matter how well prepared a team is to tactically attack a full-court press, such a defense can take too many forms to possibly prepare for each way a team might choose to apply pressure. That's why players must have a clear sense of the overall structure of the offensive system for attacking such defenses—and must be able to make intelligent choices within those parameters.

When allowed this freedom within a sound system, players will come up with some wonderful solutions to the defensive press. For example, when the vertical stack is formed and 4 slaps the ball, 2 can make the first cut if he sees an opening. If 2 takes advantage of that crack in the pressure and secures the inbounds pass, he will have done the right thing.

The reason the basketball is faked and passed, and players move to and from the ball, is to distort the defense and open up opportunities for such individual moves. When the ball is live, the inbounds passer can choose his side or move along the baseline, initiating the play from either side.

The basketball must be inbounded safely, but quickly. A good offense puts pressure on the defense, and any lull in the action will shift pressure the other way. The best way to do that is to move the ball up the floor as quickly as possible. Sound like a fast break? It is.

A press should be considered as a fast break opportunity. In fact, one of the most useful and effective tools for teaching press break is teaching the fast break. Both systems work against a full-court defense and are identical in player and ball movement.

Last but not least, when finishing the press break, the fourth player to enter the frontcourt yells, "trailer," and the last shouts, "safety." "Trailer" lets the ball handler know where an additional passing option is. "Safety" informs all teammates that the protector is in position.

Part V

SPECIAL PLAYS AND OPTIONS

Through the years, and even today, some basketball coaches have used a system where a play is called on each possession. To a degree, this type of strategy can be effective, providing the plays are based on sound principles. However, as a general rule, "play calling" will limit individual initiative no matter how much the coach may emphasize it. A specific play is designed to get the basketball to one player in one spot on the floor. Any time the focus is on one result, the other intermediate possibilities become less clear to the players and are often missed. With that said, an offensive system without set plays for selected individuals in the right situations is incomplete. In almost every game, there will be at least one time when the coach recognizes a defensive weakness and wants to make sure that weakness is exploited.

The importance of scoring on out-of-bounds plays is overemphasized. At times, a defensive player may make an error that opens up a quick pass and score opportunity. But generally speaking, too much emphasis is placed on creating tricky screening maneuvers to get a player open for the layup. These may work against inexperienced teams but certainly not against teams that have devised similar plays of their own. Of primary importance is simply getting the basketball inbounds. That should be the main focus of every player. With that in mind, the inbounds passer must be carefully selected and fully trained, and he must be provided with multiple passing options all in succession.

The following special plays were all used at one time or another. You will recognize that they are similar in structure and principle to the main offense. This is by design. Special plays that are either an already existing option or a creation based on already learned balance, spacing, cutting, and ball movement are easier for players to learn and actually aid them in the execution of the regular offense.

CHAPTER 11

SPECIAL HALF-COURT PLAYS

I have mentioned before that elaborate Xs and Os, alone, are not a solution to a team's scoring problems. A new handful of plays picked up at a coaching clinic might fortify a playbook, but will they make a difference on the court? If those plays are used in a selective, timely manner, the answer is yes.

One of the endearing features of the game is the ability of a team, at any point, to execute a play so perfectly and with such surprise to the defense that a basket is converted with little opposition. When the situation is right and a team has proven it can perform a special play with precision, such plays can serve a purpose. Perhaps a particular player has a hot hand and the team wants to get him a favorable shot at a key point in the game. Or, maybe with a modified attack, a certain defensive matchup can be exploited to the offense's benefit. In such situations, it is perfectly fine to depart from the standard offense and work a special play to score what might be a game-deciding basket.

The danger of using special plays is that, when used too often, players come to depend on them to produce easy shots, as if by magic. In reality, all an offense can do during a given possession is to create opportunities for players to make plays. It is the players that make plays, not the plays that make players. A team should never rely on special plays to the extent that they become a major part of its offense.

SPECIAL PLAY OPTIONS

The central ploy of a special play is decoying a team by leading them in one direction, making them think the play is going there, lulling a defender into a false sense of security, and making a quick change of direction or cut back. It is more than the element of surprise because it exploits human tendencies. Plays that use deception create the best openings for the quick score. For that reason, I have found the use of the basic set and some elements of the regular offense to be very effective. The repetition of our plays throughout a particular game can condition the opponent to anticipate our next move within a play. This is human nature. We take advantage of that by luring the opponent toward our normal sequence of passes and cuts and then moving the ball to an unexpected receiver.

To heighten team spirit and present more defensive challenges, each offensive position should be the target of at least one special play. It might be employed after a time-out, as the first play of the second half, or in the game's last minute. The important thing is that the play chosen isn't so predictable that it can be stopped with the defense's standard coverage. Of course, it's always wise to reserve a few plays for special times during a game when a score is essential.

Special plays can be called with a hand signal or a verbal call. During the first part of a season, the coach should call the plays. However, when the players become familiar with them and understand not only how, but why they work, the guards can be given permission to call certain plays whenever they like, providing they don't use the ones reserved for the surprise.

Kentucky

This play is designed to get a good outside shooting forward an open baseline jump shot or three-point shot. Kentucky uses a forward-to-guard pass and a cut across the top of the key to make the defense think the objective of the play is going inside.

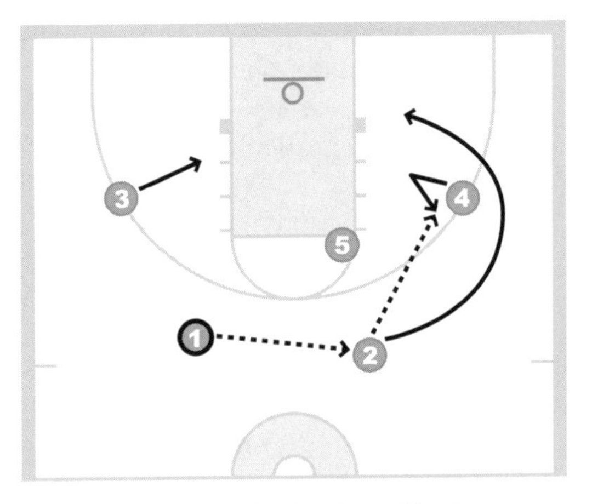

Figure 11.1 Kentucky begins with the guard to guard to forward with outside cut.

From the high-post offense set, the play begins exactly like the guard to guard to forward, outside cut (see chapter 4). The shooter (3) lines up at the left wing, opposite the side on which the play is run. Player 1 passes to 2, who passes to 4. Player 2 fakes a cut down the lane and cuts outside 4 to the baseline, about eight feet from the basket (see figure 11.1).

The opponent may recognize the play. Normally, if 4 passes out to 1, a side-post game occurs involving 1 and 3. But in this case, after the pass to 1, 4 fakes toward the low post and cuts over the top of 5 and down the key (see figure 11.2). He runs straight at 3's defender as 3 fakes a cut to the high post.

As 4 moves around 5, 5 and 2 squeeze down to the low post and set a double screen as 1 fakes a pass to 4. Player 1 may also take a dribble or two to the weak side to set the play up even better. When his man is occupied with 4, 3 makes a thrust and comes off the double screen. Player 1 passes to 3 for the jump shot (see figure 11.3). Player 5, 2, and 4 are inside rebounders, 3 is the long rebounder, and 1 is the protector.

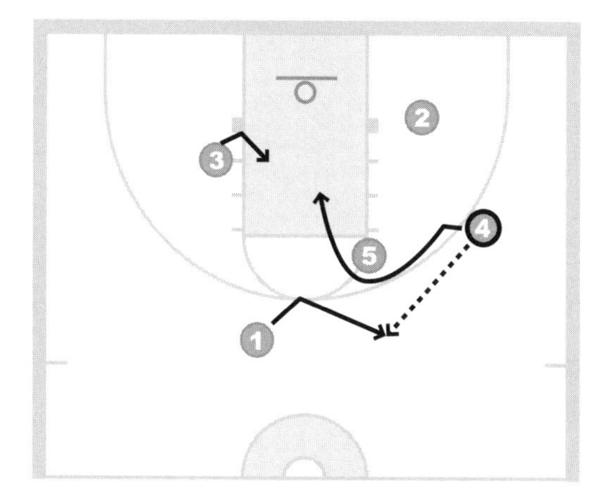

Figure 11.2 After passing to 1, 4 fakes toward the low post and cuts over the top of 5 and down the key.

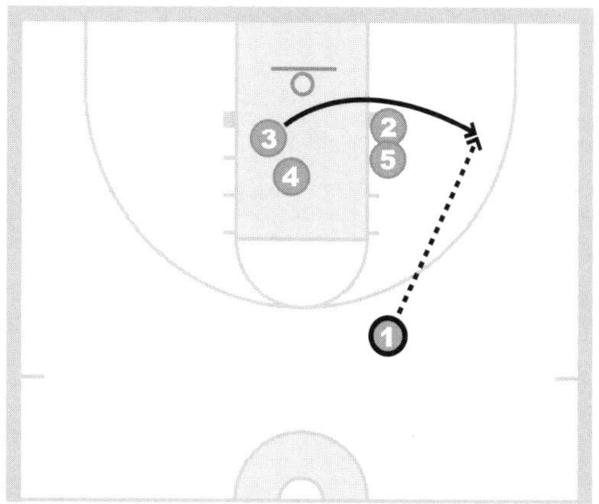

Figure 11.3 Player 1 has faked a pass to 4, drawing 3's defender. Player 3 then comes off 5 and 2's double screen for the pass from 1.

Indiana

Indiana can provide a backdoor basket for a most unlikely candidate. Player 1 passes to 2, who passes to 4 (see figure 11.4). Player 5 turns his back to screen. Player 2 fakes coming off the screen, causing his man to anticipate the cut and drop toward the basket. Player 2 pops back out to the perimeter and receives a return pass from 4 (see figure 11.5).

Player 2 passes to 1, and 4 cuts over the top of 5 and heads down the lane toward 3's defender. It looks as if a situation is being set up for 4 or 3. Player 2's defender will relax, thinking he is on the weak side and out of the play (see figure 11.6).

Because 2's defender will likely turn and look at the high-post action, and because he is playing weak-side defense, he may relax a bit. Player 1 quickly passes to 5 at the high post. As the pass is in the air, 2 makes a backdoor cut, and 5 delivers the pass (see figure 11.7).

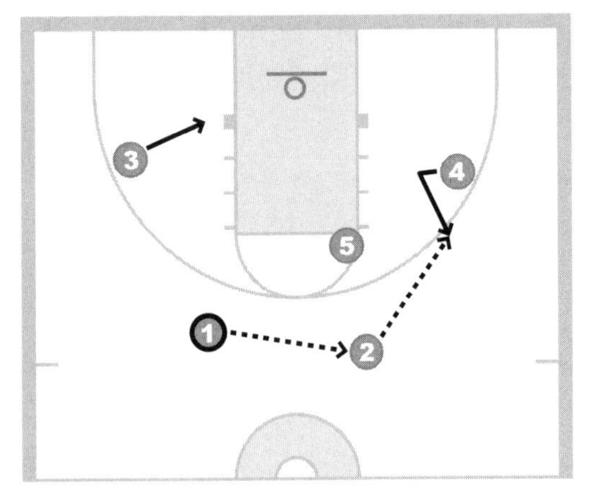

Figure 11.4 Indiana starts with a pass from 1 to 2 to 4.

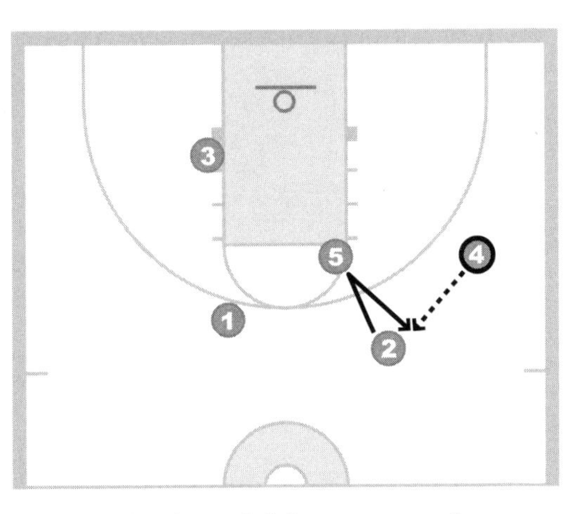

Figure 11.5 Player 2 fakes a cut to the basket and pops back out for the pass.

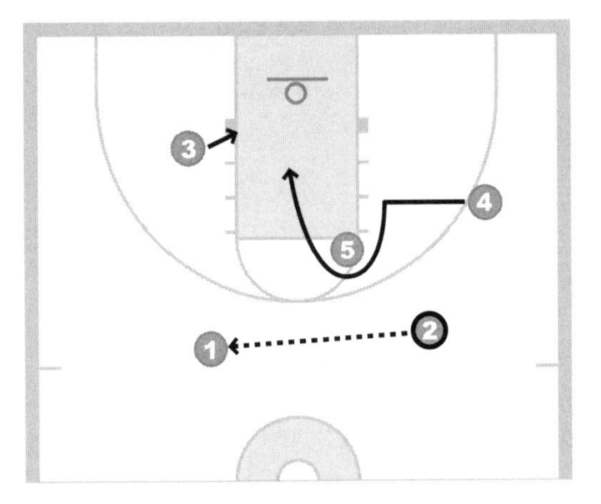

Figure 11.6 As 2 passes to 1, 4 cuts around 5 toward 3's defender.

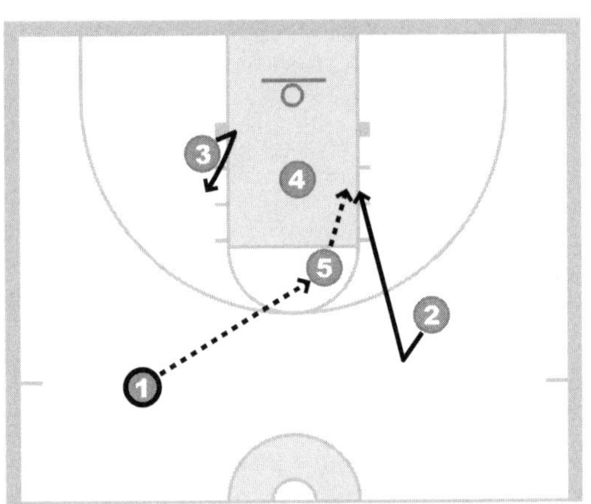

Figure 11.7 Player 1 gets the ball to 5, and 5 passes to 2, who has cut backdoor.

Santa Barbara

Santa Barbara is really nothing more than the fourth option of the four-options set. As in Kentucky, this play is designed to get the ball to an accurate shooting forward.

Player 1 passes to 2, who passes to 4. Player 5 turns his back, and 2 runs the UCLA cut (see figure 11.8). At this point, the play usually continues with 4 passing to 5, who looks for 3 in the key for the flash cut.

Instead, 4 fakes a pass to 5 and dribbles hard at 1, who reverses to the basket. Player 3's defender has already anticipated a pass to the high post and is ready to defend the flash (see figure 11.9). Players 5 and 2 set a double screen, and 3, after faking in the key, sprints off the double screen. Player 4 passes to 3 for the jump shot (see figure 11.10).

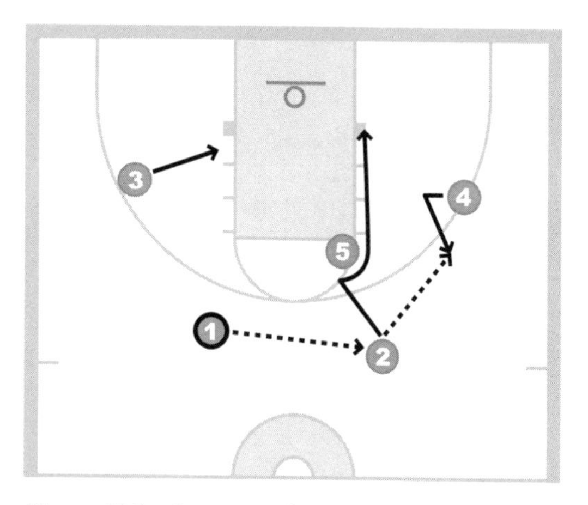

Figure 11.8 Santa Barbara begins with the guard to guard to forward with UCLA cut.

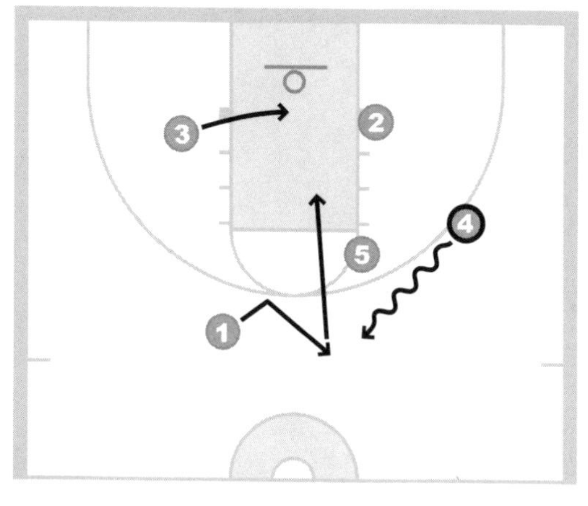

Figure 11.9 Player 4 dribbles at 1, who reverses to the basket.

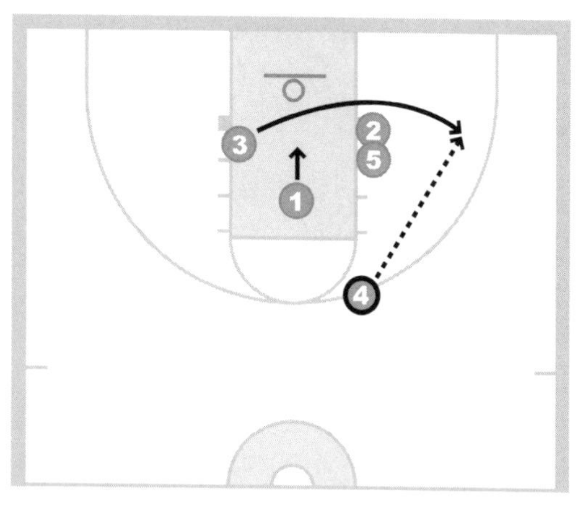

Figure 11.10 Players 5 and 2 set a screen for 3, who comes off it for the pass from 4.

Down

Down is intended to get an inside shot for the best post player. In this example, the player designated for the post is 3, but any player who can score consistently in the lane area can be assigned this position.

Player 1 passes to 2, who passes to 4. Player 5 turns his back to screen. Player 2 fakes the UCLA cut and cuts over to 4 to receive a handoff (see figure 11.11).

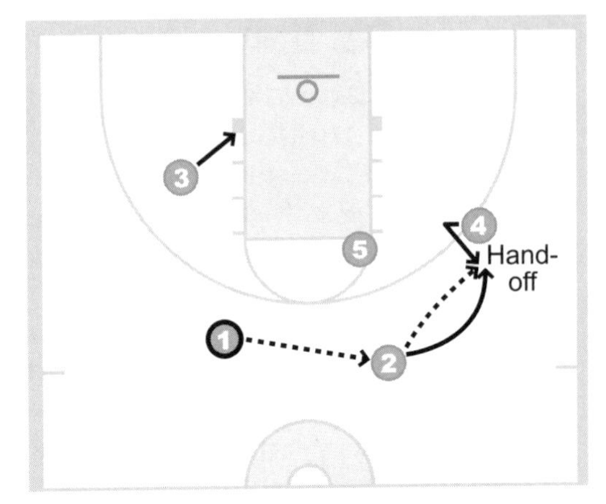

Figure 11.11 After the pass to 4, 2 fakes the UCLA cut and receives a handoff from 4.

Player 3 changes positions with 1. Player 4 cuts directly at 5 and comes chest to side so his defender is forced to move to the low side or high side. If 4's defender stays high, 4 cuts to the basket, receives a pass from 2, and has a layup. In most cases, that will not happen; 4's man will protect against the basket cut. Player 4 moves out to the three-point line (see figure 11.12).

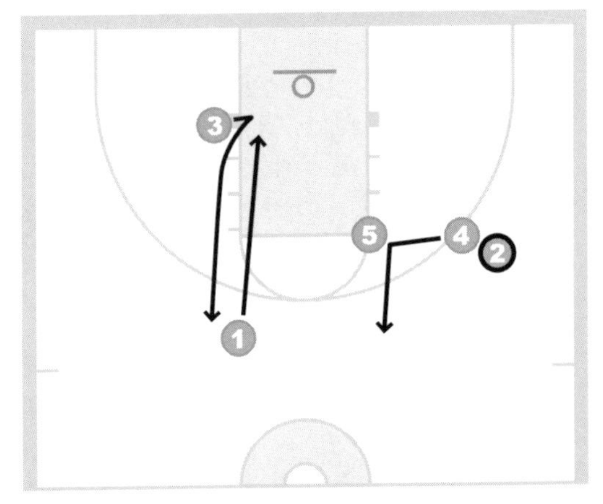

Figure 11.12 Players 1 and 3 change places. Player 4 moves to the three-point line.

This is followed by a series of three quick passes. Player 2 passes to 4 while 3 moves into the lane to down screen for 1. Player 4 passes to 1, who passes to 3, who has stepped in front of his man (see figure 11.13). The passes from 2 to 4 to 1 to 3 should be so quick that they are almost touch passes. Because 5 is involved in the down screen, his defender will not be ready to play the passing lane as 1 passes 3 the ball.

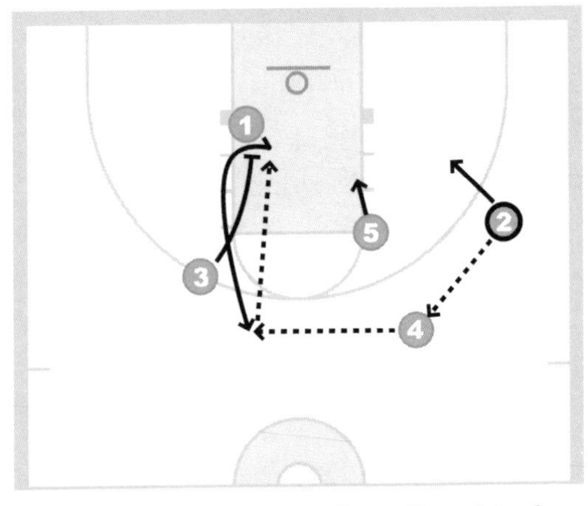

Figure 11.13 The passes from 2 to 4 to 1 to 3 need to be very quick, almost touch passes.

There is no rule that the play must be run with these players in these particular positions. Any good post player can be positioned in 3's spot, and all other players can be repositioned to take full advantage of individual abilities.

Green

Green is designed to get a strong post-up guard the ball on the block. This play was named after Johnny Green, a very skilled and cunning low-post guard who played for UCLA from 1959 to 1962. Generally, entry passes are made in a strong-side triangle alignment from the wing, which has the best passing angle to the post. This play may take the defense by surprise.

Player 1 passes to 2, who passes to 4. Player 2 makes a UCLA cut (see figure 11.14). Player 4 passes the ball out to 1. (If that pass is denied, Santa Barbara can be run.) 4 cuts over the top of 5 and heads down the lane, calling for the ball (see figure 11.15).

Player 1 fakes the pass to 4. Player 2's defender has relaxed and dropped toward the key, thinking the play is going the other way. Player 2 cuts into the low post and receives a bounce pass from 1 for the score (see figure 11.16).

Running Green immediately after Indiana may be effective; 2's defender may anticipate a backdoor and sprint toward the basket, allowing 2 to reverse and gain post position.

All but the end of this play bears similarity to Kentucky. For that reason, if Kentucky is run prior to Green, 2's defender, when he sees 4 cutting over the top and down the lane, may think 2 is about to help set a double screen for 3 and be out of position to deny 2 the ball. In addition, if 5's screen retards 4's defender, 2's defender may help prevent the lob, making the pass to his man even more viable.

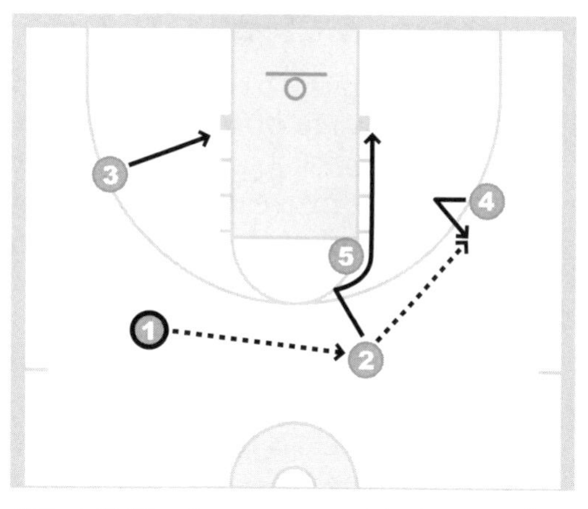

Figure 11.14 Green starts with the guard to guard to forward with UCLA cut.

Figure 11.15 Player 4 passes to 1, then cuts over the top of 5 and heads down the lane.

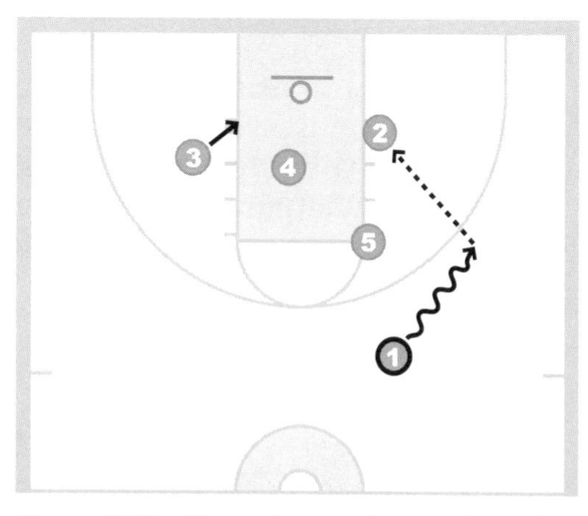

Figure 11.16 Player 2, who has cut into the low post, receives the pass from 1.

Forward Clear

When 4 appears to have a one-on-one advantage on the perimeter, the Forward Clear will provide him with more than normal spacing and time to make an individual move. The initial set is the same, but the movements are somewhat out of the normal pattern.

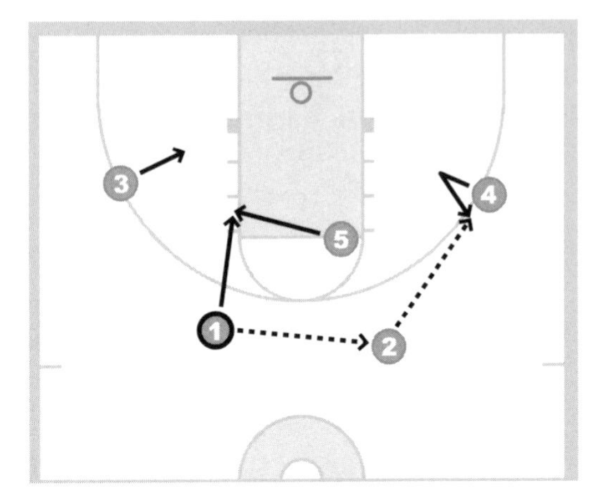

Figure 11.17 The ball goes from 1 to 2 to 4. Then 1 and 5 meet near the opposite elbow to set a screen for 3.

Player 1 passes to 2, who passes to 4. Player 1 takes a step forward and hesitates, then cuts toward the lane on his side while 5 moves away to the opposite elbow. Player 1 meets him there to set a double screen for 3 (see figure 11.17).

Player 3 comes across the lane toward the strong-side block. The moment 3 cuts off the screen, 2 is there to set a down screen for 1, who comes to the top of the key, appearing to look for a pass for the shot (see figure 11.18).

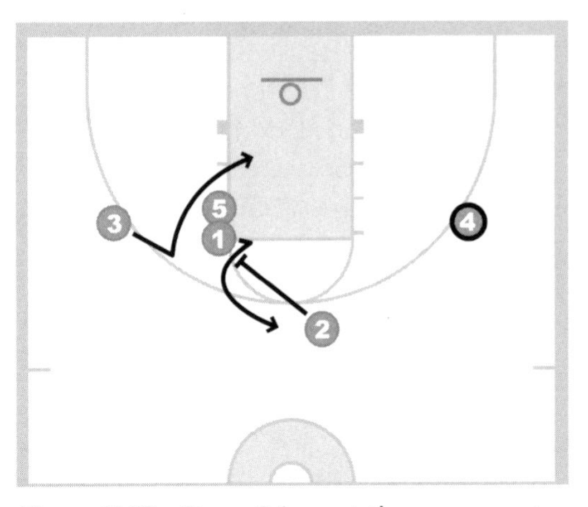

Figure 11.18 Once 3 is past the screen set by 5 and 1, 2 arrives to set a down screen for 1.

From the point of view of 4's defender, it appears that the weak-side action is actively producing open players. His teammates are kept very busy attempting to stop a layup for 3 and a jump shot for 1. In other words, all defenders are engaged in derailing what they think is a play in their area. The situation is ripe for 4 to make his individual move with significantly less than normal defensive help. Spacing is maintained, which provides 4 with passing opportunities, and rebounding and defensive balance is also good.

Guard Clear

This play is identical to the Forward Clear but with 2 and 4 exchanging assignments through a handoff pass. It is understood that 2 is a good one-on-one player and has an advantage. However, for 2 to be effective, 4 must be a good outside shooter or his defender will help on 2.

Player 1 passes to 2, who passes to 4 and then comes over and receives a handoff pass (see figure 11.19). Player 4 takes 2's original position. The play continues the same as the Forward Clear (see figure 11.20).

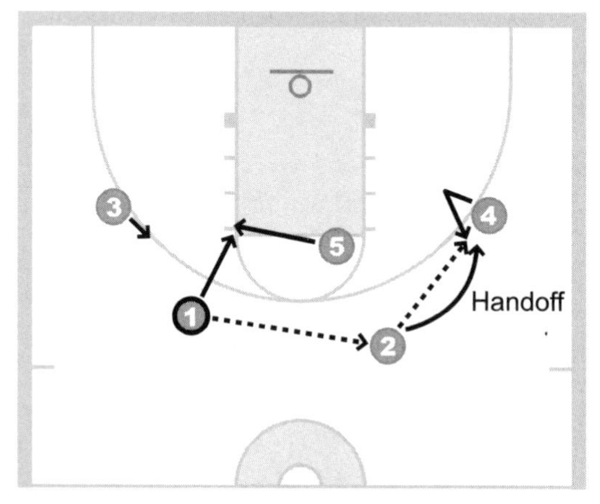

Figure 11.19 The ball goes from 1 to 2 to 4, and then 2 comes to 4 for the handoff.

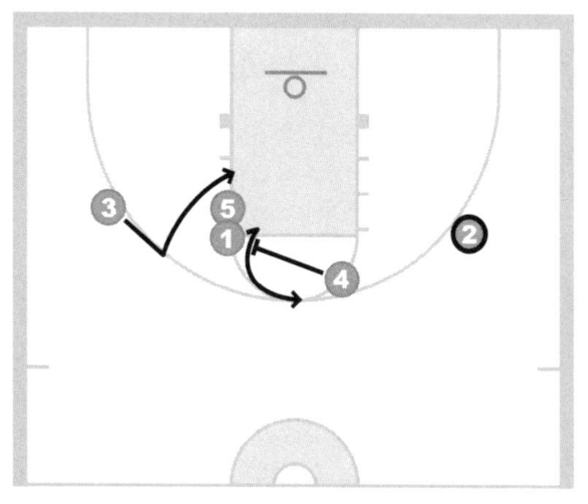

Figure 11.20 Player 4 moves to where 2 was and then screens for 1 after 3 comes off the double screen.

Screen and Roll for the Guard

For any screen and roll to work effectively, two things must take place: good weak-side action to make it appear the play is going there and a quick screen for the ball handler at the proper time. This play can be run from either the high-post or high-low beginning set; it is presented from the high-post set here. To initiate it from the high-low set, a simple adjustment is made: The center begins at the low post.

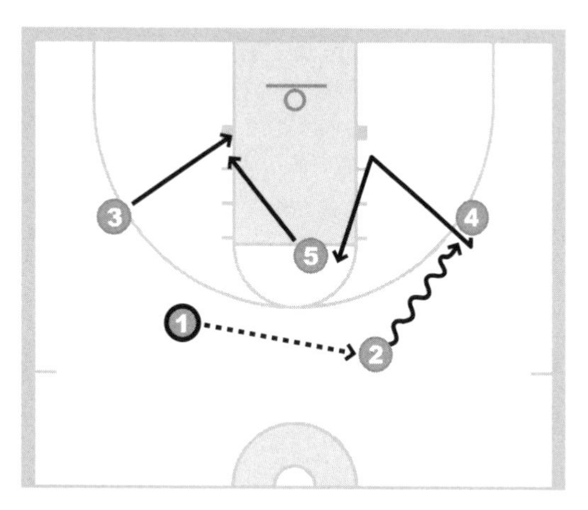

Figure 11.21 Player 2 receives the pass from 1 and then dribbles at 4, who makes a backdoor cut and changes direction to the high post.

Player 1 passes to 2, who dribbles hard at 4, reversing him to the basket. Player 4 makes the backdoor cut and changes direction to occupy the high-post area. Player 3 and 5 move to the low post and set the double screen with 3 on the bottom side no lower than the block (see figure 11.21).

Player 2 passes back out to 1, cuts toward the basket, and then makes a cut toward the weak-side double screen. Player 1 looks in the direction of the double screen and fakes a pass—before 2 comes off the screen—making his defender lean that way. Player 4 quickly comes from the high post and sets a ball screen, turning his back to 1's defender (see figure 11.22). Player 1 comes off the screen, and 4 rolls to the basket or moves to an open spot if his defender helps on 1.

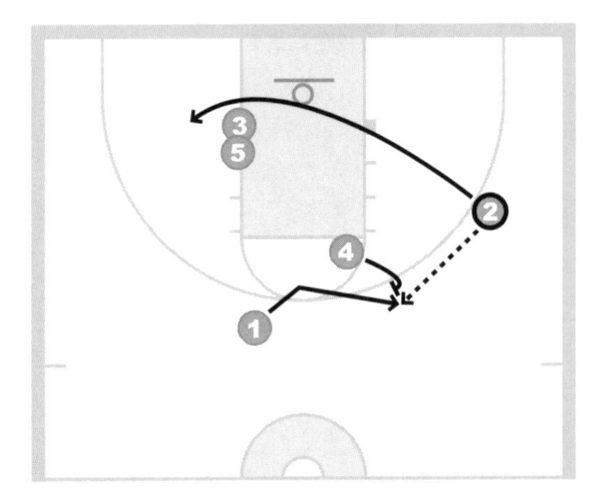

Figure 11.22 Player 2 passes to 1, then goes toward 5 and 3's double screen. Player 4 screens for 1.

Weak-Side Double

This is an effective play for a forward to go one on one. Ample space is created through deception. Player 1 passes to 2, who passes to 4. Immediately after the pass, 2 makes a hard cut down the middle, forcing his man to play him rather than double-team or help on 4. Player 2 continues to the weak-side block, where he and 5 set a double screen. Player 3 cuts down below the screen, ready to use the screen for a jump shot on the wing (see figure 11.23). Player 1 cuts in and comes back out, calling for the ball and making the defense think that the play is for 3 coming off the double screen (see figure 11.24). All weak-side defenders are kept occupied while 4 makes his move.

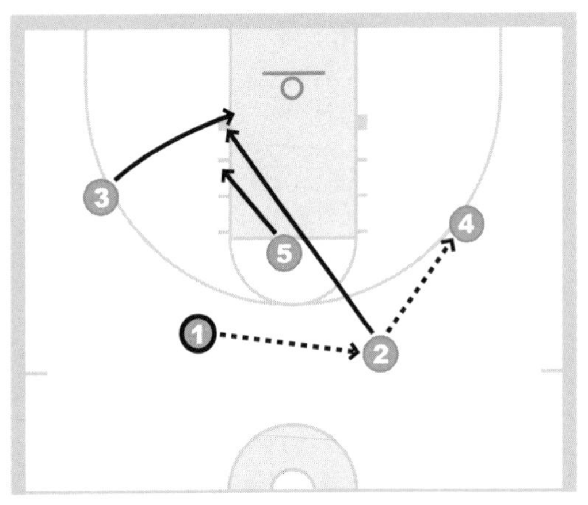

Figure 11.23 Player 2 receives the ball from 1 and passes to 4, and then he cuts down the middle, drawing his defender with him.

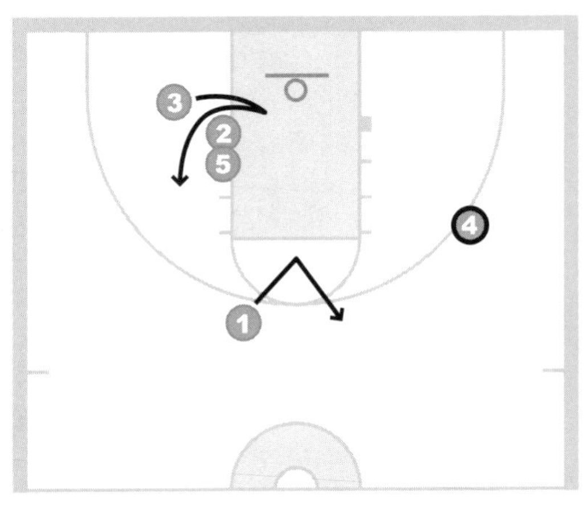

Figure 11.24 Player 1 cuts in and back out and deceives the defense into thinking the play is for 3.

MR. CLUTCH

During the 1970 to 1971 season, the Pacific 10 road trip to Oregon proved extremely taxing as both the University of Oregon and Oregon State University were well prepared for the Bruins. In both games, the score was extremely close going into the last two minutes of play, with UCLA slightly ahead. With no 35-second clock at the time, the opponents were forced to call a time-out in order to devise a way to gain possession of the ball. This enabled us to set up a one-on-one situation for Sidney Wicks to ice the game. The Weak-Side Double was used in both instances. Sidney didn't let us down.

The quickness of Sidney Wicks allowed him to get a jump shot past a defender even if that defender was much taller.

CLOSING POINTS

All special plays can be, and should be, initiated from either side. Player positions for any given play can be assigned to optimally utilize the talents of the team's personnel. For example, a left-handed guard may be more effective if the Screen and Roll for the Guard is initiated on the left side of the floor.

When teaching a special play, coaches should remember to emphasize individual initiative as well as the objective. No matter whom the play is for, all players should never cease to look for the high-percentage shot. If an opportunity is missed, that player must be constructively corrected. This will pay off because a future opponent may be familiar with the play and have a ready plan to stop the shooter. As a result, there may be openings in other areas.

Including special plays in the offense's arsenal will help improve execution of the regular plays in at least two ways: deception and timing. Defensive players who are anticipating a play to be run one way can be easily duped with effective deception. And because special plays are more structured than plays and options within the regular offense, their timing will likely be more precise.

Plays that are unexpected options of the existing offense, such as Green, should be saved for key scoring situations. Such plays are usually executed the best because the players are already familiar with the standard version within the offense, and they will readily grasp the purpose of the alternative.

CHAPTER 12

OUT-OF-BOUNDS PLAYS

The one time the team in possession of the ball is at a numbers disadvantage is when inbounding the ball. With the passer out of bounds, the defense has a five-to-four advantage on the offense. Therefore, I've always emphasized that the chief purpose of out-of-bounds plays is to enter the ball safely so that the offense maintains possession and evens out the on-court player matchups to five on five. Teams that are inclined to want to accomplish much more than that will try to force the ball to a particular player and often commit turnovers doing so. For that reason, players should be discouraged from making a quick score the primary objective when they inbound the ball, unless the game or shot clock dictates otherwise.

Simply getting the ball into play to run the offense might not provide the same immediate gratification of a made basket, but neither does it exact the penalties associated with turning the ball over to the opponent. If the team is well drilled and confident in its offensive attack, as it should be, then it is best to forgo the risky pass that might lead to a basket, and instead run the primary plays and options of the offense. Attempting to stop several cuts, screens, and passes for 20-plus seconds is much more taxing than defending a single play. And, remember, the offense is attempting to run that play at a four-to-five player disadvantage.

Establishing the priority of initiating the offense safely when inbounding the ball does not diminish the scoring value of out-of-bounds plays. Some players and teams do a poor job of defending in those situations and almost invite the offense to exploit their weaknesses. In that case, an offense is negligent if it fails to look for a quick strike for a score. In fact, the players should always look for the score. Inbounding the basketball safely is contingent on creating catch-and-score opportunities close to the basket, because this collapses the defense, opening up the outside.

INBOUNDING THE BALL

Veteran coaches and teams will be familiar with most of the standard out-of-bounds plays, and those teams will make it difficult for the offense not only to score but to even inbound the ball. To maximize the chances of inbounding the basketball safely, the inbounder must be chosen carefully. As mentioned in full-court pressure release, I recommend that one player and one substitute be selected and trained to take the ball out in all situations—under the offensive goal, on the sideline, and under the opponent's goal.

Qualifications for the inbounder role include adequate height to see over a defender who might be guarding the ball, good court vision to size up the defense and spot a teammate breaking free, and unshakable poise to keep cool all the way to four and a half seconds on the referee's count. The inbounder should have a very keen sense of time. Ideally, the offense would never be required to expend a time-out because of an inability to enter the ball into play within the allotted five-second period. But when the only alternative to a time-out call is a likely turnover, the inbounder must be capable of asking the official for time before committing a time violation.

The inbounder should stand about three feet from the out-of-bounds line to allow some space between himself and the defender. When his teammates are in position, the inbounder signals to start the play. The cue that sets the play in motion might be an oral one such as shouting a number or name, a physical one such as lifting the ball overhead, or a combination of the two such as slapping the ball.

It was my experience that coaches typically have many more out-of-bounds plays in their playbooks than can be learned and executed proficiently by their players. Goodness gracious, there are not enough games in a coaching career to run all of the ones we think are good! And, it serves no purpose to teach dozens of out-of-bounds plays for every possible contingency if players are too confused to run them.

The key is to keep it simple by identifying a small assortment of plays with options that will work in most situations and take advantage of the team's strengths. Then it's essential that the coach teaches those plays well and that players become proficient at reading the defense and executing the plays instantly, under pressure. For the most part, I used only two alignments for under the basket and sideline inbounds situations. However, the options available and player initiative to break the pattern when they see openings provide sufficient variety to be effective at all levels of competition.

All plays presented are illustrated from the left side of the floor, but they can and should be practiced and run from both sides. And, to avoid a forced pass or shot attempt on any play, each diagram indicates how players can transition smoothly into the high-post offense when a play is voided by the defense.

UNDER OWN BASKET PLAYS

Simply by its proximity to the goal, inbounding the ball underneath your own basket can present a high-percentage scoring opportunity. A lapse by the defense, such as a defender turning his head the wrong way for a split second, should be exploited for an open shot. If players are well trained in execution, a quick score will occur once in a while. But, for the most part, inside scoring threats serve as decoys to free players as receivers of the inbounds pass. As tempting as the quick score is, the inbounder must never forget that his primary responsibility is to get the ball inbounds safely, to the first open player, and within the five-second limitation.

With the ball safely inbounds, the continuity of a quick and smooth transition into the offense—as opposed to taking the time to get players into the initial set—is important because continued ball movement shifts the defense and quickly exploits mismatches and scoring opportunities. Also of utmost importance for inbounds plays is maintaining defensive balance at all times, in case a turnover occurs.

Horizontal

4 takes the ball out of bounds. Players 2, 5, 3, and 1 line up in a tight horizontal stack, with 2 just inside the elbow (as shown in figure 12.1).

4 to 1 Pass

On the signal, 1 makes a move over the top of his teammates and heads toward the strong-side corner. His defender may choose to go under the stack or follow over the top. In most cases, he will go under. For that reason, 2, 5, and 3 take one step toward the basket, in unison, to slow 1's defender down. If they do, the man guarding 2 may help on 1, often leaving an opening for 2 to cut to the basket for a score. After 2's cut to the basket, he moves to the weak side, looking for the pass from 4.

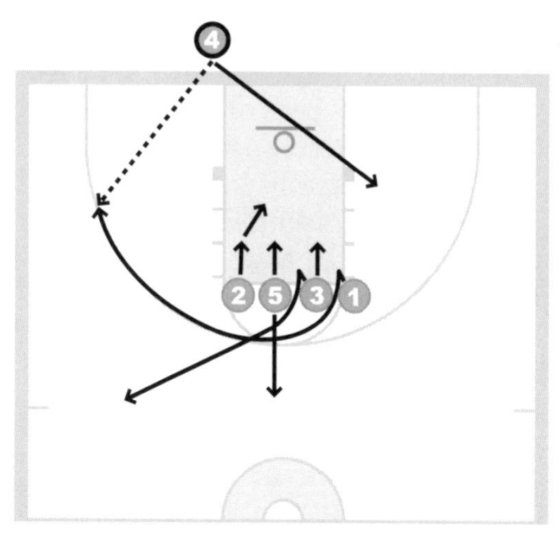

Figure 12.1 Player 1 moves over the top of the others for the pass from 4.

Player 3 fakes in and comes off 5 to the strong-side perimeter area as a potential receiver and the protector. Player 5 waits as a potential receiver. Player 4 passes to 1 and cuts toward 2 on the weak side (see figure 12.1). Player 2 moves to the weak-side guard position. The floor is balanced. All players must time their moves so 4 has plenty of time to consider each option.

Player 1 passes to 3, who passes to 2 (see figure 12.2). Players 1 and 3 change positions, and the offense is ready to begin any play. For example, 2 passes to 4 and initiates the UCLA cut (see figure 12.3).

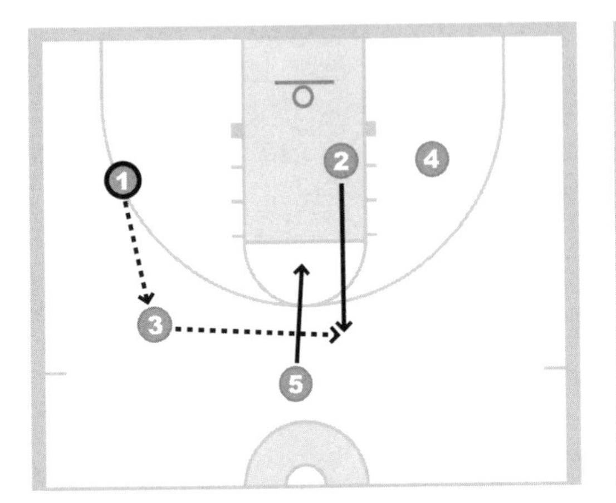

Figure 12.2 The ball goes from 1 to 3 to 2.

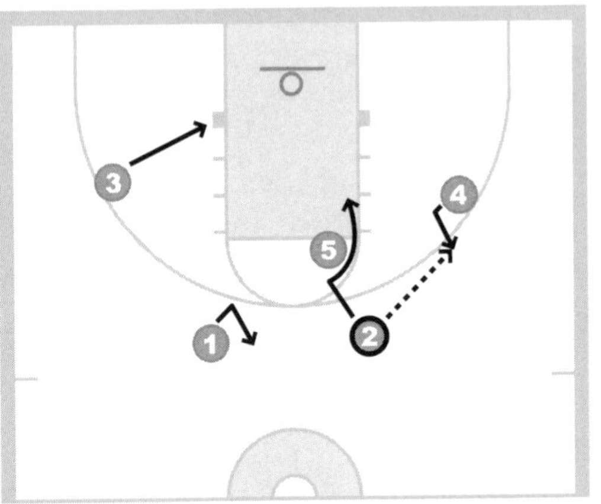

Figure 12.3 Players 1 and 3 switch places, and then a play such as the UCLA cut can be run.

4 to 2 Pass

Player 1 is covered, and 4 passes to 2 on the weak side. If 2 has an opportunity to score, 4 and 5 become inside rebounders, 1 is the long rebounder, and 3 is the protector (see figure 12.4).

If 2 elects not to shoot, he dribbles out toward the wing, and 5 cuts down the middle looking for a pass and score. To transition directly into a play, 2 passes to 3, who has faked in and come to the strong-side guard position. Player 1 takes the other guard position, and 4 moves to the weak-side wing (see figure 12.5). The offense is set.

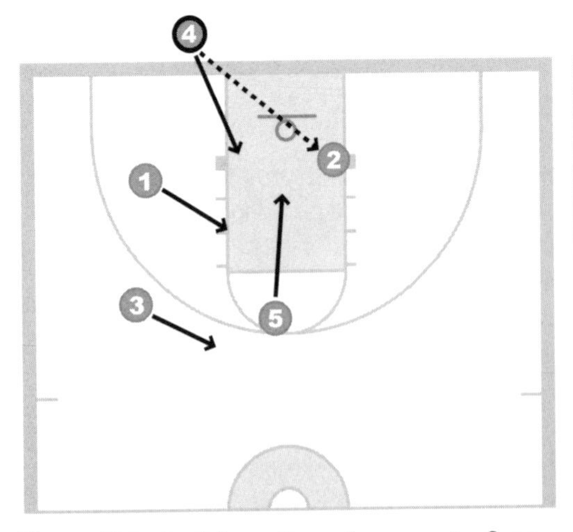

Figure 12.4 In this option, 4 passes to 2 on the weak side.

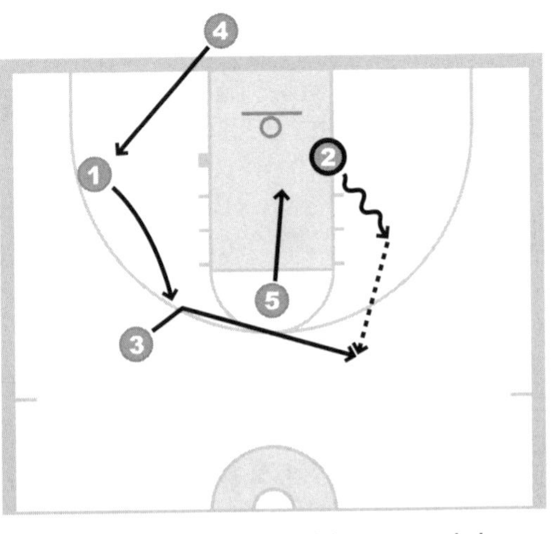

Figure 12.5 Player 2 dribbles toward the wing and passes to 3.

Special plays can be run off inbounds plays. For example, after the pass from 4 to 2 to 3, 4 comes directly to the weak-side side post and receives the pass from 3. Player 1, a good outside shooter, cuts backdoor and comes off a double screen set by 5 and 2, with 2 on the low side (see figure 12.6). Player 4 also has a one-on-one situation. The backdoor pass could very well be open because often 1's defender, seeing 1 moving toward the weak-side guard position, may either be playing the passing lane or be unsuspecting of a quick ball reversal. Incidentally, this option is available when 4 makes the inbounds pass to 1 as well.

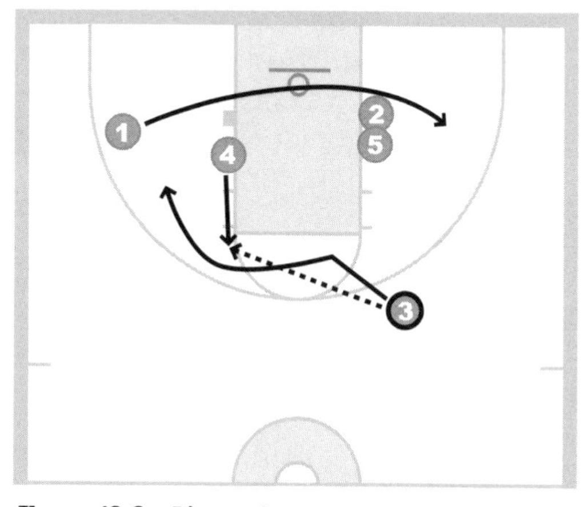

Figure 12.6 Player 3 passes to 4, and 1 cuts backdoor and comes off the screen set by 5 and 2.

4 to 5 Pass

After the passes to 1 and 2 are explored in sequence, 5 makes his move to get open. Although a quick catch and score may be available at times, generally speaking, 5 fakes in and comes back out to the elbow area to receive a high pass from 4 (see figure 12.7).

Player 4 immediately makes a cut to the basket on the weak side, looking for a pass from 5. Player 2 moves out to the weak-side guard position. Player 1 sets a back screen for 3, resulting in the two players exchanging positions (see figure 12.8). A pass back out to any guard will reset the

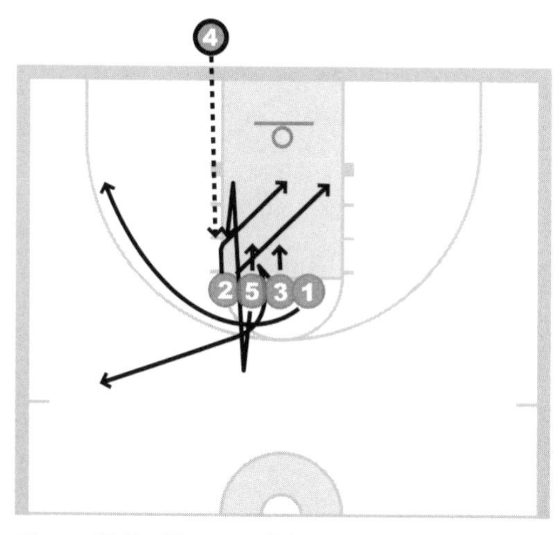

Figure 12.7 Player 5 fakes in and comes back out to the elbow for the pass from 4.

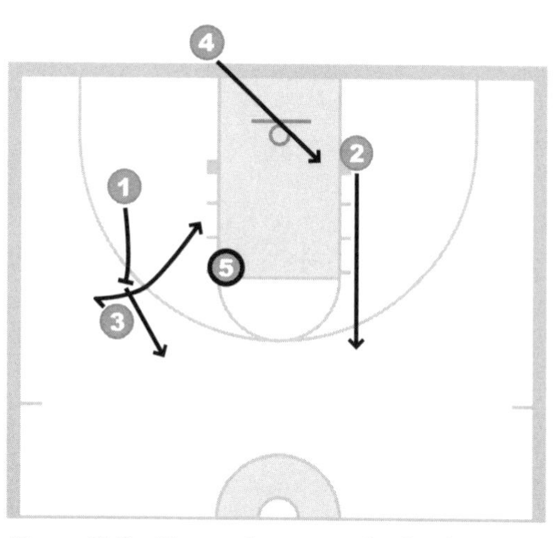

Figure 12.8 Player 4 cuts to the basket, 2 moves out to guard, 1 screens for 3, and then takes 3's place.

offense. If 5 has caught the ball above the free throw line, the "guard to guard to center" play can immediately be run (see figure 12.9).

However, 1's back screen for 3 may have created a switch and, therefore, a mismatch for either player. If 3 has a size advantage, he drops to the low post, 1 takes the wing, and the triangle should get 3 the ball for a shot.

If 1 has a quickness advantage, 5 passes him the ball, 3 cuts to the basket, and 5 sets a ball screen for 1 (see figure 12.10). At the appropriate time, 3 comes off a double screen set by 4 and 2. As will often happen, his defender, seeing the play develop, may stay inside the key to offer help should 1 drive. At that moment, 3 comes off the screen to the weak-side perimeter. He should be open. The ball screen is optional because 1 may be able to take his man without it. In that situation, 5 is a potential receiver.

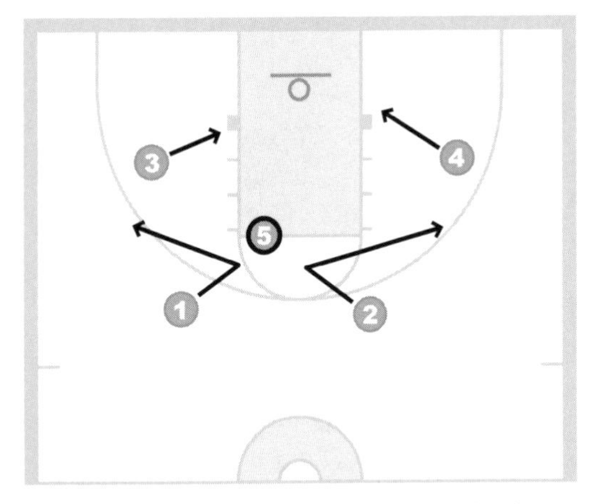

Figure 12.9 If 5 has the ball above the free throw line, the guards meet and flare, running the guard to guard to center.

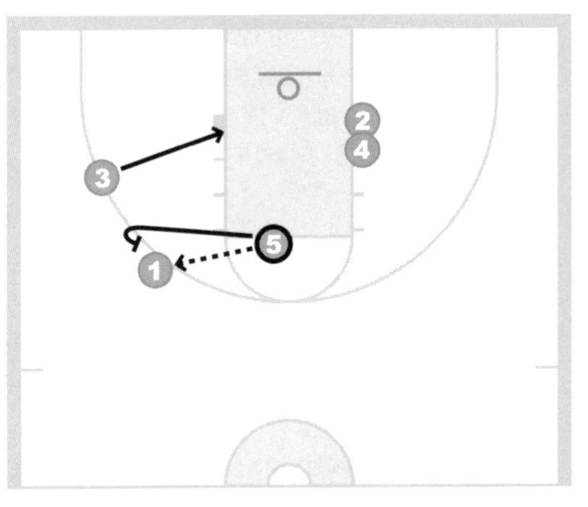

Figure 12.10 Player 5 passes to 1 and then sets a ball screen for 1 as 3 cuts to the basket.

4 to 3 Pass

If 4 makes the inbounds pass to 3, his last option, 3 passes to 2, who has moved out to the weak-side guard position. Player 4 takes the wing on that side, and 3 changes positions with 1 (see figure 12.11). A quick transition to any play is available.

Player 2's hard cut to the guard position may prompt his defender to deny the pass or even attempt a steal for a breakaway basket. Players 3 and 4 must be alert to take advantage of this aggressive

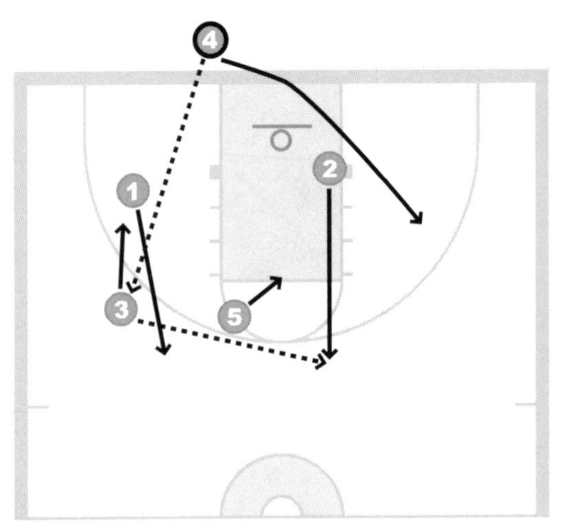

Figure 12.11 In this option, 4 passes to 3 who passes to 2. Then 4 goes out to the wing, and 3 and 1 change places.

defensive play and run a guard reverse for 2. Player 5 must also be alert to go backdoor, should he be pressured.

Vertical

Players 1, 5, and 2 line up along the strong side of the lane, with 1 closest to 4 and standing just below the elbow. Player 3 starts above the top of the key.

On the signal, 1 makes a move to the strong- or weak-side corner, depending on how his man is playing him. Next, 2 makes a responding move opposite 1. Player 5 cuts straight toward the ball, calling for the pass. Player 4 passes to 1 and cuts toward the other wing (see figure 12.12).

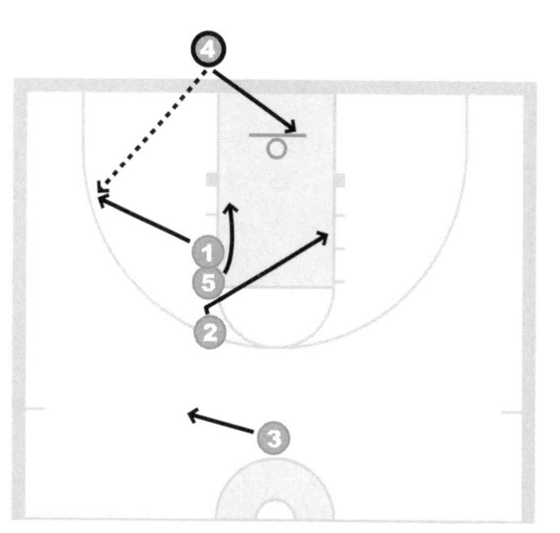

Figure 12.12 Players 1 and 2 cut to the opposite sides, with 5 going straight for the ball. Player 4 passes to 1.

Player 1 passes to 3. Player 2 comes out to the other guard position and receives the pass from 3. Players 1 and 3 change positions. Without a hitch, the offense is ready to begin any high-post offense play (see figure 12.13).

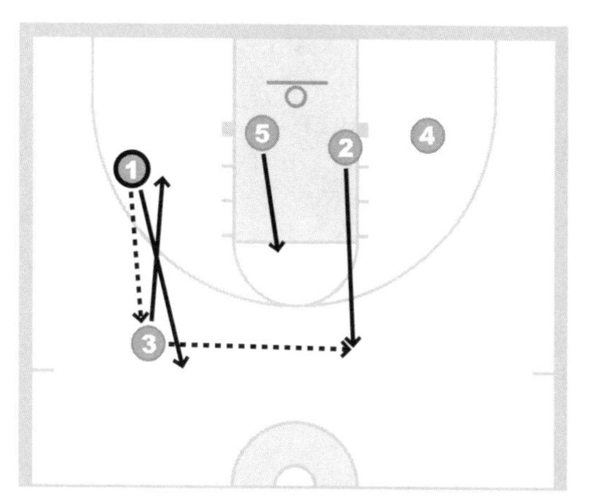

Figure 12.13 Player 1 passes to 3 who passes to 2, then 3 and 1 trade positions.

You will notice that at this point in the play, the positions of the players are the same as in the horizontal alignment, with the possible exception of 1 and 2, who may have changed positions because of 1's initial read and cut. For that reason, all transitions into half-court offense that exist for the horizontal alignment also exist for the vertical.

SIDELINE PLAYS

With more room to operate than when under the basket, it would seem that sideline out-of-bounds plays are less difficult to execute. They should be, but an often thrown cross-court pass can easily be stolen for a breakaway score. Again, the players need to be reminded that the primary objective is to get the ball inbounds to the first available receiver.

Tandem

Player 4 stands three feet back of the sideline. Players 1 and 2 are positioned at the two guard spots with the better ball handler farthest away. Players 3 and 5 are in a double stack at the elbow, with 3 on the bottom (see figure 12.14).

4 to 1 or 2 Pass

On 4's signal, 2 turns and screens for 1, who comes to the ball. Player 2 occupies the spot vacated by 1. If 2 thinks it will get the ball inbounds, he fakes the screen and comes back to the ball. In other words, 2 and 1 do whatever the defense dictates to get open. Player 3 moves to the corner, and 5 goes directly to the ball, in sequence (see figure 12.14). After a pass to either guard is explored, 3 or 5 may move to an open spot at any time.

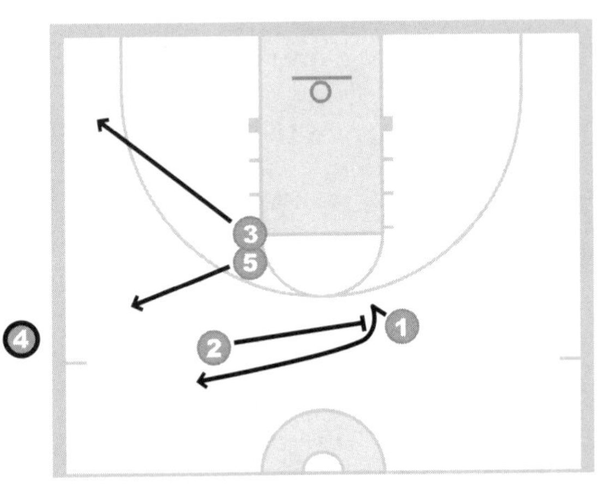

Figure 12.14 Player 2 screens for 1, who comes to the ball, while 3 goes to the corner and 5 to the ball.

Player 4 passes to 1 and makes a penetrating cut to the opposite wing. Player 3 is already on the other wing, and the guards are in position to begin any play. Player 1 passes to 2. Player 2 makes the pass to 5 at the high post to begin a play in the "guard to guard to center" series (see figure 12.15).

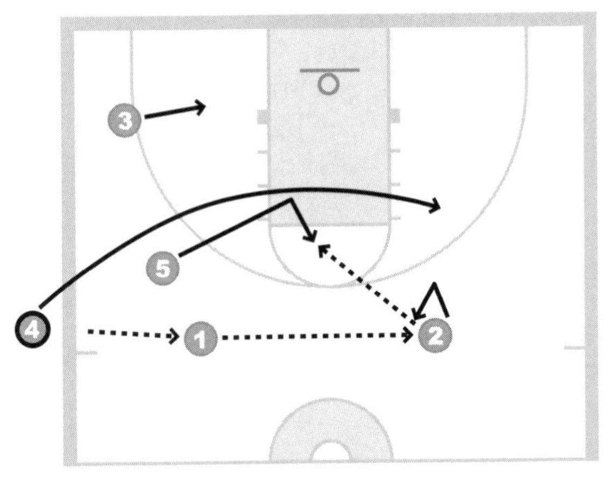

Figure 12.15 Player 4 passes to 1 and then cuts to the opposite wing. Then 1 passes to 2, who passes to 5 at the high post.

4 to 3 Pass

Player 2 has screened for 1. Player 4 passes to 3, who has cut to the strong-side corner, and cuts quickly to the weak-side block. At this point, any offensive play can be initiated with a pass from 3 to 1 (see figure 12.16). For example, a pass from 1 to 2 to 4 can be immediately followed by a UCLA cut (see figure 12.17).

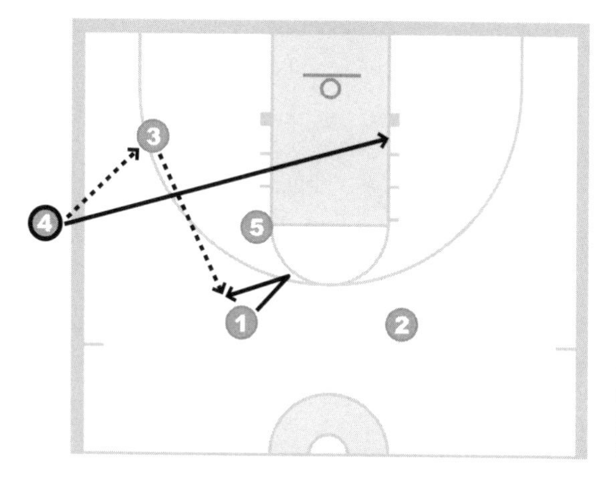

Figure 12.16 The ball goes from 4 to 3, and then 3 passes to 1 to initiate any offensive play.

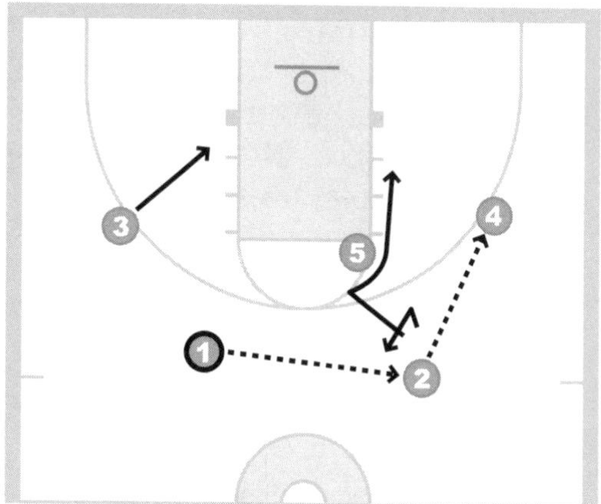

Figure 12.17 With 1 in possession, the guard to guard to forward with UCLA cut can follow.

4 to 5 Pass

Player 4 passes to 5 because 1 and 3 are overplayed. The most logical play is a backdoor pass to 3; the entire basket area should be vacant. If no pass is made, 3 continues to the opposite wing while 4 replaces him. As all coaches know, the most dangerous player in a sideline out-of-bounds play is the inbounder. If 4 is a good shooter, he may have a three-point shot. In either case, because the guards and forwards are in position, a pass back out to any guard makes the offense ready for a smooth transition into any play (see figure 12.18).

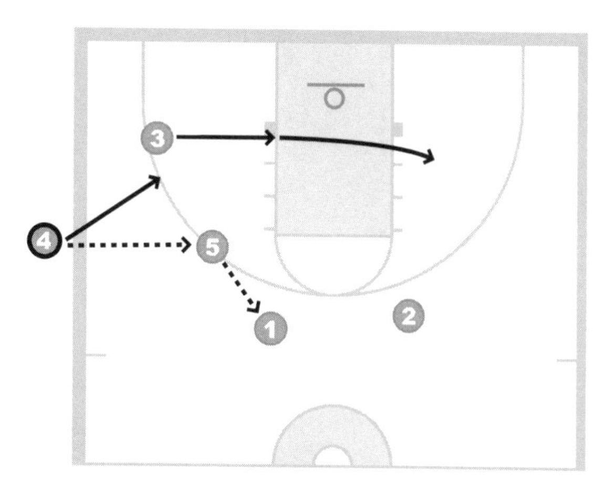

Figure 12.18 If 1 and 3 are overplayed, 4 passes to 5, and a pass to either guard puts the offense in position for any play.

Horizontal

Players 3, 1, 5, and 2 line up along the free throw line, with 3 closest to 4, and 2 farthest from 4. All four players should be in direct alignment with 4.

4 to 1 Pass

On 4's signal, 3 makes the first move by coming around his teammates and cutting down the key, looking for the lob. Player 4 fakes the lob pass. Player 1 makes the next move. If his defender is playing to the inside, he cuts toward half court; if to the outside, he cuts to the corner. Player 2 follows his lead and takes the other position. Player 5 is the last cutter and moves directly toward 4, calling for the ball. Player 4 passes to 1 and steps in (see figure 12.19).

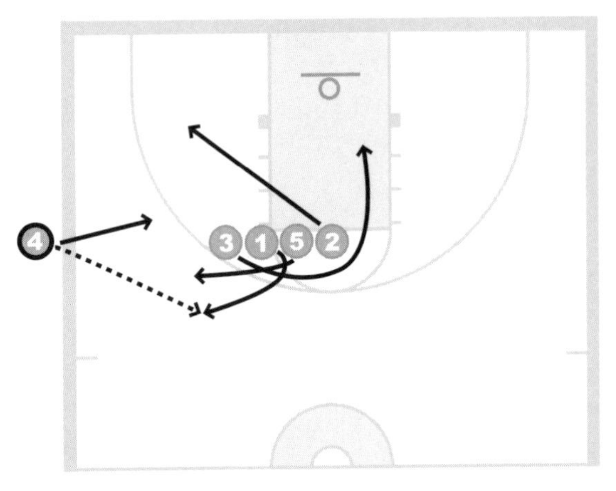

Figure 12.19 Player 3 cuts down the key; 4 fakes a lob to him but instead passes to 1.

Player 1 looks for 4, because he may have an outside shot, while 2 uses 5's screen to sprint to the weak-side guard position (see figure 12.20). The offense may be in an ideal position to run the forward reverse play because 4 may be pressured (see figure 12.21).

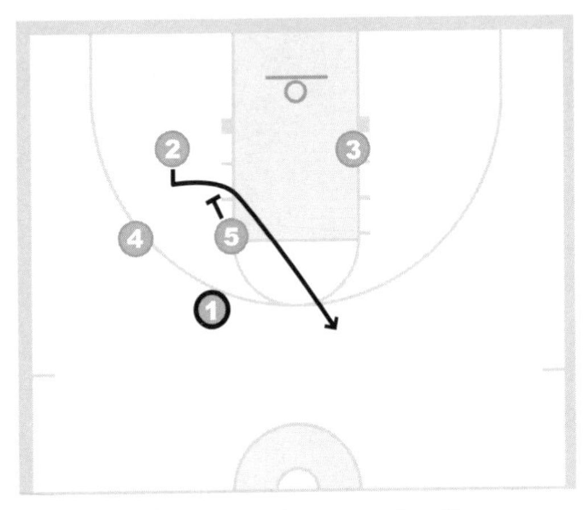

Figure 12.20 Player 5 screens for 2, who sprints to the weak-side guard position.

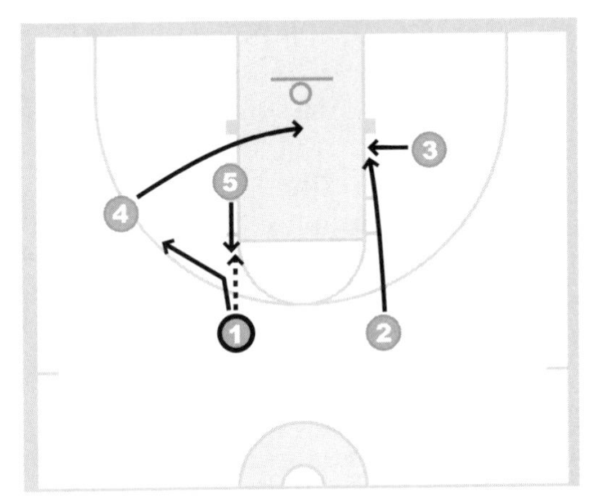

Figure 12.21 If 4 is pressured, the offense runs the forward reverse.

CUNNING CONNECTION

Without question, the two key players for creating a quick high-percentage shot off the horizontal alignment of the out-of-bounds play under your own basket are the guards. If the play is executed properly, the defender guarding the point guard, or first cutter, will be slowed down by his three teammates taking one step toward the basket, directly in his path. Player 2 then simply watches his defender for any movement toward 1, and if an opening occurs, he slips in for the catch and score.

No guard combination was better at this than Ron Livingston and Don Johnson (for the 1951 to 1952 UCLA team). On the inbounder's signal, Livingston, a crafty player, often took a small step back toward half court before cutting to the corner, causing his man to follow him. This made his cut to the corner even more effective because his defender was often trailing him. When Livingston reached the corner and Johnson's defender did not switch, the left-hander was able to receive the ball and go up for a quick jump shot. Johnson, a resourceful individual, had a great sense for knowing when he was open to cut into the middle, if his man switched out to cover Livingston.

© UCLA Photography

If there was an opening in the defense, Ron Livingston usually found it. Here, Ron drives between two defenders.

CLOSING POINTS

The primary goal of out-of-bounds plays is to get the ball inbounds. Cutting players must be taught to execute with timing and economy. The inbounder must be taught to recognize the first available, and safe, opportunity.

The second goal is to transition smoothly into the offense. Set plays can be called as the team huddles quickly before inbounding the ball. The use of special plays for three-point shots or to spring particular players open is an option to consider in certain situations.

Coaches and players should avoid getting so caught up in the Xs and Os of a play that they lose sight of executing the fundamentals. Cuts, screens, fakes, and passes must be performed properly and quickly to get the desired high-percentage shot or to initiate the offense.

Part VI

TECHNIQUES, TACTICS, AND TEAM PLAY

From the perspective of coaching responsibility, the success of any team will be determined largely by three important functions: the teaching of fundamentals, the skill of using strategy, and the development of teamwork.

Much has been discussed about the importance of good fundamentals to execution. I believe it cannot be overemphasized. A significant amount of practice time should be reserved for explicit teaching of the basic building blocks of any offense. Also, drills should be created that help reinforce those fundamentals for an entire season.

The chance of winning any game can be greatly enhanced by adjusting the focus of the offense in accordance with the upcoming opponent. This involves a coach making the most of his own player matchup advantages as well as minimizing those of the opponent.

It is not enough for the coach to believe in his system. If he is to be successful, he must sell his players on it, especially in the area of team play. At any level, there will be those who know they are not stars and those who believe they are, or should be. If the coach does not truly believe in the absolute and irreplaceable importance of players who are not skilled scorers but set screens and pass the ball effectively, he will not be able to sell his players on it. He must use tactical methodology for creating an atmosphere where the weaker players are strengthened and the stronger players are eager to share the glory.

CHAPTER 13

FUNDAMENTALS AND DRILLS

It has been said that a talented player with poor fundamentals cannot become a great player, but a player with average talent who is well grounded in the basic building blocks of the game can be a very good player. While this is true for individuals, it is also true for teams.

The UCLA offense works, not because of brilliant Xs and Os, but because the players have mastered quick and proper execution of a variety of passes, dribbles, cuts, fakes, and shots, as well as the art of obtaining offensive rebound position. Mastery means more than excellence; it means excellence with automaticity.

When fundamentally sound players are well drilled, their execution of the basics of the game is correct, quick, and unconscious. In offensive basketball, that means the physical actions necessary to carry out a play become second nature, and that the player is able to devote complete concentration to the movement of the ball and to other players on the court.

A team with players who, collectively, have few fundamental weaknesses can be very good, even if the overall talent on the squad is average. Such teams can compete with and often defeat teams with superior talent.

Because modern offenses, such as the motion offense, require players at all positions to do many different things, it's advisable that players learn the full array of fundamentals, not only those that are traditionally associated with their position (guard, forward, or center). This will allow players to move interchangeably from one spot to the next, making the team as a whole more versatile and harder to defend.

UCLA offenses are structured to create proper spacing and balance, sequenced options, and plays that take advantage of all defensive stunts. However, they are not rigid offenses; they leave options open for individual initiative if any player sees an opening or a better opportunity to score other than the original play design. Players who are part of a system in which individual moves are encouraged and expected, especially from the more talented athletes, must be able to adeptly and consistently pivot, turn, pass and receive, shoot, fake, and rebound.

ESSENTIAL SKILLS

The first objective of every coach should be to ground the players in the automatic execution of the fundamentals of the game. The second objective naturally follows—to integrate fundamentally sound players into a smooth-working unit. These priorities are often, mistakenly, reversed.

Coaches who have little time to prepare their teams for a first game—sometimes two weeks or less—are tempted to emphasize team defense and offense at the outset. This is a mistake. No system of play will be effective unless it is based on sound execution of the fundamentals. Yes, that may mean the team will look a bit out of synch at times early in the season. And it might even cost the team an early win or two. But, over the course of the season, and certainly through those players' careers, the patience to prioritize the fundamentals over scoring output will pay off.

Following are the fundamentals required to execute offense. They are listed in no order of importance. Passing is the most important because an offense is rendered useless without movement of the basketball to those in scoring position.

Stops

A good stop is necessary before making any pivot. Two types of stops are used when receiving the ball. The two-footed jump stop is best employed for moves away from the basket, such as when the forward breaks to the high post in the side-post game. The stride stop is preferred when the defense is slack and a quick turn for a shot is available.

When executing the two-footed jump stop, the feet should hit the floor simultaneously, and the entire surface of the sole should hit the floor, although most of the impact will be on the front. The feet should be parallel and a little wider apart than the shoulders. The head should be directly above the midpoint between the two feet, the chin up, the elbows tucked in, the knees slightly bent, and every joint flexed and relaxed. We prefer that the back be arched, not bowed, but some players appear to be in good balance doing the latter. The ball should be close to the body. The center of gravity is now low and in tight, allowing for quick turning and cutting.

The stride stop is primarily used when the wing player receives the ball. The wing player's trailing foot lands first as the catch is made, and it is the pivot foot. The front foot swings around to square the player to the basket. The pivot foot should be the left foot for right-handers and vice versa for left-handers.

Turns and Pivots

It is best to teach one style of pivoting. We prefer the reverse, or inside, pivot because it is generally applicable in more situations than the front pivot. Situations that require pivoting include coming out to the wing from the block to receive the guard-to-forward pass and coming to the high post from the inside for the guard reverse, forward reverse, or side-post game. The reverse pivot is executed by swinging the nonpivot foot behind. The feet are parallel and a bit more than shoulder-width apart, allowing for quick and balanced pivots. As the player turns, he stays low and maintains his center of gravity. The player's head remains directly above the midpoint between the two feet, and the chin and eyes are up (see figure 13.1).

Figure 13.1 Reverse, or inside, pivot.

Passing and Receiving

Passing is the most important offensive fundamental because high-percentage shots usually result from a series of good, quick passes. It is no surprise that teams that pass the ball best shoot more accurately than those that rely on the dribble. Passing practice should emphasize passing and receiving the exact passes used in the offense. Improved ball movement and timing will also give shooters more time to release.

Passes should be made quickly and accurately, and when possible, with some deception. The offensive player must avoid telegraphing the direction of the intended pass and allowing the defense to intercept the ball or get in position to deny the receiver any operating room.

Two-Handed Push Pass, or Chest Pass

The two-handed push pass is used when the defender has no chance of deflecting it. It is a straight pass, and the flight of the basketball remains parallel to the floor. It should be thrown quickly with a snap of the wrists. Backspin is provided when the hands turn inward so the palms end up facing out and the thumbs are pointed at the floor (see figure 13.2).

Figure 13.2 Two-handed push pass.

One-Handed Push Pass

From the crouched position, the offensive player checks the positioning of the defender's hands. If the hands are up, the player uses the head, lead foot, or the ball to fake up, then points the throwing hand by the defender's waist and delivers a bounce pass (see figure 13.3). Bounce passes generally should land two-thirds the distance to the receiver. If the defender's hands are down, the passer will fake down and throw a one-handed air pass. Although the player may take a forward step when executing the one-handed push pass, it is more deceptive if no step is taken.

a

b

Figure 13.3 One-handed push pass (bounce).

Handoff Pass

Figure 13.4 Handoff pass.

In the high-post and high-low offenses, the handoff pass (sometimes referred to as the "flip" pass) is used only during the side-post game and the guard reverse. The guard passes to the forward, who has cut to the high post, then cuts off and looks for the handoff pass.

No spin is required nor should the ball be thrown up at the receiver. The passer simply releases the ball into the hands of the receiver with the two players never touching the ball simultaneously (see figure 13.4).

Two-Handed Overhead Pass

Figure 13.5 Two-handed overhead pass.

With the hands toward the back of the ball, the passer fakes down, the hands go straight up (never behind the head because it will delay the pass), and the passer snaps the wrists to deliver the pass. The feet remain a little wider than shoulder width; no advanced step is required because it will telegraph the pass. Since this pass is used often, it must be practiced to improve quickness, deception, and accuracy. In the guard reverse, the guard will generally fake down and use this pass to deliver the ball to the forward (see figure 13.5), because it is quicker than a bounce pass. However, there will be times when the bounce pass is appropriate.

Shooting

Players should work on a variety of shots, and the bulk of their time should be spent on the shots they will get in games. That is why some time should be reserved in almost every practice session for guards working together, forwards working together, and centers working together.

All players should be taught to be quick shooters. Also, the saying "Shoot by the defender, not over him" is true. When a defender is ready to put pressure on the shot, drive fakes and pass fakes are essential to getting him off balance for a quick shot or drive. The set, jump, and hook shots are the most commonly used shots in the offense.

Set Shot

Many set and jump shot styles have been used through the years. What we have learned is that the exact technique in preparation for the shot is less important than what happens at release. All good shooters keep their elbows moving up as they snap their wrists for the follow-through. In addition, the head follows the shot. The motion is similar to a nod. This action transfers momentum into the basketball. Nonetheless, proper preparation can put a player into a more favorable position for the release. Good balance, proper position of the elbow through the shot, and the movement of the head are important. The elbow should start directly above the knee with the wrist wrinkled, signifying the wrist is cocked. As the ball moves up, the elbow continues on a path in line with the basket. As the shot is released, it continues up and ends up above the ear. The most important function of the elbow is that it is moving up when the ball is released. This makes it a "lift" rather than a "push."

On the set shot, the feet don't leave the floor until the shot is released. This allows all body momentum to be transferred into the ball, making it easier to get the ball to the basket, especially on three-point shots.

Jump Shot

The fundamentals of the jump shot are the same as for the set shot. However, balance is even more important on the jumper. Ideally, a jump shooter's feet will land in the same spots from which they left the floor. Shooters must watch not to float or shoot off balance, because this will reduce jump shot accuracy and consistency. Regaining balance is particularly important to players coming around a screen to receive a pass for a jump shot (see figure 13.6).

Figure 13.6 Jump shot.

Hook Shot

The technique for the hook shot begins with the ball tucked in below the chin, the pivot foot closest to the basket, and a long step that does not increase the shooter's distance from the goal. At the start of the jump, the player extends the ball up first, then slightly out, rather than a swinging motion where the ball is extended out first, then up. The release is made by a flip of the wrist and the entire arm following through to the basket. The player's body should turn during the shot so he is squared up to the basket when landing (see figure 13.7).

Figure 13.7 Hook shot.

Faking and Footwork

A very valuable skill is to make the opponent think you intend to do one thing, and then do something else. Such fakes can involve the head, the ball, and the feet, with the ball being least important. Movement on a pass fake should be limited to a few inches while the elbows remain in close proximity with the body. Extension of the arms too far both exposes the ball for possible deflections and takes longer to bring the ball back to a position where the player can use it. Every fraction of a second is important because opportunities open and close quickly.

Jabbing with the foot and faking down with the head, without much leaning, will cause a defender to retreat or step over, perhaps making room for the shot or clearing a path for the drive.

The shot fake should replicate the exact preparatory movements of a shot. Too many times we see only the ball going up when it should be the ball, the head, and the shoulders. The knees must be bent to keep a quick drive as an option.

Rebounding

Notice how rarely the leading rebounder on a team or in a conference is the player with the highest vertical jump. That's because a great sense of timing and a knack for anticipating the spot and angle of the missed shot are more important than jumping ability to excel as a rebounder.

Rebounding skills are developed through effective drills and a relentless "the ball belongs to me" attitude. Then, through practice, players can hone their anticipation and timing. From there, all that is needed is the determination to get in an advantageous position to rebound the ball.

An offensive rebounder must establish position at a good location—where a teammate's shot is likely to land. (A true rebounder assumes all shots will be missed.) When the shot is in the air, or before if possible, the player fakes away from the desired spot, moves his inside hand past his opponent's shoulder and toward his target, and follows with a step in the same direction. The hands should come up to shoulder height in case the ball caroms off the backboard or rim quickly.

Paul Silas, Dennis Rodman, and Ben Wallace are among the best offensive rebounders ever to play the game. They each had three things in common—an instinct for where the ball was going, a great desire to claim it, and the quickness to beat their opponent to the basketball.

The offensive fundamentals that have been presented in this section should be taught systematically, first in isolation and next combined with other fundamentals. This building process provides the foundation for the offensive system's success. A strong foundation is developed through effective and repeated practice activities that approximate game situations.

PRACTICE DRILLS

After isolated skills are mastered, technique combinations, more complex tactical maneuvers, and even gamelike scrimmage situations serve as the building blocks for player and team development. Proper sequence and timing of this progression are essential for successful learning.

IMAGINARY SHOOTING

Preparation

All players are in lines facing the coach, ready in crouched positions with the feet a little wider than the shoulders, the imaginary ball tucked under the chin, the knees bent, the back straight, the chin up, and all joints flexed and relaxed.

Procedure

When the coach blows the whistle, all players shoot an imaginary jump shot and return to the original position without standing to rest. The coach blows the whistle as many times as necessary, depending on the physical condition of the players, to get enough work in.

Teaching Points

- Players should be continually reminded to jump their highest.
- The quick release must be insisted on. Some players shoot what some call "two-count shots," where the ball is brought up behind the head, stops, and is then pushed forward. The ball must never stop but, rather, continue up and forward.
- The position of the elbow should be watched and corrected. It should start directly above the knee and continue up. Most important, it must continue up at the point of release. To ensure this happens, when returning to the original position, the hand should retreat along the identical path it used to release the shot. This helps eliminate dropping the hand and arm toward the floor after release.
- The head must follow the shot, though slightly.
- Players should return to a balanced position.
- As an extension, the shot fake, one-dribble drive, and pull-up jump shot should be taught.

IMAGINARY REBOUNDING

Preparation

The setup is the same as for imaginary shooting, except the players are crouched with the hands at shoulder level.

Procedure

The coach throws a ball straight up into the air, and the players jump and reach, as if pursuing an actual rebound. Variations of this drill involve blocking out, outlet passing, or making a move to get to an offensive rebound.

Teaching Points

- In the crouched position, a player's hands should be no lower than shoulder height, and they must not drop below that level at any point.
- Players must work on timing, reaching their highest points when the ball is obtainable.
- If working on defensive rebounding, the players should be instructed to turn their heads and make the imaginary outlet pass when obtaining possession of the ball. Outlet passes to the right and left side must be taught.
- When returning to the floor, a player's feet should flare to create space.
- When obtaining possession, the ball must be quickly pulled to just below the chin, with the elbows spread wide.

POSITION FUNDAMENTALS

Preparation

Guards, forwards, and centers are stationed at separate baskets.

Procedure

The coach and assistants teach offensive fundamentals that are priorities for specific positions.

For example, three centers are working on hook shots, turnaround jump shots, and drop steps to the baseline. The players rotate in turn, and the coach is passing the ball to the players. No defense is provided in the first phase as each player shoots five consecutive shots (e.g., the hook shot across the key). When all three have finished, they are ready for the second phase—three-quarters defensive pressure. The last phase is full defensive pressure. When work on all three moves is completed, the players play one on one, selecting the appropriate move based on reading the defense.

The guards are at a separate basket working on receiving the handoff pass in the side-post game. They receive explicit instructions on reading their defensive men. First, they practice the various options: the back cut, the drive, and the pull-up jump shot. Then defense is added to help in their decision making.

At another basket, the forwards are also working on the side-post game. With no defense, they learn to come to the elbow of the key, receive the pass, and come to a two-footed jump stop, providing the possibility of using either pivot foot for a move. They learn how to hand off and roll, hand off and pop out for the jump shot, and make the one-on-one move if they elect not to hand off. When defense is added, they learn to take what the defense gives them.

Later, the guards and forwards are combined to practice the side-post game, first with no defense and later with full-on defensive pressure. It is during all-out competition when players are encouraged to improvise and discover individual moves that work and don't work.

REBOUND AND PASS-OUT DRILL

Preparation

One player is positioned at each wing, and a line of no less than two and no more than three players is at the top of the key. The basketball is held by the first person in line at the top of the key. Players are instructed to fake away before receiving any pass, fake before passing, move without the basketball, and catch the ball and then pivot correctly.

Procedure

Player 1 passes to 2, who has faked away and come back out on the wing. Player 2 makes an inside pivot, swinging his right foot back (toward the low post), and assumes triple-threat position. Player 1 fakes away by touching the opposite elbow with his left foot and changes direction toward the opposite block. Player 2 fakes down and delivers a two-handed overhead pass to 1 in the key (see figure *a*).

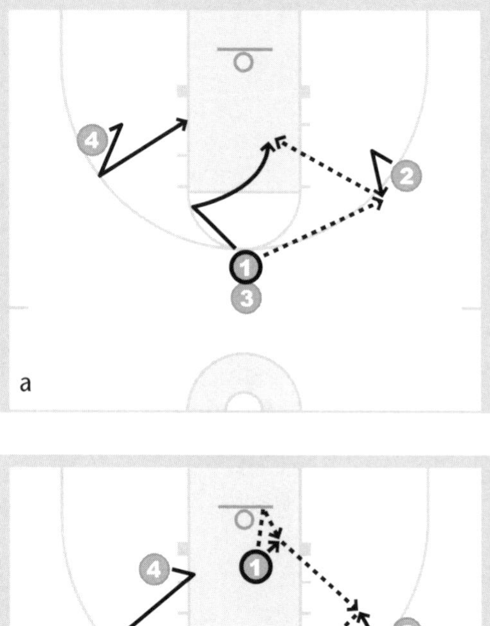

Player 1 throws the ball onto the backboard while 2 takes one or two steps toward half court. Player 1 rebounds and outlets to 2, who has come back to receive. Player 2 passes to 3, who has cut away and come back. Player 3 passes to 4, who has cut toward the block and come back out (see figure *b*). The play is now run on the left side and will alternate until time is up.

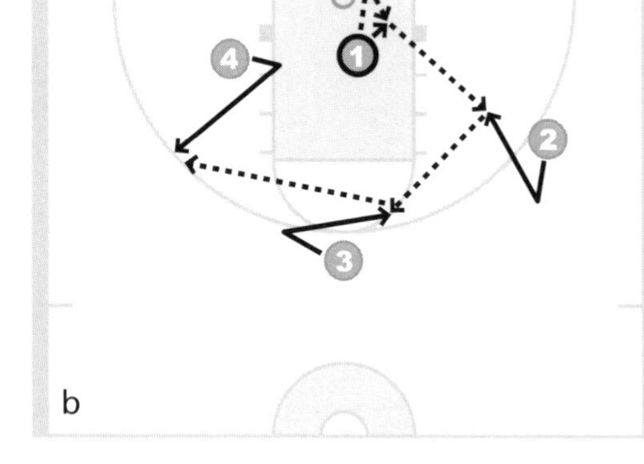

Teaching Points

- Every receiver must make a move to get open before receiving the ball.
- After receiving, every receiver shot fakes, drive fakes, or pass fakes before making the pass.
- Players should work on passing, receiving, and timing. Timing must be perfected so the ball keeps moving with no player waiting for another to get open.
- Each player should keep his hands around shoulder level at all times.

FOUR-PLAYER PASS, RECEIVE, AND CUT DRILL

Preparation

The players are positioned in a two-guard front with one forward on each side. (One substitute is waiting at each position.) The ball is in the hands of the guard on the left side.

Procedure

Player 1 passes to 2, who passes to 4. Player 2 makes a UCLA cut off an imaginary high-post man, calling for the ball. Player 3 moves to the weak-side block (see figure *a*).

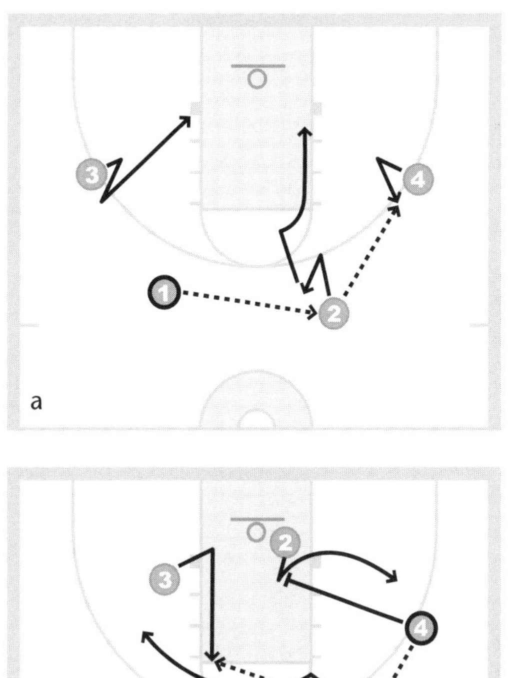

a
b

Player 1 fakes away and comes back to the ball. Player 4 passes to 1, takes one step toward the high post, and begins a down screen for 2. Player 3 comes to the side post. Player 1 passes to 3, and they run the side-post game (see figure *b*). Player 3 keeps the ball, turns, and looks at the down screen set by 4. Player 2 comes around the screen, and 4 slips into the key. Both players call for the ball. Player 3 passes out to the next player in the guard line opposite where the play started. Players 1, 2, 3, and 4 quickly exit the court and get in a line. The play is now run in the opposite direction with four new players.

Teaching Points

- As in the Rebound and Pass-Out Drill, the coach should teach the proper execution of passing, receiving, and the timing of the two.
- The high-post player involved in the side-post game may hand off and receive a return pass from the guard before passing out to restart the drill.
- The guard involved in the side-post game may vary his cuts when he comes off the high post: backdoor cut, over the top, fake backdoor cut, and pop-out.
- All players without the ball should be working on the proper cutting fakes to keep their defenders occupied.

FIVE-PLAYER PASS, RECEIVE, AND CUT DRILL

Preparation

The players are positioned in a two-guard front, with two forwards on the wings and the center at the high post.

Procedure

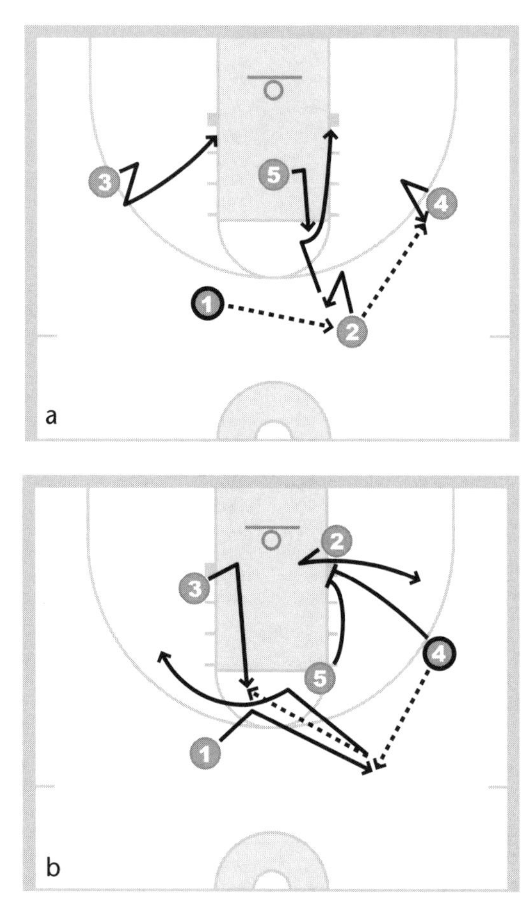

Player 1 passes to 2, who passes to 4. Player 5 turns toward the baseline. Player 2 makes a UCLA cut, using 5 as a screener and calling for the ball. Player 3 moves to the weak-side block (see figure *a*).

Player 1 fakes away and comes back to the ball. Player 4 passes to 1, takes one step toward the high post, and begins a down screen for 2. Player 3 comes to the side post. Player 1 passes to 3, and they run the side-post game (see figure *b*). Player 3 keeps the ball, turns, and looks at 5 and 4 setting a double down screen for 2. Player 2 comes around the screen, and 5 and 4 pop the stack with 4 coming in front of 5 and to the high post. Player 3 passes out to the next player in the guard line opposite where the play started. Players 1, 2, 3, and 4 quickly exit the court and get in a line. Player 5 may stay for three or four possessions before being replaced by another post player. The play is now run in the opposite direction with four new players.

Teaching Points

- The high-post player involved in the side-post game may hand off and receive a return pass from the guard before passing out to restart the drill.
- The guard involved in the side-post game may vary his cuts when he comes off the high post: backdoor cut, over the top, fake backdoor cut, and pop-out.
- All players without the ball should be working on the proper cutting fakes to keep their defenders occupied. This includes the center as he cuts toward the basket and returns to the high post.

FORWARD REVERSE DRILL

Preparation

One low-post, wing, and guard player are positioned on one side of the floor, with one substitute waiting at each position, out of bounds, on the same side of the floor, ready to come in. The ball is in the hands of the guard up top.

Procedure

Player 3 is overplayed (but no defense for the drill). Player 5 comes to the high post and receives a pass from 1, who has faked down and passed up using the two-handed overhead pass or the bounce pass. Player 3 makes a backdoor cut toward the block, and 5 delivers the pass. Player 1 replaces 3. Players 1, 3, and 5 move to the other side of the floor as 7, 8, and 9 begin the drill. Players 2, 4, and 6 will go next.

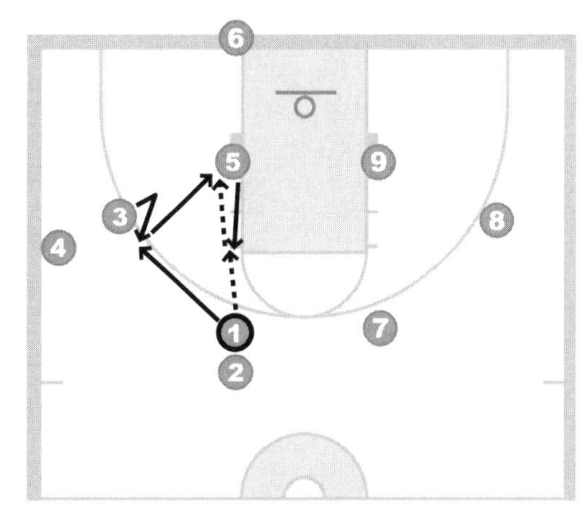

Teaching Points

- The coach should watch post footwork for traveling violations.
- An air pass is most appropriate to a tall player.
- The forward should be well on his way to the basket when the post player receives the ball. The backdoor pass should be caught about three feet above the block.

WING SCREEN DRILL

Preparation

On one side of the floor, a guard is on top, a center is at the high post, and a forward is on the wing. (One substitute is waiting at each position, out of bounds and on the same side of the floor.) The ball is in the hands of the guard.

Procedure

Player 2 passes to 5, fakes the UCLA cut, and screens for 4, who comes around the screen to the high post and around 5. Player 5 can hand off to 4 or give 2 the backdoor pass. Players 2, 4, and 5 move to the other side. The substitutes run the play and then move to the other side.

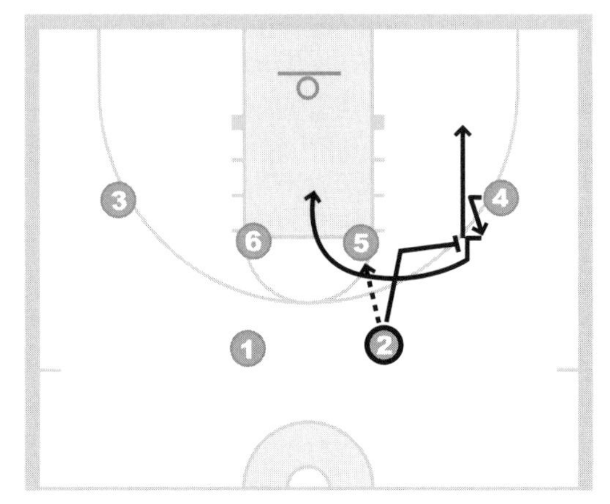

Teaching Points

- The guard should have his back to the forward when setting the screen.
- The guard should roll or pop out after setting the screen.
- Players should work on the guard slipping the screen.
- The post player can fake the screen for the slipping guard before handing off to the forward.
- The post player can fake the handoff pass to the forward and drive to the basket.

SIDE-POST GAME DRILL

Preparation

A guard is positioned at the top, opposite a forward at the weak-side wing. The guard has the ball. (Substitutes are waiting at each position.)

Procedure

Player 4 fakes away and comes to the side post. Player 1 passes to 4, cuts inside, and comes over the top. Player 4 can hand off and pop or roll, keep the ball for an individual move, or pass to 1 for the give-and-go.

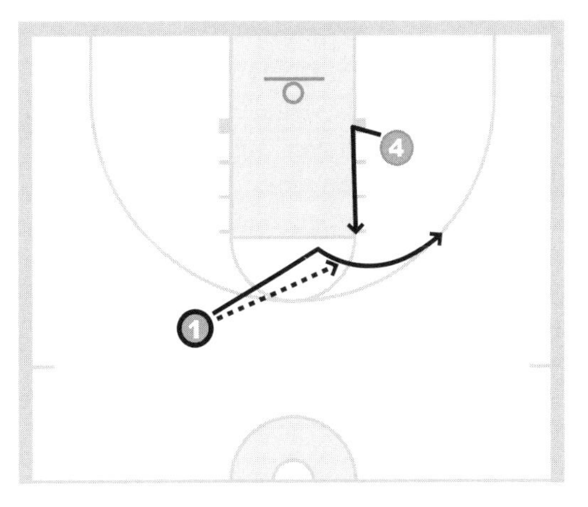

Teaching Points

- The guard can vary his cuts off the post.
- The coach should watch post footwork for traveling violations.
- Players should execute all options, including the give-and-go.
- Players should execute the screen and roll off this play.

GUARD REVERSE DRILL

Preparation

Three players are involved—a two-guard front and one weak-side forward. The ball is at the 1 guard position.

Procedure

Player 2 is overplayed (but no defense for the drill). Player 4 cuts toward the baseline and comes to the high post. Player 1 passes to 4, and 2 cuts backdoor. Player 1 cuts toward 4 and comes over the top, looking for the handoff. Player 4 may pass to 2, hand off to 1, or make the individual move.

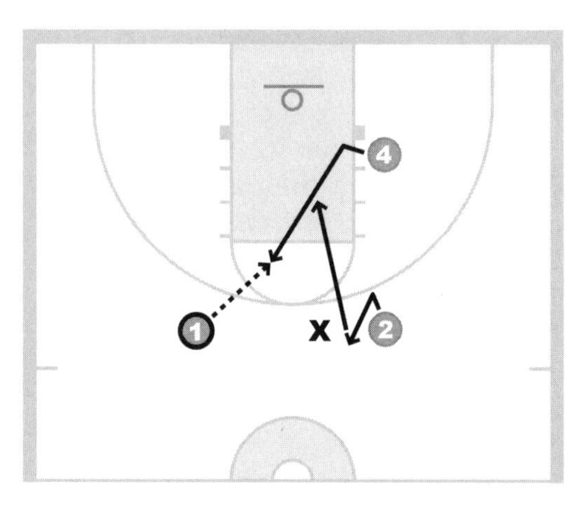

Teaching Points

- Players should work on timing of the backdoor pass from 4 to 2. Player 2 should begin to accelerate to the basket just before 4 receives the ball.
- The coach should watch the forward's footwork for traveling violations.

GUARD TO GUARD, LOW-POST CUT DRILL

Preparation

Four players are involved—a two-guard front, a center at the high post, and a forward at the wing. The ball is at the 1 guard position.

Procedure

Player 1 passes to 2, who hits 5 at the high post. Both guards head for the top of the key and split. Player 1 cuts down to the block and screens for 4, who has come down. Player 5 passes to 4. Player 4 fakes the shot and passes the ball out to 1, who has faked away and come back.

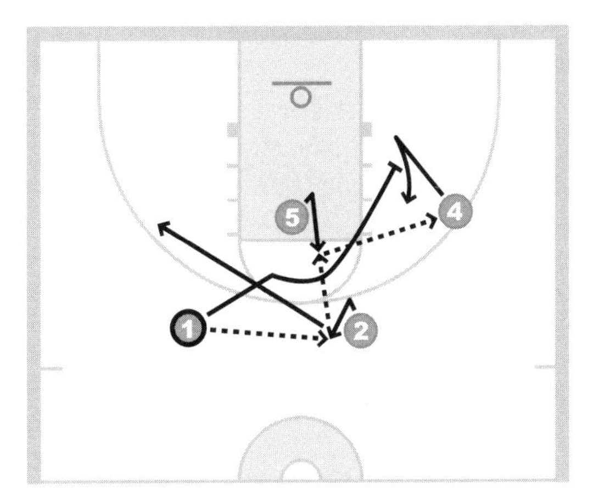

Teaching Points

- The passing guard cuts first.
- The coach should make sure that 4's timing is good coming off 1's screen.
- After screening, 1 should move into the key. At times, he can also slip the screen.
- Player 5's pass fake to 2, when 2 cuts off the post, may open up a handoff for 1.

POP THE SCREEN DRILL

Preparation

Double screen stacks are set on both sides of the lane. One player is positioned in the lane, ready to use the double screen to come to the wing for the jump shot. Each group has one guard out front with the ball. Groups alternate running plays.

Procedure

On the signal, 2 comes off the double screen to the wing. Player 3 comes in front of 4 to the high post as 1 passes to 2. Player 2 may shoot, pass to 4 inside, or pass to 3 at the high post. The other group starts their play.

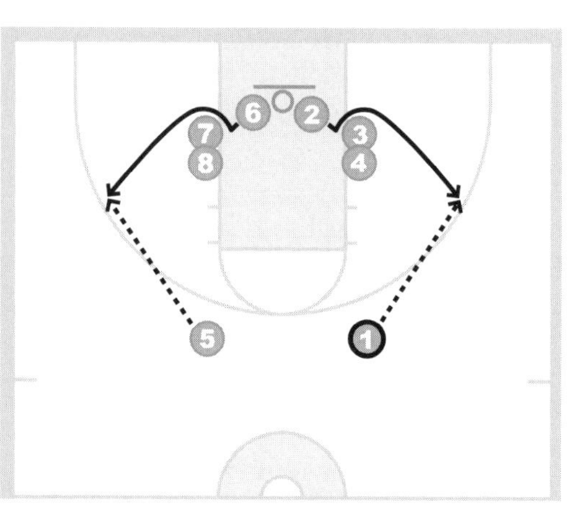

Teaching Points

- If well executed, players should be able to get a good shot just about every time a double screen is attempted. However, the receiver's read of the defense is key to obtaining a high-percentage shot. The receiver should practice curling off the screen, popping to the baseline, popping to the wing, and making a reverse cut to the basket after coming off the screen. Either screener in the stack can slip the screen at any time.

ANTI-OVER REBOUND DRILL

Preparation

This drill can be run with more than three players, but we recommend using three because it gives players more work and better simulates game conditions. Two players line up on one side and close to the basket, with the first holding the ball, and one player lines up on the other side.

Procedure

Player 1 tosses the ball over the basket so it makes contact with the top, far corner of the backboard rectangle. Player 3 times his jump to catch the ball high, and while in midair, he sends it back across to the far corner of the square while 1 cuts inside behind him (see figure *a*). Player 2 times his jump and does the same as 3 cuts inside and behind him (see figure *b*). The drill continues until the whistle blows. After a player tosses the ball to the other side, he cannot slide to the opposite side to get in position. He must sprint.

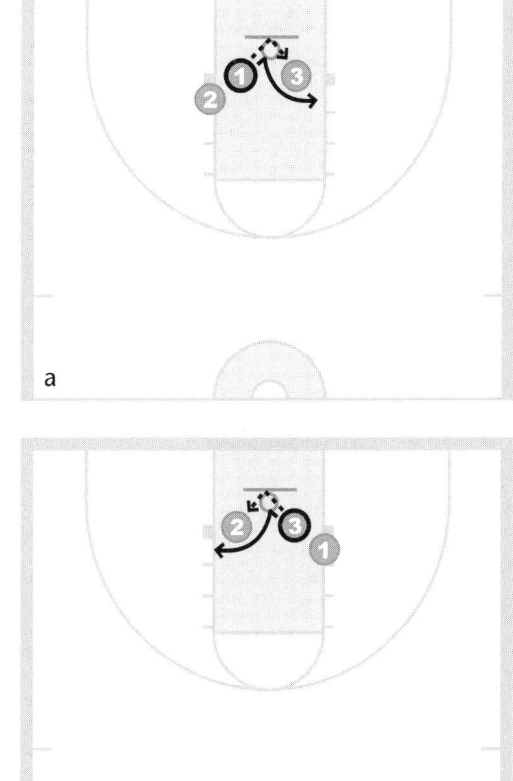

Teaching Points

- The players' hands should be at about shoulder level at all times.
- Players should learn to jump quickly, with elevation and their backs straight.
- Each player should work on catching the ball at the highest point of his jump.
- After passing the ball over the basket, the player should sprint behind the player on the opposite side.
- Begin with players using two hands to catch and pass the ball over the basket. Progress to one hand—the left hand on the left side of the board and the right hand on the right side.
- Players should count passes out loud. The 10th pass is a bank shot off the glass into the basket.
- This drill is often followed with each player shooting a one-and-one free throw situation, which is followed by another session of anti-over.

THE PRACTICE SESSION

One key to success is proper practice planning. Often, the amount of time spent planning each practice will equal or surpass the length of the practice session. The plan should include only those activities that are directly related to the program's system of play. Anything beyond that is wasted time. It does not make sense to include a shooting drill that has no relation to game shots, to run a breakdown drill that is not part of the offense, or to spend time practicing behind-the-back dribbling if it is not allowed in games. In short, each activity must be relevant. If not, it must be replaced.

UCLA practices included an unusual method for practicing free throws. Unlike most teams that devote a period of time to individual or team free throw shooting, at UCLA, every player shot two free throws 10 times at the conclusion of selected drills. After the two foul shots, each player would then do five fingertip push-ups and race to the next activity. Free throws were also integrated into the five-on-five scrimmage conducted toward the end of practice, after the drills.

When the scrimmage began, substitutes would shoot free throws at side baskets. When a sub made a certain number of free throws in a row, he would replace a player who was playing his position in the scrimmage. That player would immediately begin shooting free throws, and the cycle continued until the scrimmage ended. Practicing free throws in this way made each attempt more gamelike, made players concentrate more, and meant that we didn't have to devote additional time to them outside of the other practice activities.

Practice plans should be followed to the minute. Each activity should have a specified duration that is not compromised. Although it's tempting to let a drill continue longer than planned because players seem to just be grasping it, or they aren't performing it well and you want them to have success before moving on to another drill, you should resist that notion. If the length of a drill is problematic, make a note of it and adjust its length, if necessary, the next day.

Every practice session should start on time and end on time. To send that message, announce that practice will begin at, say 2:59, and end at 4:29. Then start and stop the session exactly on the designated minutes. This will benefit the team in several ways. Players will gain a greater appreciation for promptness, the coaching staff will gain greater respect from the players who see that the plan is being adhered to, and players will practice harder the last 30 minutes than they might otherwise if unconsciously pacing themselves for an unknown duration.

The practice session should be divided into the following sections:

1. Warm-up and stretching. Imaginary shooting and rebounding, full-court change of pace, change of direction, defensive sliding, one-on-one, and weaves.

2. Fundamentals. Jump stops and pivots, four-person passing drill, anti-over drill, and rebound and pass-out.
3. Special situations. For example, protecting a lead with ball-control offense—working for a high-percentage shot against a very aggressive and gambling defense. All fundamentals are observed closely and corrected.
4. Breakdown drills. Fundamentals and effort are emphasized.
5. Scrimmage. Players should demonstrate a solid grasp of the fundamentals and tactics, and they should execute them within a team attack.
6. Final notes. Practice should always end on a positive note, perhaps with an activity players will find fun.

PLAYER INSTRUCTION

Drills don't teach; they only provide a platform for instruction. It is the proper teaching of the fundamentals that helps players understand their importance and makes the difference between poor and excellent individual and team execution.

It has been said, "You have not taught until they have learned." The coach who takes full responsibility for transferring basketball skills to his players is a true teacher.

Winning is dependent on several things, some of which are out of the coach's control. But a coach can make certain that players are properly taught the skills and tactics of the game. If the coach also gets his players in top physical condition and prepares them mentally to play as a unit and compete until the final whistle, positive results will follow.

When introducing a particular play, it is best to first reveal what it should look like when it is complete. Then break it into parts and work on those parts at separate baskets, dividing the team into two or three groups. After those breakdown drills, assemble the parts back together into the whole, working with five-player units executing the various parts within the entire play and its options. This "whole-part-whole" method enhances players' understanding of the purpose of each part of the play as it relates to the whole.

For example, let's take the UCLA cut play (guard to guard to forward). Take five players and walk them through the first two passes, explaining how receivers are to get open and describing the fakes that can open up passing lanes. Next, show how the guard executes the UCLA cut and how the center gets open at the high post. Then move on to the forward's pass to the center, and show how the weak-side forward gets open on the flash move inside the key. Correct any lapses in timing, reading screens, moving to get open without the ball, and making passes very catchable so that the receivers can do something immediately with the ball if an opportunity is available.

Then the team breaks up into groups. At one basket, the guards work on the pass from guard to guard to forward and the UCLA cut. No forward is present; guards take the forward spot. At another basket, the center is working with the forward on delivering the pass into the key. Halfway through the drill, the center will leave his group and work with the guards on setting the screen at the high post.

Finally, we bring all players back to one basket and work on the play without defense. Then we add defense and correct all fundamental errors until time is up. We continue the next day with more breakdown drill-sand five-on-five work.

THE FOUR LAWS OF LEARNING

When teaching an offensive fundamental or play, a coach should apply the Four Laws of Learning to enhance players' comprehension and ability to perform automatically.

Law 1—Demonstration and explanation. Players are shown the correct performance (slowly at first) while it is being described to them.

Law 2—Imitation. Players imitate the model.

Law 3—Correction. As players attempt to replicate the performance, they are provided with corrective feedback. Perfection is demanded.

Law 4—Repetition. Players continue to practice (with correction) until the skill or play execution becomes automatic. This may take several days or weeks.

CLOSING POINTS

Every action in basketball is—at its most basic level—a fundamental or a combination of fundamentals. Follow a player for an entire game, and what you'll see is a series of fundamentals linked sequentially to accomplish a certain objective. For example, the UCLA cut involves a chain of passes and catches, and stops and pivots, all intended to free a particular player for a high-percentage shot. A lapse in any fundamental along the way will likely render the play ineffective. So stress the learning, drilling, and practice of fundamentals in the offensive attack. For it is true that a chain is only as strong as its weakest link.

CHAPTER 14

GAME PREPARATION AND ADJUSTMENTS

The coordination of skills, tactics, and talents of five offensive players on the floor versus the schemes and efforts of a defensive unit is what makes basketball competition so fascinating. And, it is true that wise strategic decisions in preparation for, and during, games can enhance a team's ability to outperform the opposition.

But even the best offensive tactics require a team that can execute them; otherwise, they are rendered ineffective. That is why tactical instruction and adjustments should be emphasized only after the offense is well taught and drilled. It is when plays are run with intelligent purpose, and when players are familiar with one another's idiosyncrasies, that strategic maneuvers become relevant.

The offensive schemes presented in the previous chapters are flexible and effective, capable of dealing with all types of defensive tactics. Adjustments can be made quickly to each tactical challenge the opposition might present simply by running the offense correctly. Triangles will form repeatedly as the offense flows, making for advantageous passing angles. And, because of the multiple passing options and the freedom to exploit a defensive lapse with a dribble or shot, every player will have an array of possibilities every time he handles the ball.

Thus, the individual initiative and spontaneous decision making encouraged in the offense are two chief reasons why it's so difficult to defend. This enables players to transition swiftly from one method of attack to another (e.g., from guard-to-guard-to-forward entries to guard reverse pressure release entries) without missing a beat. For example, if we wanted to use two offenses within the same game, our players had little difficulty doing so because the same principles and fundamentals applied to all of our tactical options. With any offense, success hinges not so much on the particular positioning and movement patterns of players, but on how well it is taught, absorbed, and embraced by all team members.

PREPARATION FOR DEFENSES

In preparing for games, we focused primarily on just this type of precise execution of our offense as a whole, and of certain plays, specifically. We were not overly concerned about what the opponent might do or how certain positions would match up. The options and special plays took care of exploiting advantages. The sound structure of the offense and the principles it was founded on are a great foundation for making tactical adjustments to take advantage of defensive weaknesses. In fact, in most instances, little adjustment needed to be made.

However, being well aware of the defensive challenges our teams would face during the season, and having full knowledge of each opposing coach's strategy from past experience, I knew that additional tactical preparation was needed. The following are some of the challenges I knew I had to get my teams ready for:

1. Pressing and trapping half-court defense
2. Pressing three-quarter-court defense (man-to-man and zone)
3. Pressing full-court defense (man-to-man and zone)
4. Pressing defense on out-of-bounds plays
5. Trapping defense such as the 1-3-1
6. Switching defense
7. Box-and-one defense to stop the star player
8. Defense with good shot blockers

To prepare the team for particular defensive alignments and schemes, players need to know and embrace a set of defense-specific tactical guidelines. For best results, players should be taught these tactics at the start of the season; the coach can then make them a point of emphasis in practices leading up to the games in which they apply.

Against athletic teams that press and trap in the half court

- Keep in mind that the ultimate goal is to get the ball inside and get fouled or score.
- Use the passing attack rather than the dribble.
- Reverse the ball to get the defense moving. Then attack the middle.
- Get the basketball to the high post as soon as possible. Then advance it to the block or inside.
- Run the guard reverse and forward reverse, penetrate, and look inside first and then to the perimeter. Make reverses your first three or four plays of the game.
- Remember that patience is a virtue. Except for the quick reverse, getting a good shot may require more passing and take longer against pressing defenses.

Against three-quarter-court pressure

- Simply extend the offense.
- Use a passing attack before dribbling.
- Look for the pass to the forward before going guard to guard.
- Get the ball to the middle of the court (safely) as early as possible. Then look down the middle for the next receiver.
- Make vertical cuts after a vertical pass. Getting the ball to the middle and making vertical cuts are key to attacking an extended defense.
- Bring the weak-side forward to the middle.

Against full-court pressure

- Use a sound inbounds alignment to get the ball in safely.
- Follow the inbounds pass with an immediate vertical or diagonal cut to draw the defense back.
- Use a passing attack.
- Follow all the principles listed previously for use against three-quarter-court pressure.
- If the center is not a good decision maker, place him around the offensive basket area. He should float from side to side, looking for the pass and score when the press is broken. Layups discourage teams from continuing to press.

Against pressing defense on out-of-bounds plays

(e.g., The defender guarding the inbounder is playing shortstop. He turned his back on his man and is zoning the basket area.)

- Make the opponent guard the basket first by making a cut down the middle. If you don't, you could be in trouble because the defense will extend into all passing lanes (see figure 14.1).
- Provide sequential passing options for the inbounder.
- Use the pressure release pass (the pass over the top toward the half-court line) as a last resort—but use it.

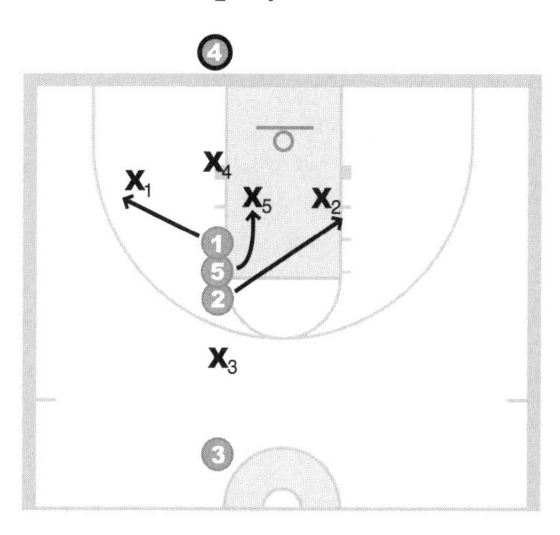

Figure 14.1 If you don't make the opponent guard the basket first by making a cut down the middle, this situation results: defenders block all possible passes.

Against a 1-3-1 half-court trap

- Keep in mind that the goal is to create one-on-one situations.
- Use the high-low offense to get into the 1-3-1 alignment by dribbling the forward to the high post (see figure 14.2). This will make it difficult to trap as well as create one-on-one situations.

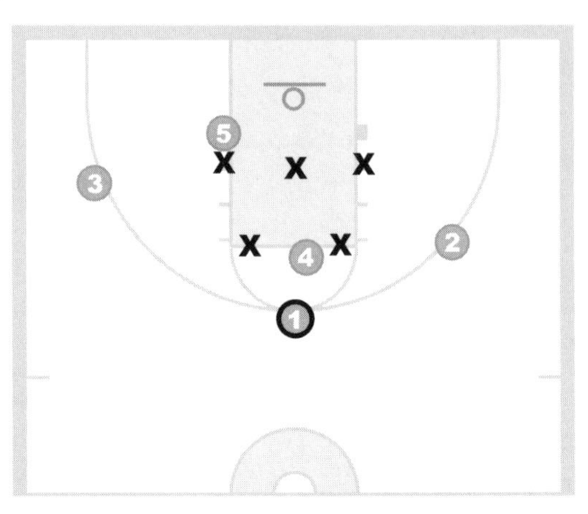

Figure 14.2 The 1-3-1 alignment makes it difficult to trap.

- Remember that an offensive advantage against zones is that the offense can create any matchup they like. Get the ball to the player with the mismatch.
- Get the ball to an athlete at the high post, and place two shooters on the wings. You may ask, "What shooters? I have shooters, but I need makers." I understand.

Against switching defenses

- Be aware that teams use switching defense to play the passing lanes. Run the guard reverse, and run a defender off the double screen. Switching on a double screen usually leaves the top player open momentarily because the double stack's top defender will usually switch to take the cutter (see figure 14.3).
- Keep in mind that the screener is more likely to be open than the cutter. Slip the screen, especially on down screens (see figure 14.4). The down screen will also produce a size advantage for the screening forward.
- Run the UCLA cut. If the defense switches, the guard should clear, and the center should cut to the low post (see figure 14.5).
- Run the side-post game and roll to the basket. On the handoff, the guard may be open for an outside shot or may have a quickness advantage (see figure 14.6).

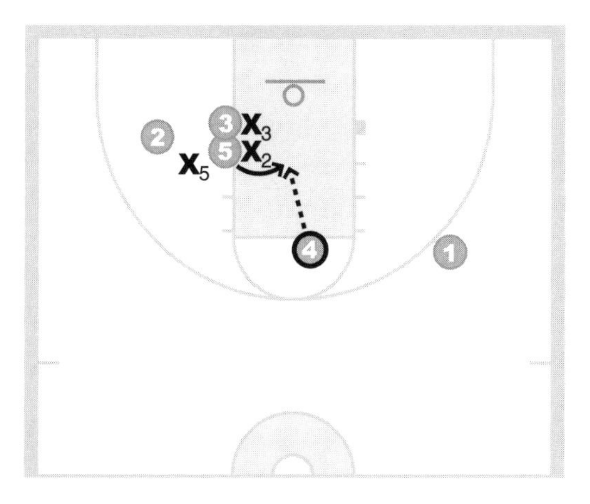

Figure 14.3 The top player in the stack is open for the pass.

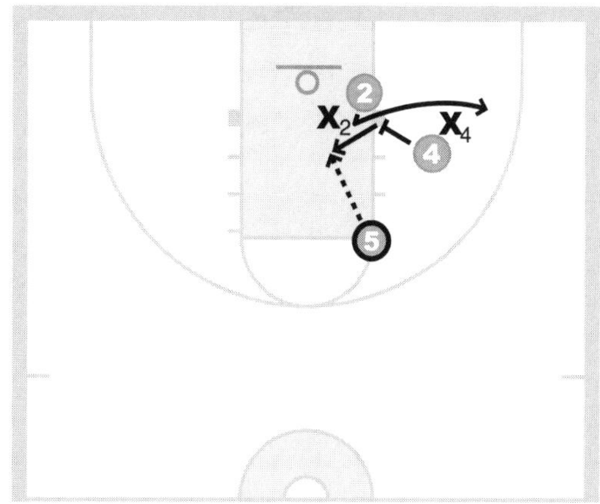

Figure 14.4 The screener, 4, is more open than the cutter, 2.

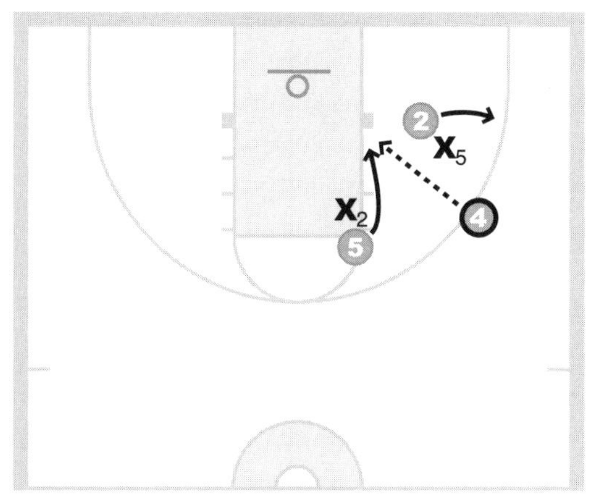

Figure 14.5 The guard clears and the center cuts to the low post.

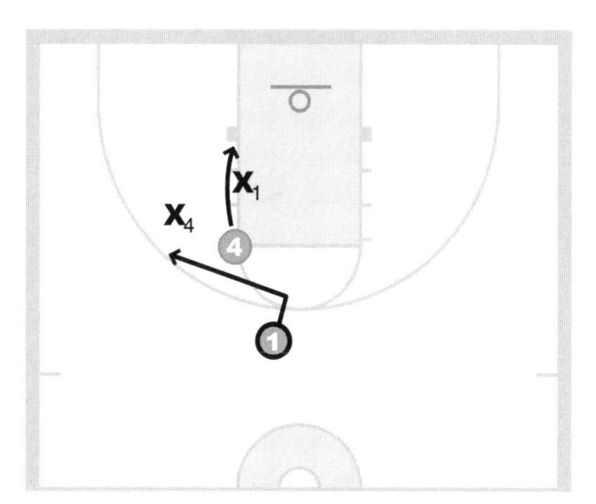

Figure 14.6 The guard may be open for an outside shot or have a quickness advantage.

Against box-and-one defense

- In the high-post or high-low offense, have the target player (2) set the down screen after the UCLA cut. No one will cover the shooter (see figure 14.7).
- Run the guard reverse and place the target player at the bottom of the double screen. When the reversing guard comes off the double screen and a bottom defender moves out to guard him, the top man in the double screen is wide open (see figure 14.8).

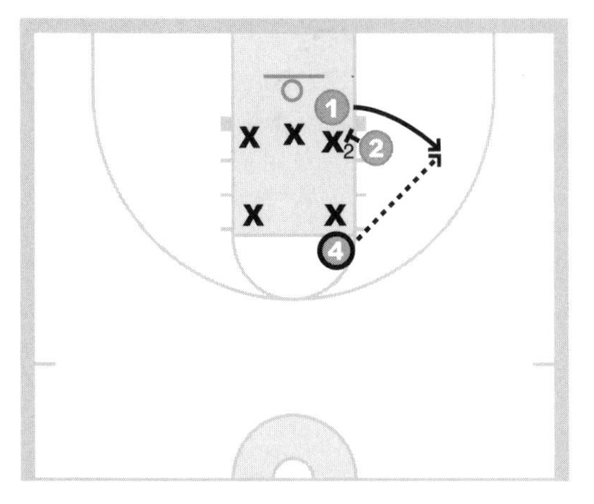

Figure 14.7 Player 2 sets a down screen for 1, who gets the pass.

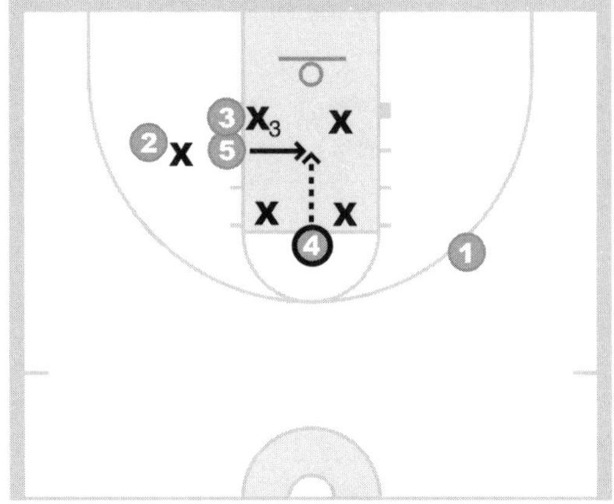

Figure 14.8 Player 5 is open, as his defender is distracted by the reversing guard.

- Also look for action off the forward—when he comes to the high post to receive the ball—when running the guard reverse. When the passing guard comes around the forward, replacing the cutting guard, no player is available to guard him quickly. It's a two-on-two situation, but the defense is far out of position when the play occurs, because the bottom defender must either come from the inside to the high post or all the way to the wing (see figure 14.9).

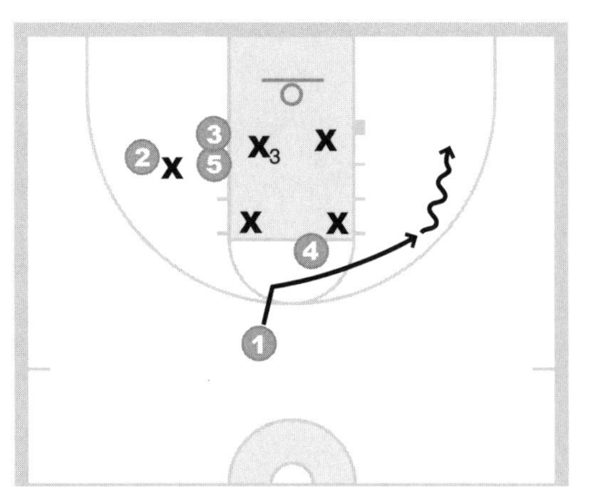

Figure 14.9 The bottom defender must either come from the inside to the high post or all the way to the wing.

Against a shot-blocking center

- Drive at a shot blocker, not as a primary strategy, but in the flow of the game. Mix it up by stopping for 10-foot bank shots.
- Select drivers who are good "finishers" and skilled at drawing the foul.
- Keep in mind that shot blockers depend on shooters leaving their feet early and releasing the ball away from the rim. Teach players to take it all the way to the nook between the basket and the backboard.
- Make the extra pass to the shot blocker's man when the shot blocker moves to block a shot.

- If attacking the low post, use ca one-on-one plays where the offens shot.
- Involve the shot blocker in screen ar He is more likely to foul on the mo and can time his jump to the shot.
- Make the shot blocker guard the high not the only player who can play the

GAME PLANNING

The temptation of any coach is to overcoach. And on offense. Several factors contribute to this, but perhaps the that Xs and Os just seem to be in a coach's lifeblood. We love sketching this and that play while in our mind's eye imagining how the diagram we've illustrated would actually manifest itself on the court. In short, we enjoy the mental gymnastics.

The opportunity to outfox an opponent is also appealing, especially to coaches whose teams appear to face a size or skill disadvantage. This prospect feeds into the coach's ego, as the silly notion of "outscoring" the opposing coach takes hold. If a coach carries this mind-set into a game, it is quickly altered after tip-off. Players score points and win games, not coaches.

Still, members of the media are fond of bestowing the label "genius" on certain successful coaches because their offense looks very organized, often gets uncontested shots, and shoots a high percentage.

The point is that overcoaching a team offense when it comes to strategy is based on a false premise—that tactics alone determine success or failure. In fact, players with too much tactical information to learn and remember are more inclined to be hindered than helped. A player trying to recall just what options to use off of just what play against just what defense is going to suffer paralysis by analysis. That's why the UCLA offense was kept simple enough for all players to learn completely, yet complex enough to meet all challenges.

A few good plays with two or three options for individual initiative, when mastered, will promote fluency and ball movement. If in doubt, it is better to lean toward the side of simplicity. This will instill confidence in players that the offense will work if executed properly. It will also promote team play.

Nearly every offensive strategy requires team play. The coach can prepare a team to handle opponents by teaching them to rely on each other. When all players become convinced, in theory and practice, it is amazing what a team can accomplish; when no one cares who gets the credit, they become teachable.

g can also take the form of providing the team with a secret to defeating an upcoming opponent. This turns nto competitiveness. For example, a coach who thinks s superior in physical conditioning might tell his players opposing coach is too nice to work his players hard, and ey should take advantage of this by maintaining a high pace he entire game. The coach's confidence will be assimilated by players. And that confidence converted to competitiveness will nake players more aggressive, which is especially important against defensive pressure.

Let us not forget that player input can also play a key role in tactical planning. Once they begin to see the rationale behind the coach's offensive adjustments to counteract defensive stunts, players often begin to see potential alterations of their own. The fact that they are physically involved in the action helps them come up with possibilities the coach may not even think of. Although the practice session is the authorized setting for creativity, the time-out may also qualify. Coaches who allow their players to chat for the first portion of the time-out, while the coaching staff is preparing to address the huddle, are pleasantly surprised to find some valuable propositions once they get there. Asked earnestly and frequently, the question "What do you guys think?" may pay substantial dividends.

SITUATIONAL ADJUSTMENTS

Once the proper balance of fundamental and tactical preparation is achieved, a coach is much better able, within the normal flow of practice, to help prepare his team to meet specific situations.

When perusing books on basketball instruction, it is no wonder that little is found on game strategy; the amount of pages dedicated to fundamentals, conditioning, team play, and offensive patterns far outweighs those on game strategy. Most of the tactical information deals with various defenses to stop a dominant center or make the opponent play a style of game it is not accustomed to. However, offensively speaking, few tricks are needed. Within the already existing high-post or high-low offensive system, there are plenty of options available to create a variety of shots for a player who has an advantage or the hot hand.

Forward with an inside advantage

In the vernacular of the day, when Sidney Wicks received the basketball anywhere inside 10 feet, "school was out." Against USC, Wicks scored five consecutive times from the low-post area.

- The UCLA cut (away from his side). Hit the high-post player, and duck the forward on the weak-side block.

- The UCLA cut (to his side). Get the ball to him after he has down screened for the guard.
- Guard reverse (away from him). He will be part of the double screen. After the guard comes around the screen, the center comes to the high post, leaving the forward to post up.

Forward with a hot hand

Gary Cunningham, a six-foot-seven forward, was a great outside shooter. When he was hot, which was often, the rest of the players honed in on opportunities to get him open. Gary dominated several games for UCLA.

- Kentucky.
- Guard to guard to forward, outside cut. Run him off the double screen.
- The fourth option of the four-options set.

Forward with a quickness advantage

Sidney Wicks was also a great one-on-one player. He may be the only UCLA forward who was allowed to go one on one at will. Against Oregon State, he won the game with the following isolation play. The other plays listed are options that were used for him in other games with great success.

- Guard to forward, UCLA cut. The guard cuts through to the other side, and the forward goes one on one. The floor is balanced for passing options, triangle rebounding, and defensive protection.
- Guard to guard to high post. Run the play to his side so he can reverse to the basket.
- Side-post game. This will isolate him for the one-on-one.

Guard with an inside advantage

Johnny Green was, without question, the best posting guard in UCLA basketball history. He received the basketball in a variety of ways.

- The UCLA cut. Use this play to hit him at the low post from either guard position. Johnny often got himself open by cutting behind the center into the low post from the weak-side guard position.
- Guard to guard to high post. Have him cut down the lane and down screen for the forward, who comes to the wing.
- Green.
- Guard to guard to forward, outside cut. The center screens away for the weak-side forward while the strong-side forward delivers the ball to the guard inside.

- Same play but the forward passes the ball out to the guard, the beginning of the double screen play for Gary Cunningham. Instead of Gary coming off the screen, the guard moves into the block, and the ballhandling guard dribbles to his side and delivers the pass.

Guard with a hot hand

John Vallely was particularly skilled at getting open on the perimeter when cutting off the center after passing there from the guard position. Against the University of Minnesota, he used a variety of ways to get free for a jump shot, two of which were crossing with the other guard and faking the cross and flaring to the same side.

- Guard to guard to high post. Read the defense to either cross the guards or flare them to their sides. The high-post player must know who has the hot hand and direct his attention to that side of the court.
- Side-post game. Run a play through so he's involved in the side-post game, taking the handoff from the forward.
- Guard reverse. Run him off the double screen.

Guard with a quickness advantage

The 1975 championship team had two quick starting guards: Pete Trgovich and Andre McCarter. Although few plays were run specifically for them (because of the powerful inside presence of Marques Johnson and Richard Washington), the team did look for opportunities to benefit from their quickness.

- Guard to guard to forward, UCLA cut. The other guard cuts if he thinks he has an opportunity. Make the quick guard the one who passes to the forward or center.
- Guard reverse (for the quick guard).
- Indiana.

Center with an inside advantage

The 1972 NCAA finals had UCLA matched up against Memphis State. Memphis State chose not to double-team Bill Walton. It was rather simple to get the ball into him that night; the first two of the following plays were just about all we used. The rest are options off the high post that can be effective if used here and there within a game.

- High-low offense: guard to high post. Look for the center on the duck move.
- High-low offense: guard to left wing to post. The high-post player reverses to the basket in case his man helps on the post.

- High-post offense: "Down."
- High-post offense: guard reverse. The center is open after the double screen splits.
- High-post offense: guard to guard to forward. Have the center screen across for the weak-side forward. The pass goes to the forward, who hits the center on the duck move.

There is one additional point concerning Indiana and Kentucky. While those plays work well during the flow of the game, they can also be strategically used after time-outs and halftime, because their deceptiveness may catch the defense by surprise.

Plays directed to a hot player should not be run in succession or the element of surprise is eliminated. The guards who initiate the plays should run another option once or twice and then look for him in another setting. Let the opposing player who is being exploited, as well as the rest of the opposing team, gain a little false security when the play is run away from his man. Then hit him with another, different challenge.

However, tactical sequencing of plays and options based on matchup advantages may not be a coach's primary concern. He may not have any one-on-one advantages at all. Rather, he may be more concerned about preparing the team to meet an opponent with a dominant center who is a master shot blocker, a team with a distinct height advantage at almost every position, or in many cases, a team that is more athletic and will press from end line to end line.

PRACTICING TACTICS

Practice is the time for guards to put in extra work on timing the reverse cut, reading the defense when coming around double screens, and passing to a forward who has come across half court to receive the ball against a three-quarter-court press. Forwards may need to polish up on receiving the ball against pressure and making the right pass to the next player, passing into the post, or flashing in the key. Centers may need help finishing a press break, accelerating to the ball against pressure, or successfully completing a backdoor pass. However, some players may require supplementary teaching. If time is available before practice, this is a good setting for individual instruction, because what is taught can be immediately applied.

Those one-on-one moments can also be used for coaches to consider informing individual players of particular strengths they may have or maneuvers they can make against upcoming defenders. This instills confidence and is a good preparatory strategy. For example, the coach may anticipate a mismatch when the opposing reserve forward (a weaker defender) enters the game and may tell his player to take advantage of it. He may tell another player that he has heard that the man who will be guarding him turns his head toward the ball on the weak side; the coach may encourage his player to watch for this and move to an open spot. These "tips" can transfer confidence from coach to player.

CLOSING POINTS

Generally, the first organized practice session is three to six weeks before the first game. Study the schedule and prepare accordingly. Know what teams you will be facing early and what defensive tactics they're likely to employ so your squad will have some familiarity with those schemes.

On the first day of practice, emphasize the main offensive plays but also introduce and teach pressure release plays, such as the guard reverse or forward reverse. Opponents often begin a season with aggressive and extended defense. You'll want to have your players ready to successfully handle pressure. If they are, the opponents will back off and you'll be able to run all the plays you want. If they don't handle it, you may face pressure all year.

During the season, rarely does a team have more than five or six days to prepare for the next contest. Within those time constraints, you need to prepare your players as best you can for what they will encounter, based on the information available. Plan your practices so that all necessary offensive options are covered before the first league game.

In teaching tactics, never sacrifice the fundamentals. You might lose a game or two against some specially contrived defensive attack, but in the long run, training players to execute the basics quickly, properly, and at high speed will enable you to come out on top.

CHAPTER 15

TEAMWORK

The beauty of the high-post and high-low offenses is that all five players are involved in passing, catching, screening, and cutting to make the plays. In most cases, all players handle the ball and have scoring opportunities at one time or another.

More-talented offensive players, because they can create and make a high percentage of shots, will naturally score the most points. But in doing so, they should not hinder the continuity and flow of the offense.

Teaching and understanding the proper boundaries of individual play within the structure of the offense are perhaps the coaches' and players' greatest challenge in executing it properly. Players must be encouraged to develop their resourcefulness, all the while making wise judgments about when an individual move is appropriate, and when to keep the ball moving to help create scoring opportunities for teammates.

The elements required in the high-post and high-low offenses to allow sufficient individual expression while still maintaining continuity, team play, and execution are

- equal opportunities among players to positively affect the action;
- situations of advantage that lend themselves to singular initiatives; and
- trust and unselfishness among all members of the squad.

BUILDING COHESION

The morale of most teams is enhanced when all positions have approximately the same number of "touches." No formal count or statistic is kept to document exactly how many times each player handles the ball. Rather, it is a sense gained both by participants and observers that the ball, moved primarily by the pass, could well wind up in any open player's hands—that is, of course, if the team is disciplined enough to follow plays through, making a sufficient number of passes to produce high-percentage shots.

Much of the success of the high-post and high-low offenses hinges on the actions of the "stars." If the one or two more-gifted players take shots almost every time they receive a pass, it will undermine the purpose and flow of the offense and could result in other team members adopting the same "me first" mind-set. However, if the star athletes integrate their talents effectively into the offense, moving the basketball, cutting, setting screens, and making individual moves in situations the offense has created, the rest of the team will do the same. That's not to say that each player will average the same number of points per minute played. The more-talented offensive players will, and must, score more for the team to be successful. What is important is that all five players on the court contribute to that result.

The coach plays a key role in striking this fine balance of teamwork and individual initiative by more-talented offensive players. The first priority, as mentioned, is to teach an offense where all players genuinely think they are essential contributors to each score. Four other effective measures are to make the stars play defense, to set up plays for the other team members, to correct fairly, and to praise the supporting cast.

Insist That Offensive Stars Play Defense

If a coach allows a great offensive player to give less than his all on the other end of the court, he will destroy the team concept. Nothing justifies an athlete with the tools to be highly successful on offense playing defense poorly or with anything less than full effort. Any player who can dribble and make individual moves to score has the quickness, balance, and footwork to play good defense. In fact, offensive players benefit from being equally focused on their task on the defensive end of the court. Their speed and quickness, attention to fundamentals, and overall alert play as defenders carry over to when their team has possession.

Run Plays for Lower Scorers

Enter each game with a handful of plays designed to get high-percentage shots for players that the defense least expects to score. Then, when the time is right, direct the offense to run those plays. The key is to treat the use of such plays not as an act of charity, but as a sound tactical maneuver that will deceive the defense for easy scores. Furthermore, it will force the defense to respect all offensive players as potential threats, rather than directing most of their efforts toward stopping the one or two top offensive players on the team.

Another plus of employing such plays is that it reinforces in a very tangible way the point that all five players on the court are critical to

TEAM PERFECTION

I have awed at a solo performance
And spectacular flashy display,
    But I crave for the best
    And my eyes are *more* blessed
When an unselfish team makes a play.

A play that's so perfect and simple,
With the weaving of role with a role—
    Every piece partly seen
    Like a fine-tuned machine,
And you notice not one, but the whole.

Every wild one, once blinded by glory,
Is now cured and is one of the tame.
    He receives his esteem
    As a part of the team
And is eager to sacrifice fame.

It's amazing what teams have accomplished.
It's astounding how much they have done,
    When the ultimate call
    Is when one is for all,
And the credit is reached for by none.

–Swen Nater

the offense's success. Just watch how a low-scoring player who converts a basket after his number was called responds afterward. With a potent reminder of his accountability, he will have a renewed commitment to contributing to the team every subsequent trip down the floor. Whether called on to set a screen, make a pass, or crash the boards, his effort level will be extremely high.

Correct Fairly

One sure way for a coach to be labeled unfair is to aim the bulk of corrections at the nonstars. Worse yet, some coaches antagonize less-talented players by making them the targets of their ill humor. No player should ever be subject to such derision by a coach, especially not in front of others.

The proper approach is to correct errors constructively and fairly. That does not mean that corrections will be distributed evenly across the team. It does, however, mean that whenever one of the top scorers commits an error or violation, he is corrected just as other players would be had they erred in the same manner. Indeed, depending on the temperament and talent level of the star, he might receive even less margin of error because more is expected.

Acknowledge All Who Contribute

Box scores and newspaper articles generally provide a great deal of positive reinforcement for top scoring players. And the impression conveyed by them is that the statistical leaders were most responsible for the victory. That may or may not be true.

Players should be taught to appreciate the contributions of all teammates, regardless of points, rebounds, or minutes of playing time in any given contest. Even those players who never left the bench during the game had a role in helping to prepare the starters and reserves who did play, including challenging them on the practice court.

Both in communications with the team and in public with the media and fans, a coach should take the opportunity to praise those whose contributions to proficient offensive performance may not have been noticed as much as scoring or rebounding. This type of acknowledgment not only sends the message that the work of the supporting cast has been noticed and appreciated, encouraging those players to maintain their efforts, but it might also prompt the statistical leaders to work even harder at the little things that can raise their—and the team's—performance to a higher level.

FINE-TUNING EXECUTION

I have always favored identifying 7 or 8 players who will play in each game until the outcome has been decided. That won't always be easy, because the 9th and 10th players might have very positive qualities that could help the team in particular situations. And it is sure to disappoint the 7 or 8 team members who will primarily be practice players and spend most games on the bench. But, especially for offensive teamwork, it is usually the right thing to do.

Identifying five starters with one substitute for the guards and one for the forwards and center will allow more practice time for those combinations. The more practice working together, the more fluid timing, cutting, and passing become.

The goal is to achieve perfection on each possession. Yes, true perfection is unattainable, and the journey toward perfection has no end. But that must be the ideal for the team—to run the offense with precision in each cut, pass, screen, and shot. That is why we work for hours on the practice floor, correcting miscues, refining good but not great moves, and becoming more familiar with each teammate's preferences and tendencies. All these efforts are intended to help players execute the offense, individually and collectively, with ultimate precision.

Even if we fall a bit short, as we inevitably will, we'll have moved up the ladder of improvement by challenging ourselves to the highest standard. And the thrill of improvement, and the experience of becoming even more in synch as a unit, will inspire further efforts and closer approximations to the perfect game.

So, never become completely satisfied with the team's performance. Once a player or coach is fully satisfied, complacency will set in and performance will most assuredly decline. It has been said, "Once you're through trying to improve, you're through."

The proper attitude is best expressed as "Let's see how good we can get." This approach creates energy and motivation to continue improving, for both the regulars and reserves. It also shifts a team's focus from grading itself on a curve—comparing itself to opponents—to the effort it is making to become the best it can be. When this type of thinking is believed and practiced, outscoring the opponent becomes a by-product of the pursuit of excellence.

A SPECIAL TEAM

I have always had a special place in my heart for my first championship team at UCLA, not because they won the crown, but for other reasons. A team filled with very strong-willed individuals, they played with tremendous hustle, drive, and determination. I'm doubtful if the word *defeat* ever entered any of their minds. The 1963 to 1964 team met every challenge head-on. They had a good balance of courage and poise.

Above all, the magic of this team was how well they played together at both ends of the court. The 2-2-1 press was a weapon that paid eventual dividends. When the ball was stolen, each player knew exactly where the others were and often moved the ball for an easy score, adding to the pressure they placed on the opponent by stealing the ball. All players possessed the killer instinct; the intensity and quickness of the press increased with every turnover.

Their teamwork on the other end of the court was equally beautiful to watch. They believed in the system. More than once, I was tempted to make a structural or tactical change, but this team's ability to execute the basic offense and, equally as important, to augment the offense with

continued »

» continued

cunning improvisations left my pen in my pocket. And, although Gail Goodrich and Walt Hazzard were the main scorers, the others—Keith Erickson, Jack Hirsch, Fred Slaughter, and valuable reserves Doug McIntosh and Kenny Washington—were completely sold on the team concept and worked hard to get them the ball. But it took time for this team to jell completely.

Goodrich, a very competitive and confident guard, and ever conscious of Hazzard monopolizing the ball, felt he could do so much more with the ball if he had it. But he soon discovered that if he worked hard to get open without the ball, Walt would get it to him. This type of sacrifice, in my opinion, is the essence of teamwork because it made both Walt and Gail better players. In addition, Gail's eagerness to play the team game may have been a contributor to the unselfishness of the entire team. I have always felt that when the more valuable players play team basketball, it often filters through the entire squad.

Walt Hazzard was an effective passer because he was deceptive. Here, no one knows the pass is made except Walt and his receiver, Fred Slaughter.

But the most remarkable transition from individual play to teamwork may be the one made by Walt Hazzard. A native of Philadelphia, Walt was a very talented ball handler and passer. With an excellent sophomore year behind him, as a junior, he began to revert to his old habit of fancy dribbling and blind and behind-the-back passing. Allowing our team to develop into the Walt Hazzard show would have destroyed teamwork and, eventually, the ability of the team to reach its full potential. For that reason, in two consecutive games, I pulled him out. We lost both games—one rather handily.

Concerned for his feelings, I telephoned his father, a minister in Philadelphia, and discovered that Walt had already called him and told him he was coming home. His father assured me that he had explicitly told his son not to come home and that adversity is something to face rather than avoid. Walt made the right decision. He came to understand what I wanted to accomplish and refined his offensive approach. He was my kind of guard.

CLOSING POINTS

Years ago, when attempting to choose a word that would express my exact feeling for team play, I chose *teamwork*. However, that never quite settled with me. It suggested more of the act of individuals involved in performing their own responsibilities rather than the give-and-take required for performing within those responsibilities. I replaced *teamwork* with two words—*team spirit*. My definition for team spirit was a willingness to sacrifice personal glory for the welfare of the team.

But still I felt something was missing. Willingness implies reluctance. Reluctant sacrifice will ultimately resurface as selfishness. The word I was looking for was *eagerness*. Gail Goodrich was not willing to sacrifice handling the ball more; he was eager to do so. Eagerness implies an enthusiastic commitment and will seldom result in a change of mind.

Finally, thoroughly thought-out Xs and Os, based on sound principles all tailored to the talent available, are necessary for success. But the coach will never see the full effectiveness of plays and options if all players are not sold on team play. Then, and only then, will all elements of offense jell for a fluent attack. With this in mind, the goal of every coach should be to develop a group of players whose play proves they believe "the star of the team is the team."

BIBLIOGRAPHY

Allen, Forrest C. 1937. *Better Basketball.* New York and London: Whittlesey House.

Bee, Clair. 1942. *Zone Defense and Attack.* New York. A.S. Barnes.

Bunn, John W. 1964. *Basketball Techniques and Team Play.* Englewood, NJ: Prentice-Hall.

Lambert, Ward L. 1932. *Practical Basketball.* Chicago: Athletic Journal.

Meanwell, Walter E. 1924. *The Science of Basket Ball.* Self-published.

Nater, Swen, and Ronald Gallimore. 2005. *You Haven't Taught Until They Have Learned.* Morgantown, WV: Fitness Information Technology.

Nater, Swen, and James A. Peterson. 1995. *The Complete Handbook of Rebounding.* St. Louis: Coaches Bookshelf.

Newell, Pete. 1962. *Basketball Methods.* New York: Ronald Press.

Rupp, Adolph F. 1948. *Rupp's Championship Basketball.* New York: Prentice-Hall.

Winter, Fred (Tex). 1962. *The Triple-Post Offense.* Englewood Cliffs, NJ: Prentice-Hall.

Wooden, John R. 1966. *Practical Modern Basketball.* New York: Macmillan.

Wooden, John R., and Bill Sharman. 1975. *The Wooden-Sharman Method.* New York: Macmillan.

Wooden, John R., and Jack Tobin. 1972. *They Call Me Coach.* Waco, TX: Word.

Wootten, Morgan. 2003. *Coaching Basketball Successfully.* 2nd edition. Champaign, IL: Human Kinetics.

INDEX

Note: The italicized *f* following page numbers refers to figures.

L

M

N

O

P

ABOUT THE AUTHORS

Photo by Todd Cheney/UCLA Photography

John Wooden is simply the most successful basketball coach in the history of the sport. In his 40 years as a head coach, Wooden compiled an unparalleled 885-203 overall career win-loss record (.813). Wooden's UCLA teams registered 620 wins and only 147 losses, won a record 10 NCAA championships, and achieved one of the most amazing winning streaks in all of sports with 38 straight NCAA tournament victories. His Bruin teams also set the all-time NCAA record by winning 88 straight games over four seasons, including consecutive 30-0 seasons in 1971-72 and 1972-73.

As a high school basketball player in Martinsville, Indiana, Wooden won all-state honors three consecutive years. At Purdue University, he won letters in basketball and baseball his freshman year and later earned All-American honors as a guard on the basketball team from 1930 to 1932. He captained Purdue's basketball teams of 1931 and 1932 and led the Boilermakers to two Big Ten titles and the 1932 national championship.

Shortly after graduating from Purdue in 1932, Wooden began his teaching career at Dayton High School in Kentucky and then went on to South Bend Central High School two years later. His impressive 11-year prep coaching record was 218-42. After serving as a full lieutenant in the U.S. Navy from 1943 to 1946, Wooden went to Indiana Teachers College (now Indiana State University) as athletic director and basketball and baseball coach for two seasons before moving to UCLA.

Wooden was the first person to be inducted into the National Basketball Hall of Fame as both a player and coach. In 1999, ESPN named Wooden the Greatest Basketball Coach of All Time. He was also named *The Sporting News* Sportsman of the Year in 1970 and *Sports Illustrated* Sportsman of the year in 1973.

Photo by Todd Cheney/UCLA Photography

Swen Nater was a UCLA player under Wooden and the first and only college player in history to be drafted in the first round of the NBA draft without ever having started a college game. Despite this fact, Nater went on to a 12-year professional career spanning three leagues: the American Basketball Association (ABA), National Basketball Association (NBA), and Italian League. He was the ABA Rookie of the Year, and he is the only player in the history of professional basketball to lead all three leagues in rebounding.

After his playing career, Nater served as athletic director for 9 years at Christian Heritage College, where he also coached the basketball team to a national title. Currently, Nater is an assistant sporting goods buyer for Costco Wholesale, and he resides in the small town of Enumclaw, Washington, with his wife, Marlene.